Gift of the Estate of
Robert (1938-2013)
and Gay Zieger (1938-2013)
October 2013

Union Busting in the Tri-State

UNION BUSTING IN THE TRI-STATE

THE OKLAHOMA, KANSAS, AND MISSOURI METAL WORKERS' STRIKE OF 1935

BY GEORGE G. SUGGS, JR.

UNIVERSITY OF OKLAHOMA PRESS : NORMAN AND LONDON

By George G. Suggs, Jr.

Colorado's War on Militant Unionism: James H. Peabody and the Western Federation of Miners (Detroit, 1972)

(editor) *Perspectives on the American Revolution: A Bicentennial Contribution* (Carbondale, Ill., 1977)

Union Busting in the Tri-State District: The Oklahoma, Kansas, and Missouri Metal Workers' Strike of 1935 (Norman, 1986)

Library of Congress Cataloging-in-Publication Data

Suggs, George G., 1929–
    Union busting in the Tri-State.

    Includes bibliographical references and index.
    1. Metal-workers' Strike, U.S., 1935—History.
    2. Trade-unions—United States—Organizing—History.
    I. Title.
    HD5325.M52 1935.S84   1986   331.89′2871′0973   86-6910
    ISBN 0-8061-2012-6 (alk. paper)

Publication of this work has been made possible in part by a grant from the Andrew W. Mellon Foundation.

The paper in this book meets the guidelines for permanence and durability of the Committee on Production Guidelines for Book Longevity of the Council on Library Resources, Inc.

To Ginny,
whose love and encouragement
made this book possible

Contents

Illustrations and Maps

MAPS

Preface

FOR many years before the Great Depression of the 1930s, organized labor attempted to establish itself in the Tri-State Mining District of Oklahoma, Kansas, and Missouri, a district that was for a time the world's greatest producer of lead and zinc concentrates. For a variety of reasons, the miners and millmen there rejected the efforts of organizers from such unions as the Western Federation of Miners and its successor, the International Union of Mine, Mill, and Smelter Workers, to found permanent organizations. Despite the enormous wealth extracted from the district, it nevertheless was ravaged by a host of social, economic, and medical problems that bore heavily on the workers who, unfortunately, lacked their own organizations to address the problems and articulate their grievances. The onslaught of the depression further exacerbated the plight of the Tri-State workers and made them less reluctant to organize.

Encouraged by the prolabor legislation of Franklin D. Roosevelt's New Deal, organizers of the International Union reentered the district in 1933, established seven local unions, and sought recognition. But refusal of the mining companies to recognize it as the exclusive bargaining agent for Tri-State workers led to a great strike in May 1935. Because the thirties were marked by violent labor unrest in major mass-production industries (e.g., steel, rubber, and automobiles) that captured the headlines of the nation's newspapers, the strike of the lead and zinc workers failed to receive as much nationwide attention as it warranted, not because of any less violence, but probably because of the relative isolation of the Tri-State District. Although several historians have noted the strike in studies concerned primarily with larger themes, their treatment of the strike was limited. Furthermore, they failed to perceive the strike as a microcosm that revealed the many currents of change that greatly affected labor in the significant decade of the thirties.

Consequently, my intent has been to use the strike in the Tri-State to demonstrate the complexities of the changes besetting American workers during the Great Depression. The New Deal's prolabor legislation (especially the National Industrial Recovery Act and the National Labor Relations Act), the role of powerful companies in contesting and countering the legitimate rights of workers by using devices like the company union, the continuing role of local and state governments in supporting companies that undermined worker organizations authorized by federal law, the split of organized labor over industrial unionism into two national organizations that struggled for the workers' membership—all of these developments determined the character of the lead and zinc workers' strike of 1935. By examining the interaction of national change and labor unrest in the Tri-State, it is possible to renew one's appreciation of the struggles required to elevate American workers everywhere to a more tolerable existence.

This book would not have been possible without substantial assistance from the Grants Funding and Research Committee and the Faculty Development Committee, College of Social Sciences, Southeast Missouri State University, and the National Endowment for the Humanities. Grants from the Grants Funding and Research Committee and the Faculty Development Committee made possible a semester leave of absence during 1980–81 and research in the Library of Congress, regional libraries, state historical societies, and the Tri-State Mining District. A National Endowment for the Humanities Resident Fellowship for 1980–81 provided an opportunity to study the "New Labor History" at Brown University and supported research in the National Archives' Federal Records Center, Suitland, Maryland, and in the Tri-State District. I am deeply grateful for the assistance rendered by these agencies. To the staffs of the following institutions, I also extend my gratitude for their help in facilitating my research: the Kent Library, Southeast Missouri State University; the State Historical Society of Missouri; the Kansas State Historical Society; the Oklahoma Historical Society; the Division of Archives, Department of Libraries, Oklahoma; the Federal Records Center at Suitland; the Dobson Memorial Center (Miami, Oklahoma); the Walter P. Reuther Library, Wayne State University; the Western Historical Collections, University of Colorado, Boulder; and the Picher (Oklahoma) Museum. Their aid was indispensable.

In writing this book, I have incurred a large indebtedness to a number of individuals whose encouragement and assistance were invaluable. I acknowledge with appreciation the role President Bill W. Stacy of Southeast Missouri State University played in making possible the important National Endowment for the Humanities year in residence at Brown University. I am especially obligated and grateful to Glenn A. Hickman, former secretary-treasurer of the Tri-State Metal Mine and Smelter Workers' Union (later renamed the Blue Card Union of Zinc and Lead, Mine, Mill and Smelter Workers) and editor of the *Blue Card Record*, who in interviews, tapes, and letters generously made available to me his recollections, observations, and feelings concerning events and personalities in the Tri-State during the labor troubles of the 1930s. At this writing, Hickman is the last surviving official of the Blue Card Union, and his astute perceptions and observations were therefore invaluable. I am also indebted to James Graves, a board member of the Picher Museum, who spent inconvenient hours assisting me in my search for Tri-State records. His interest in the history of the Tri-State and his determination to preserve the extant records of that history were most gratifying. Marrion A. Parsons, director of education for the Laborers' International Union of North America, who grew up in the district, has been an enthusiastic supporter of my research and the writing of this book. I am grateful for his suggestions and references and his constant willingness to help. I am especially obligated to Joan W. Scott and to members of her National Endowment of the Humanities seminar in the "New Labor History" at Brown University during 1980–81 for their constructive criticism of a paper that I have expanded into the present work. Professor Scott gave timely and much-needed encouragement and critically commented on portions of the manuscript. My special thanks also to Jack Brennan, director of the Western Historical Collections, University of Colorado, Boulder Campus, for his help over the years.

My gratitude goes also to Harold Dugger, Lawrence Breeze, Eugene Nutter, and Charles Eagles, colleagues at Southeast Missouri State University, for suggestions that greatly improved the quality of the entire manuscript, and to Frank Nickell, former chairman of the History Department, who obligingly arranged my teaching schedules to facilitate my writing and who read portions of the manuscript and encouraged its completion. I am also obligated to Charles C. Bonwell, present chairman of the History Department, Dean Sheila Caskey, Dean David E. Payne, and Provost Leslie Cochran for their encouragement and strong support. And I thank Diane Morgan, Peggy Ebner, Sherry Baker, and Janice Hart for their patient typing of the revisions of the manuscript. I am grateful to my son Owen, an attorney in labor law, for his review of and suggestions concerning litigation in the Tri-State. Finally, I acknowledge with deep appreciation the vital role my wife Ginny played in the completion of this book.

Cape Girardeau, Missouri   GEORGE G. SUGGS, JR.

Union Busting in the Tri-State

No Blacks, No Foreigners, No Unions—No Power

FROM all directions as one approaches Picher, Oklahoma, the mountainous chat piles loom prominently in the distance, impressive testimony to the labor of thousands of miners and millmen who spent their lives extracting and milling lead and zinc ores from the Tri-State Mining District of Oklahoma, Kansas, and Missouri. The workers who were responsible for these towering vestiges of the past and who risked life and limb blasting, shoveling, and milling the rich ore deposits from underground shafts and tunnels are rapidly vanishing. Like their counterparts in the hard-rock camps of the Rocky Mountain West, time has steadily depleted their ranks, so much so that their annual reunions held in Picher to celebrate, reminisce, and rehash the old days draw only a fraction of the workers who inhabited the district when it was vigorous with the sights and sounds of a major mining and industrial center. Nevertheless, the industrial remnants—the photographs of strong-faced work crews, the rusting ore buckets now proudly displayed, the concrete pillars and foundations of old mills, the rusted-out machinery and, above all, the mountains of chat—all attest to their labor, which, for a time, helped to make the Tri-State the world's greatest producer of lead and zinc concentrates.

The district in its heyday was impressive. In a recent article in the Picher (Oklahoma) *Tri-State Tribune*, Marrion A. Parsons, who grew up in the district, described his first visit to Picher and its surrounding area in 1925 as a boy of six. Picher was then the hub of a mining industry that was enjoying its most productive years. After struggling to the top of Picher 5's chat pile, which towered over South Connell Avenue, Picher's principal street, Parsons was moved by the sweeping, panoramic view before him. Fifty-eight years later he wrote:

> I reached the top and stood in wonder—you might say in awe and amazement at what I could see from this tremendously high vantage point in the sky.
> I could hardly believe my eyes! Only twice since in my life have I ever experienced the wonderment and thrill as I had in those few moments. Once at the Grand Canyon and another peering into the vast hole of a live volcano in Hawaii. I looked and looked; the East, West, North and South, and then, almost, as in a daze, slowly rotated a few degrees at a time, each time discovering new shapes, sizes, clouds of smoke, wisps of steam, movement of trains, trucks, horses and wagons—near and far. It was a veritable land of machines, buildings, tall and short and the movements were amazing. People seemed to be everywhere.[1]

Parsons's childhood reaction to the beehive of industrial activity on the surface might have been even greater had he been able to incorporate into the panorama the hundreds of men and machines at work in the miles of underground shafts and drifts within his viewing range.

Professional observers who visited the Tri-State in its prime years were equally impressed but, unlike Parsons's recollection of boyish wonder and awe, they viewed the industrial cyclorama more critically. After three months in the district in 1920 as a representative of the Industrial Relations Department of the Interchurch World Movement, Charles Morris Mills noted in the *Survey* the ravaging impact on the land produced by the feverish exploitation of the lead and zinc ore reserves. He wrote:

> Like many other mining communities, the centers of past and present productive activity set forth a Sahara-like panorama. Mammoth tailing [chat] piles, frequently fifty to one hundred feet in height, cover thousands of acres of formerly fertile land which can never be reclaimed for agricultural purposes. The soil, contaminated with the overflow from the mills, becomes barren. Everything has been sacrificed in the

Tri-State Mining District. Map courtesy of Kent Library, Southeast Missouri State University.

feverish scramble to get as much ore out in the quickest time possible and nature has consequently suffered abortions from which she can seemingly never recover. This distinctly hideous outlook seems to be a psychological factor in the line [life?] of both miner and operator; both tend to become dwarfed and stunted by the waste and barenness [*sic*] of their environment.[2]

Mills concluded that the mining industry "*absolutely*" determined the life of the district, relegating agriculture and manufacturing into a strictly secondary position. This economic domination produced instability, a "feverish unsteadiness" that "warp[ed] the social instincts and ideals of men" and made it impossible to plan for "permanent social improvements."[3] The pursuit of underground wealth westward from around Joplin, Missouri, into Oklahoma and Kansas thus resulted in staggering human costs as mines were exhausted and workers with their families moved on to establish usually temporary residence around new discoveries. These costs soared when hard times hit the district as in the 1930s.

Located in Jasper and Newton counties of southwestern Missouri, Ottawa County of northeastern Oklahoma, and Cherokee County of southeastern Kansas, the Tri-State Mining District comprised a mineralized area of nearly twelve hundred square miles in the mid-1930s. The discovery of lead deposits in 1848 and zinc deposits in 1871 near Joplin and Grandby, Missouri, had launched the district. Subsequent discoveries of rich ore reserves in Kansas (Galena, 1876) and Oklahoma (Peoria, 1891; Quapaw, 1904; Commerce, 1906) further extended its boundaries. But the discovery in 1915 of the Picher field in Oklahoma and Kansas, the greatest bonanza discovery of all, made the district the world's leading source of zinc and lead concentrates. Between 1848 and 1934, Tri-State workers extracted nearly 18.75 million tons of ores and milled concentrates valued at $827 million, with nearly half of this production coming from the Picher field. In the thirties, the mining industry continued to undergird trade, commerce, agriculture and all other enterprises as it had in the early twenties when Mills wrote. As mining went, so went the economic life of the district. The livelihood of half the district's sixty-five thousand inhabitants in 1935 depended directly upon the continued operation of its fifty-odd mines and mills,[4] and any general disruption would adversely affect the welfare of the entire population.

The thirties were an unusually significant decade for not only Tri-State workers but all American labor. Stalking the land with its massive unemployment and other plagues, the Great Depression demoralized a generation of workers. Within the American Federation of Labor (AFL) a divisive, bitter struggle between the advocates of industrial and craft unionism produced the Congress of Industrial Organizations (CIO) and split organized labor into competing bodies—the AFL and the CIO. Concurrently, the prolabor policies of Franklin D. Roosevelt's New Deal, embodied in the National Industrial Recovery Act, the National Labor Relations Act, and other statutes, raised new hopes and expectations among the nation's workers by placing for the first time the power of the federal government squarely behind their right to organize and engage in collective bargaining. These developments produced a volatile and heady mix of despair, conflict, and expectancy among American workers that exploded into violent and highly publicized strikes, particularly in the mass production industries, when employers challenged the new labor laws in the workplace and the courts. The state was increasingly drawn into these struggles intended to redefine, establish, and legitimize the rights and interests of the working class. Nowhere were the swirling forces of change in labor-management relations more sharply focused, and nowhere were the powerful and conflicting roles of the national, state, and local governments more clearly revealed than in the strike in 1935 of the lead and zinc workers in the Tri-State Mining District.

Historically, the labor force of the Tri-State was nationally recognized as difficult to organize and was perceived as a vast pool of potential strikebreakers available for service anywhere. For example, the district's reputation as a "scab center" was notorious, especially in other hard-rock camps where Tri-Staters had frequently arrived as strikebreakers during labor unrest. The *Miners' Magazine*, the official organ of the Western Federation of Miners, which tried unsuccessfully to organize the district in the early part of the century, frequently complained about the use of district strikebreakers in the Rocky Mountain gold camps. An early example of these complaints appeared in the November 1901 issue.

> We have seen the workingmen in nearly all the large cities of the United States and visited every mining camp in the West . . . and in all our experience we saw nothing that could equal the wretched vulgarity so manifest in Joplin on Saturday evening when the agent of some mining corporation was making a canvass of the saloons for men to take the place of workingmen struggling for their rights in the mountains of Colorado, Idaho, or British Columbia. . . . Small wonder that the work-

ingmen of the West call Joplin "The Scab Incubator," as they have good reason for applying the epithet.[5]

Labor recruiters for western operators found Joplin a mecca for strikebreakers who often were lured to struck mining camps with promises of good jobs, high wages, and assurances that labor conditions were stable. Even at home the apparent willingness of Tri-Staters to play the strike-breaking role was recognized. On April 2, 1907, the *Socialist News* (Carl Junction, Missouri) described Joplin as "that great scab market."

For three decades prior to the thirties, the Western Federation of Miners and its successor, the International Union of Mine, Mill, and Smelter Workers worked unsuccessfully to establish permanent locals in the Tri-State. Disturbed by the large number of miners in the Joplin area who hired out for service as strikebreakers in the Rocky Mountain hard-rock mining camps, as early as 1900 leaders of the Western Federation of Miners attempted to organize the Joplin District in order to reduce the supply of strike-breakers available to western mine owners.[6] Between 1900 and 1905, Western Federation miners' unions were established at Joplin (No. 88, 1900–01), Aurora (No. 210, 1903 to 1905), and Webb City (No. 205, 1903 to 1905). Across the state line in Kansas, where a number of smelters had been built to exploit the proximity to the Joplin mines and the discovery of an abundance of natural gas, the Western Federation also actively organized. It established miners' or smeltermen's locals at Argentine (No. 120, 1901–02), Bruce (No. 125, 1901–02), Cherryvale (No. 149, 1902–03), Gas City (No. 147, 1902–03), Girard (No. 124, 1901–02), LaHarpe (No. 148, 1902–03), and Iola (No. 123, 1901 to 1905). Most of these locals survived for less than two years. Some were immediately reestablished, only to collapse within a short while. For example, after the death of Joplin Local 88, its replacement (No. 195, 1902 to 1905) expired within three years. Thus Western Federation leaders failed to block the flow of strikebreakers to the West through unionizing. Nevertheless they continued to try.

In 1910 they organized Local 217 at Joplin, which died shortly after birth. The new Webb City local (No. 226, 1910) suffered the same fate. But at Carterville, Local 221 lasted from 1912 to 1916, then a long life for a Western Federation miners' union in the Joplin area. In Kansas, new locals among smeltermen at Altoona (No. 238, 1910 to 1913), Carey (No. 227, 1910 to 1916), and Dearing (No. 237, 1910 to 1916) endured longer. For the first time, Western Federation unions appeared in Oklahoma smelters in locales close enough to receive ores from the expanding Joplin field. Organizers formed locals at Bartlesville (No. 132, 1910 to 1914), Collinsville (No. 133, 1912), Sardis (No. 134, 1913), and Miami (No. 137, 1914) which failed to endure.

Shortly before it became the International Union of Mine, Mill, and Smelter Workers, the Western Federation launched another vigorous campaign to organize the district metal workers. In Missouri its organizers established in 1916 short-lived locals at Duenweg (No. 207), Oronogo (No. 205), Prosperity (No. 206), and Sarcoxie (No. 219). More than half a dozen new locals appeared in Kansas (Altoona, No. 232; Cherokee, No. 237; Coffeyville, No. 246; Galena, No. 210; Pittsburg, No. 222 and No. 238; and Weir, No. 488)—all in 1916. Four new Western Federation locals were organized in Oklahoma in the same year (Commerce, No. 221; Henryetta, No. 228; Kusa, No. 227; and Sand Springs, No. 224). With the exception of the union at Commerce, the locals consisted of smelter workers. These new attempts failed to secure a foothold in the developing district, as did a later International effort in 1925, despite promising starts.

By playing upon the workers' economic distress and their nativist sentiments, by using strikebreakers and labor spies to ferret out mining union leaders, and by extending minimal wage increases and other concessions to struck men at the appropriate time, the operators over the years successfully countered the unions' attempts to penetrate the district. Like their efforts in the base metal production industry elsewhere (for example, iron and copper in

Michigan and the Southwest), the Western Federation's and the International's attempts to organize permanent locals among the metal workers of the Tri-State were notably unsuccessful in making organized labor an enduring force to be reckoned with in industrial affairs. The result was that the mines and mills were unorganized at the start of the Great Depression.

The Tri-State metal workers were an anachronism. Although the industry in which they toiled was somewhat physically isolated, the coal fields directly to the north in Crawford County, Kansas, had long been organized by the United Mine Workers of America (UMW), which had also organized coal-mining regions in Missouri and Oklahoma. Furthermore, many workers in other trades in the district, especially in the urban centers such as Joplin and in the surrounding area, had embraced unionism by the thirties. Examples of labor organizations abounded. Nevertheless, the Tri-State miners and millmen remained resistant to organization, paradoxically forming a strong pocket of anti-unionism in an industry marked locally by conditions that daily threatened their health and safety—even their lives—and offered them little chance to realize creature comforts and economic security for themselves and their families. Unlike their counterparts in the hard-rock camps of Colorado, Idaho, and elsewhere, Tri-State metal workers rejected unionization as a panacea for their problems.

Several explanations have been offered to explain why, in an area where a mining, milling, and smelting industry employing thousands had been under way for decades, the workers refused to organize. Early commentators focused on the homogeneous character of the district population, which consisted primarily of white, native-born American Protestants with strong xenophobic attitudes toward foreigners ("outsiders") and blacks. Paradoxically, instead of facilitating unionization, homogeneity obstructed it, providing deeply rooted psychic opposition. Blacks and foreigners were definitely unwelcome. During the mid-twenties, there had been a strong Ku Klux Klan movement in Oklahoma and Kansas that partly originated in the xenophobic attitudes of the native-born, white, Protestant population of the two states. With its antiblack, anti-Catholic, anti-Jew, antiforeign, and antiunion attitude, the Klan demonstrated great power for awhile in local and state politics. By the end of the decade, however, the Klan had collapsed in the two states, leaving in its wake the nativist residue that had spawned it. Although not significantly involved in the Klan issue, Tri-Staters, especially the mine and mill workers, firmly believed that foreigners carried un-American ideas about labor and property, and that blacks should be strongly encouraged to reside elsewhere. As late as the mid-thirties, for example, a generally accepted "unwritten law" prevailed in Ottawa County that barred blacks from working and living there.[7]

In 1920 when Charles Morris Mills, an industrial counselor of the New York State Industrial Commission, asked Alex Mac[   ], a Scotch-American veteran of twenty years of work in the district, why the workers had never organized, the latter responded:

> I reckon 'cause we want this to be a white man's camp. We don't want no Bolos or I.W.W.'s or labor grafters who steal the pot before the draw. And we don't have to have no union to keep out the greasers. Why, last fall, when the coal strike was on [around Pittsburg, Kansas] some dirty Austrians and hunkies tried to work here. Before you could say Jack Robinson, there was a gang ridin' 'em out in box cars right back to Kansas.[8]

After residing in the district for three months, Mills concluded that Mac[   ] was right, "that an industrial group of 12,000 miners, absolutely American, yet completely unorganized, could exert through their very individualism a potential influence upon the industrial organization of an entire mining field."[9]

Consequently, in their search for reasons why the district was so distinctly different in resisting organization, many contributors to the *Engineering and Mining Journal* and similar professional journals (whose editors naturally found the antiunion attitudes appealing and worthy of analysis) detected a definite correlation between the Americanism practiced in the mines and mills of the Tri-State and the native-born labor force. That Americanism consisted of an amalgam of racial and regional pride, values and attitudes perceived to be uniquely American, for example, hostility to unionism, and a traditional agrarianism that was reflected in a fierce individualism and independence. The journalists concluded that this essentially white and native-born labor force with its innate intelligence somehow explained not only the great productivity of the district but also the rejection of labor organizations. Writing for the *Engineering and Mining Journal* in 1921, F. Lynwood Garrison observed that

> it is pleasant . . . to record the unusually cordial and mutually helpful relations between operators and employees. Strikes are unknown, no labor unions exist in the district, and the miners are almost wholly native-born Americans, mostly boys reared on neighboring farms. Negroes are conspicuous by their absence, and are not wanted in any capacity. Many of the operators and practically all the superintendents were just common miners, who raised themselves step by step, as an intelligent native American will do when given the opportunity, freed from the trammels of restrictive unionism and the poison of specious propaganda.[10]

Thus the crucial factor in making the Tri-State Mining District different from other hard-rock camps was the absence of a conspicuous foreign element and blacks. Because historically employers throughout the nation had singled out the foreign-born as fomentors of labor unrest, radicalism, and unionism, the absence of a "foreign element" was unusually significant. In their conviction that unions were un-American and alien to the "American" way of life, Tri-State operators were no different from their counterparts elsewhere. To serve their own antiunion purposes, they encouraged the racist and xenophobic tendencies of their workers, hoping thereby to retain a docile labor force that spurned calls for unionization. In this practice, of course, Tri-State employers were not unique.

For example, long before the great textile strike of 1929 in Gastonia, North Carolina, the mill owners there had used similar techniques to control the thousands of white,native-born farm people who had flocked into their mills and villages. The homogeneous character of the mill people, like that of the metal workers of the Tri-State, was subtly used to serve employer interests.[11]

Other observers also noted the native-born character of the Tri-State labor force and emphasized its importance in determining the fate of unionization. Malcolm Ross, a staff member of the National Labor Relations Board in the mid-1930s and one certainly sympathetic to organized labor, wrote that the Ozarks had furnished an "unfailing reservoir" of "hungry hillbillies" who retained a "passion for independence and were likely to resent unionization if it required strikes and stoppage of work."[12] Ross concluded that the independent traits of the hill people from Missouri and Arkansas had infused the mine and mill workers and had been instrumental in causing them to reject organization as the best means of protecting their interests. In 1935 in an address to the American Mining Congress, M. D. Harbaugh, secretary of the Tri-State Zinc and Lead Ore Producers' Association, pointed to the rural, Ozarkian character of Tri-State labor. Extolling the Tri-State workers as "intelligent, native white Americans—independent and generally self-reliant," Harbaugh stated that most of them were "natives of the Ozark agricultural country along the edge of which the mining district lies, and many of them still live on farms. Nearly all of them have an agricultural background which sets them apart from the typical industrial workers of many localities. No foreigners and no Negroes are employed in the industry."[13] Harbaugh believed, as did Ross, that the traits of native-born, white Ozarkian farm people characterized Tri-State labor and made it resistant to appeals for unionization. As noted, workers with antiunion bias were readily available. According to Ross, one operator had informed him that "all you have to do to get fresh miners [from the Ozarks] is to go out in the woods and blow a cowhorn."[14]

Other observers rejected as a myth the view that the Tri-State labor force was essentially Ozarkian in makeup, composed of hill people attracted to the lead and zinc fields to exploit the many opportunities there. Glenn A. Hickman, a ground boss at the Black Eagle Mine who became an active leader in organizing workers into a powerful back-to-work organization during the lead and zinc workers' strike of 1935, refuted the notion that the men in the mines and mills were mostly native-born Ozarkians. Hickman stated:

> I don't know who or what gave birth to the myth that the Tri-State lead and zinc miners were Ozarkians unless the Joplin/Webb City/Carterville area was considered to be a part of the Ozarks. It is true that the miners were an independent, individualistic people, but they did not, for the most part, come from the Ozark Mountains. And certainly they did not commute to and from mountains to the mines daily as some written accounts imply. Many did come from the farms adjacent to the mines, indeed many combined the two occupations which may have contributed to the independence and individualism of the people. Hardrock mining—coal mining, too, for that matter—historically is like any craft or trade in that it draws its personnel from within its own industry. For example, many Tri-State miners came to Webb City/Carterville from the Southeast Missouri lead mines, and as dirt from the Joplin/Webb City area diminished and mines shut down operations, miners migrated to the Picher area and from there to the hard-rock mines in the Coeur d'Alenes, Butte, Illinois, Tennessee and other mining areas. My own father . . . and uncles were among those who made the migration from Southeast Missouri to Webb City to Picher. There were many others. These were the seed miners.
>
> At the time of the 1935 strike, my crew at the Black Eagle Mining Company had some of the second and third generation miners, but probably a greater number was from the farms within an hour's commuting distance from the mine, and, of course, the two categories overlapped, some of the early miners having bought or leased farms. There were no blacks or women in the workforce. There was at that time a great deal of prejudice against blacks, so much that in Oklahoma especially, there were no black residents in the towns. There were a few black families in both the towns and rural

areas of Kansas which had no intolerant laws [against them], and even larger, more or less segregated communities of them in the Joplin area.[15]

Mills's assessment of the Tri-State miners and millmen of the twenties differed little from that of Hickman. In explaining their racial prejudice and their fear that labor organizations would cause the introduction of foreign-born workers, Mills wrote:

> The average Joplin miner is of pure American stock. Indeed, the last census [1920] revealed 94 percent American-born of American parents in the chief towns. Physically, the Joplin miner is of a superior type, tall, muscular, well-built; with good, intelligent face. He is generally recruited from rural surroundings, from the "backwoods" or "sticks" of the adjacent regions of Missouri, Kansas or Oklahoma, or the nearest mining centers. He is psychologically drawn to the mines and the slogan "Once a miner always a miner" holds true. Coming from such an environment, it is easy to understand his hatred of a "foreigner." Even people from Massachusetts and New York are classed as "foreigners." A miner told me one day he "didn't want no damned foreigner from New York poking into his business." Suspicion of the outsider, therefore, has tended to maintain an American group.[16]

Although there was some disagreement concerning the origin of Tri-State labor, there was common agreement that the native character of the mine and mill workers was the source of the antiunionism and other "Americanisms" that prevailed among them.

More objective sources confirmed the native-born character of the Tri-State population and suggested that using it to explain the district's historical antiunionism was justified. Of the 7,772 men examined at the Picher clinic during 1927–28, 99 percent were "native born Americans." Only 58 were foreign-born and only 8 were Indians. Because there were no blacks in the labor force, none were examined at the clinic.[17] The population census for 1930 also reflected the absence of a significant foreign-born element and number of blacks. Of Cherokee County's population of 31,457, only 1,061 (3 percent) were blacks.

Of 38,542 residents of Ottawa County, only 252 (.07 percent) were foreign-born whites and only 2 (.005 percent) were blacks. Only 653 blacks resided in the two counties where the mining industry had come to be centered and, as Hickman indicated, these persons lived principally in Kansas and were not involved in mining and milling. For these two counties with a combined population of 69,999, 64,928 (93 percent) were American-born whites. In Jasper and Newton counties, which had a larger combined population of 102,769, 1,166 (1 percent) were foreign-born and 1,330 (1 percent) were black. For the entire district, there were only 2,479 (1 percent) foreign-born and 1,983 (1 percent) blacks in a total population of 170,968. Throughout the district, American-born whites composed slightly less than 98 percent of the population.[18]

The religious bodies in the four counties composing the Tri-State also substantiated the strong white, native character of the population. In the mid-1930s, the district was principally a white Protestant stronghold. For example, the religious census of 1936 reported 36,369 members of religious denominations, of which 2,772 (7.6 percent) were Roman Catholic. In Ottawa and Cherokee counties, where the lead and zinc mining industry was centered, the percentage of Catholics was approximately the same, that is, 992 of the 13,062 total (7.6 percent) in the two-county area. For the entire district, the census listed only 275 Jews (.08 percent), a very small group located entirely in Jasper County. The membership in exclusively black religious denominations was also extremely small. In Ottawa County, the census showed none. Directly north in Cherokee County, it reported 93 (AME) Methodists and 171 black Baptists, a total of only 264 of the 6,451 (4 percent) church members in the county. In Jasper and Newton counties only 32 black Baptists and 14 (AME) Methodists were reported (the Baptists in Jasper and the Methodists in Newton), an extremely small percentage (.02) of the two-county total of 23,307 church members. Of the reported 36,369 members of religious bodies in the district, only 310 (.09

percent) were enrolled in black churches. Throughout the entire Tri-State, the census showed only 3,357 blacks, Roman Catholics, and Jews in a total 36,369 (approximately 9 percent) members of religious bodies.[19]

In contrast, while Baptists (Southern, Northern, and Free Will) claimed 7,656 (21 percent) members, white Methodists (Episcopal and Episcopal, South) numbered 6,601 (18 percent), the Disciples of Christ counted 6,670 (18 percent), and the Presbyterians listed 3,540 (10 percent) of the 36,369 total membership. Other white denominations (for example, the Assembly of God, the Church of the Nazarene, the Church of Christ, the Lutheran Synod of Missouri) composed the remainder of the total. With a membership of 33,002 of the 36,369 members of religious bodies in the district (91 percent), white Protestants apparently dominated its religious life.[20] Yet Charles Mills observed that although the "native religion" of the Tri-State was Protestant, the church did not seem to "draw the Miner to its membership." Of the 204 miners admitted to the "accident" hospital in Picher over a five-month period in 1920, 176 indicated that they were not church members. Mills suggested that the focus of the Protestant church on a "narrow, emotional type of old-fashioned theology instead of living and serving as the social, recreational and inspirational center" may have caused the miners' apparent disinterest in religion.[21] Even so, in religion as well as in the workplace, Roman Catholics, Jews, and blacks had an extremely low visibility, particularly in Ottawa County.

Some white Protestant ministers took pride in the "American" character of the district and undoubtedly encouraged their parishioners to have the same. In his appearance in 1940 before Secretary of Labor Frances Perkins's committee to investigate the terrible health and housing conditions in the Tri-State, the Reverend Cliff Titus, minister of the First Community Church in Joplin, stated:

We have a group of laboring men in our Tri-State district which is all American. Now we say that with no aspersion at all

on foreigners, of course, but it happens to be that the men
who work in the Tri-State area are Americans, white Americans. They have quite a tradition behind them; they are pretty
independent; they don't like to be bossed very much. They
have done pretty much as they pleased; if they didn't like the
ground boss in one mine they would go across the road and
work for a ground boss in another mine.[22]

Titus's obvious pride in the white character of the population and his apologist posture concerning the extraordinar-
ily bad social conditions among workers in the district reflected the prevailing suspicion directed toward so-called
"outsiders." Such statements from a clergyman undoubtedly helped sustain the persistent belief among Tri-Staters
that they were uniquely "American" in their values and
attitudes and that their best interest was served by dis-
couraging blacks and the foreign-born from settling in the
district. But such comments also demonstrated the similar-
ity of interests, perceptions, and viewpoints among the
leading secular and religious leaders who did not want to
undermine the status quo by allowing challenges to develop from labor unions, larger numbers of Catholics,
Jews, blacks, and the foreign-born with their contrasting
cultures.

Although the predominantly white population of the
district provided a plausible explanation for the mine and
mill workers' traditional resistance to unionism, another
explanation was equally valid to contemporaries. According to it, a major impediment to labor organization was the
reputation of the district as a "poor man's camp," a reputation based on the opportunities historically available to
workers either to lease or acquire mining property and
subsequently to move from the wage-earning into the employing class. The dozens of large and small companies
that operated in the district, many of them owned by men
who had risen from the ranks of labor, confirmed the vertical mobility at work there.

As early as 1910 in an article for the *Engineering and
Mining Journal*, Lane Carter observed that one reason for

the "satisfactory labor conditions" prevailing in the district was that many workers had acquired mining leases and become operators.[23] In an editorial five years later, the *Journal* pointed out why Tri-Staters had turned a deaf ear to organizers over the years: "This district cannot be successfully unionized, for the reason that a majority of working miners are always carrying an interest in some prospect and as soon as these prospects develop into mines the miners leave their jobs and go to work in their own diggings, thus becoming employers of labor instead of employees, under which conditions they have no use for the union."[24] The expectation of becoming an operator or an owner was judged to be sufficiently strong among the workers that they refused to accept a permanent working-class status. Writing for the *Survey* in 1921, Charles Mills observed that so many miners had become operators that that generally known fact was the "commonest reason given for non-organization." He further noted: "A miner as an employee, who sees that there is a possible and even probable chance of his becoming an employer, does not rush into a labor organization. Seemingly, economic opportunity has allowed the Joplin group to go forward unorganized."[25]

The opportunity for upward mobility effectively stunted the growth of working-class consciousness among the miners and millmen by blinding them to the commonality of their interest as opposed to those of the owners and operators. The chance to rise caused them to perceive their interests and those of the owners as mutually supportive rather than adversarial. They were not class conscious. This was particularly true of the more intelligent and ambitious element of the work force who normally provided the leadership for a union movement. Such men were anxious to improve themselves, refusing—perhaps because psychologically unable—to identify with the mass of workers to provide them with the necessary leadership to differentiate and articulate class interests. The opportunity to acquire mining leases and farm property thus produced

A panoramic view of Picher, Oklahoma, surrounded by man-
made mountains of chat. Courtesy of Dobson Memorial
Center, Miami, Oklahoma.

an upward mobility that prevented class lines from solid-
ifying, a fact that worked against unionization in the Tri-
State during the early days.

In his *Wilderness Bonanza*, Arrell M. Gibson concluded
that the chance to move up and change one's economic
status was more important in explaining "labor apathy" toward organization than the native and local character of
the labor force.[26] In a recent article, Gibson returned to
and elaborated on the theme of the "poor man's camp," the
view that the "wide range of opportunities available to
miners until recent times" was a powerful inhibitor to a

A southwest view of Picher with its moonscape of towering chat
piles as seen from the Big Chief Mine. Courtesy of Dobson
Memorial Center, Miami, Oklahoma.

permanent union movement in the Tri-State. In the early days when operations were on a small scale, according to Gibson, many miners were simultaneously both workmen and operators. Two men frequently worked as partners, one operating underground and the other remaining on the surface to hoist and process the extracted ore. The partnership sometimes included a number of miners. Some were fortunate and struck it rich; others exhausted their resources in a futile effort to do the same. Gibson noted that, yo-yo-like, "Some miners moved in and out of the operator class twenty times within their life span." He concluded, as had contemporary observers, that the easy movement from "wage earner to capitalist status account[ed] in a great measure for the lack of a vigorous labor movement in the district in the period before 1910." Even so, worker and operator organizations sporadically and temporarily appeared. But with the emergence of

larger, heavily capitalized companies, the range of opportunities for the average worker narrowed, forcing many of
them who had acquired small properties and leaseholds
back into the ranks of wage-labor as they succumbed to
more powerful competitors. Consequently, the level of
capitalization and industrialization required to extract the
deeper ores led to the inevitable demise of the Tri-State's
"poor man's camp" character.[27]

Nevertheless, the native-born character and the agrarian
attitudes of the Tri-State mine and mill workers should not
be too readily discarded as explanations for the failure of
unionism to grow, for the operators repeatedly used them
to undermine the work of union organizers and to establish and maintain the "open shop" throughout the district. Furthermore, and perhaps of greater importance, the
gradual destruction of the "poor man's camp" tradition by
the influx of heavily capitalized, industrial-type mines and
mills employing hundreds of workers did not result in a
permanent union movement before the 1930s, despite the
reduction in vertical mobility stemming from diminished
entrepreneurial opportunities. The failure of organized
labor to establish itself in the district concomitantly with
the rise of large mining and milling companies and the demise of personal opportunities to betterment there suggested that the values and attitudes of the native-born
labor force was the more important inhibitor to unionization. With a collective mind-set characterized by xeno-
phobia and fierce independence, the response of the lead
and zinc workers to the call of union organizers was usually short-lived. Not until the Great Depression when an
organizational movement emerged among them that was
compatible with their outlook was there any likelihood of
permanency in labor organizations.

Tri-State workers were hard-hit by the depression. Production had peaked in 1926 when the value of marketed
concentrates was nearly $55 million, produced by a labor
force that averaged 10,200. From 1926 to 1933, which was
the nadir year of the Great Depression, the value of output

dropped drastically to $4 million, and the number of workers, many of whom labored only part time, sank to 2,100 as the industry adjusted to shifting market trends, changing technology, and the depression. Although by 1935 production and employment had risen (the value of concentrates to $9 million and employment to 4,300), conditions remained extremely precarious for workers, especially for those employed on properties operating only part-time in response to market demands. Adding to their uncertainty were the changing personnel policies of the larger companies, such as Eagle Picher Mining and Smelting, which refused to rehire many seasoned miners and millmen because of age or alleged physical impairments. Thus scores of workers found themselves unemployable when an upturn began during 1933.[28] Forced onto direct relief, work relief, or odd jobs for reasons that they judged to be unfair, their bitterness and discontent increased the instability in the work force.

Throughout the 1930s, Tri-State mining remained unsettled. Production and wages were tied to a fluctuating market demand and the price for lead and zinc concentrates. When demand fell companies either shut down or operated part-time, dividing the available work among their employees. When prices fell, wages followed. In the autumn of 1935 common underground labor earned $2.80 and surface labor $2.50 for an eight-hour day when working. Skilled labor, such as machine men, blacksmiths, and carpenters, received $3.75 to $4.75 per day. Shovelers, who constituted the bulk of underground labor and who contracted their work on a per-can basis, received approximately $4 to $4.50 per day, depending on their rate of shoveling.[29] Shutdowns and part-time operations reduced annual incomes. The average annual income of 74 miners and millmen employed at Eagle Picher properties at Cardin, Oklahoma, was $536.58 for the three-year period of 1932 to 1934. Their average weekly wage was $10.31.[30] Such low wages and income plagued Tri-State workers during the 1930s. Furthermore, periodic shutdowns threw hundreds out of work at a time when alternative employment was nonexistent. Unemployment figures for 1937 in Ottawa and Cherokee counties, the center of the mining industry, revealed the grimness of the workers' situation. In Cherokee County, 1,321 men were out of work, 1,023 were on work relief, and 719 worked part-time. Directly south in Ottawa County, 1,469 workers were jobless, 608 were on work relief, and 737 had partial employment.[31] Ironically, an estimated six thousand men then worked in the mines and mills, the largest number for any year between 1931 and 1939. Yet, as with workers elsewhere in the nation during the decade, unemployment was a constant threat, generating anxiety and apprehension about the future.

The depression accentuated other long-standing problems of the working class in the Tri-State. In 1935 the Kansas Commissioner of Labor and Industry reported that the majority of miners in the Kansas portion of the Picher field occupied "entirely inadequate and substandard living quarters."[32] That same year in a speech to the Metal Mining Convention, M. D. Harbaugh, secretary of the producers' association, stated that "living conditions in some parts of the mining field are far from satisfactory." He was quick to disclaim company responsibility for the pathetic state of housing. Poor roads, a desire for proximity to jobs, a boomtown mentality, company and Indian ownership of homesites, the temporary nature and primacy of mining—all were used by Harbaugh to explain why substantial numbers of lead and zinc workers and their families lived in deplorable housing.[33]

Four years later, after surveying thousands of homes in thirteen mining communities throughout the district, the Tri-State Survey Committee, a New York-based group interested in improving the social and economic welfare of Tri-State workers and their families, reported that "the chance is two-to-one that any particular miner lives in a house not fit for [human] habitation." Such housing was said to have "characterized the Tri-State mining communities from the beginning" and was not attributable to the depression. An investigator for the committee observed 4,867 houses in the thirteen mining towns—eight in Oklahoma (Picher, Commerce, Cardin, Hockerville, Douthat, North Miami, Quapaw, and Zincville), three in Kansas (Treece, Galena, and Empire), and two in Missouri (Chatwood and Smelter Hill). Of the 4,867 houses, 3,541 were classified as "unfit for habitation." Some 1,785 of the total had had "makeshift repairs," that is, broken windows covered with tin sheets or boards, and roofs and walls mended with tar-paper. In addition, 1,754 houses had "visible holes in the walls or roof" and broken windows stuffed with rags.[34] When made public, the report of the Tri-State Survey Committee focused national attention on the social conditions in the district. It also sparked rebuttals.

When Glenn A. Hickman, who in 1939 was a public relations officer for the Eagle Picher companies, heard that newscaster Walter Winchell was planning an exposé of the conditions in the Tri-State, he contacted Quentin Reynolds, a writer for various national magazines, and asked that he inform Winchell about his (Reynolds's) observations made during a recent visit to the district. Hickman wrote:

> If your notes indicate it, I would like you to point out to Mr. Winchell that no one who works in the mines or mills for a living is compelled to live within miles of any chat piles, but does so by choice and convenience because it is close to his job. As you noticed, there is plenty of room in the towns of Commerce, Miami, Baxter Springs, Joplin and many others. You visited Mrs. Hickman and me in our 5-room, modern home in Baxter Springs. You saw hundreds more of these homes equally good or better which have been bought or rented by my friends and neighbors who work at every job the mines have to offer. These homes sell for from $1,000 to $2,000; not too much money for the average miner who makes around $30 per week to pay. They can be bought on most any reasonable terms proposed by the purchaser, or they can be rented for from $15 to $20 per month.[35]

In his testimony before Secretary of Labor Perkins's committee, the Reverend Titus indicated that Tri-State workers who lived in substantard housing did so by choice. In his opinion:

> Most of them [the workers] own automobiles of some character. They could live, if they wanted to, in some town; they might live in Baxter Springs, in Joplin, or Miami, or some place else. Most of them prefer to live down close to the mines, near the chat piles, because they would rather spend their money for something else.
>
> They are not so much concerned about owning a house or renting a home that might furnish a lot of conveniences. Most of them live where they do because they want to live there.[36]

Nevertheless, as early as the 1920s observers had noted the poor state of housing in the district and the possible adverse effect it had on the health of workers and their families. For example, during 1927 and 1928 doctors at the Picher clinic, while examining 7,782 men, discovered that 75 percent of them slept in rooms with at least one other person, 20 percent in rooms shared by two others, and 10 percent slept in a room with more than three persons.[37] These figures suggested that overcrowding further complicated the medical problems of silicosis and tuberculosis, which plagued the district.

Substandard housing and unemployment exacerbated deep-rooted health problems of the Tri-State. Silicosis, a debilitating occupational disease commonly called "miners' con" or "miners' consumption," was rampant, predisposing workers and their families to more dangerous threats from diseases such as tuberculosis. In 1914 the United States Bureau of Mines and the United States Public Health Service began more than two decades of investigating and reporting about silicosis and tuberculosis in the district. Their comprehensive study during 1914–15 revealed 433 silicotics among the 720 miners who were examined in the Joplin area, then the center of mining activity. Of the silicotic cases, 103 were complicated by the onset of tuberculosis. Another 39 of the 720 miners had tuberculosis without other pulmonary complications.[38]

In 1927 the United States Bureau of Mines, the Metropolitan Life Insurance Company, and the Tri-State Zinc and Lead Ore Producers' Association established a clinic at Picher, Oklahoma, to develop diagnostic methods for silicosis and to educate workers and industry how to prevent and combat the disease. For five years (1927 to 1932), companies belonging to the producers' association required thousands of their employees to visit the clinic for examinations. The results revealed a labor force riddled with silicosis and tuberculosis. As part of this extended study, in 1929 clinic doctors carefully examined 8,853 men (5,114 employed in the mines, 3,739 unemployed). Among the 8,853 were found 1,557 silicotics, of whom 1,116 worked in the mines. The physical examinations also discovered 220 individuals who had silicosis complicated by tuberculosis, 138 of whom worked in the mines, and another 121 men who had uncomplicated tuberculosis, of whom 46 were employed in the mines.[39] Reporting in 1938 on the full five-year study, Dr. R. R. Sayers indicated that "of the 27,553 individuals examined, 5,366 had silicosis, 742 had silicosis plus tuberculosis, and 320 had uncomplicated tuberculosis." The study revealed a definite relationship between work in the mines, poor housing, and the massive health problems of the district.[40]

Although the larger companies attempted to reduce the dust in their mines, which was recognized as the major causative factor, there was evidence as late as 1937 that these efforts were less than vigorous.[41] So extensive, persistent, and devastating were the problems of disease, housing, and working conditions in the Tri-State that Secretary of Labor Frances Perkins called and presided over a conference in Joplin, Missouri, on April 23, 1940 to consider possible solutions.[42]

Tri-State workers emerged from the disastrous winter of 1932–33, the nadir of the Great Depression, unorganized and without their own organization to address the staggering problems that engulfed them—massive unemployment, low and uncertain wages and annual incomes, hazardous and unhealthy working conditions, poor housing, and widespread, chronic disease. Because the district was situated within several political jurisdictions (three states, four counties, and approximately a dozen towns), there was no single, responsible agency with district-wide authority to act in their behalf. Silicosis and tuberculosis, for example, were problems that required a district-wide solution. Instead, scattered jurisdictions fragmented the effort to control, treat, and eradicate the diseases. Although the Tri-State Zinc and Lead Ore Producers' Association had made commendable contributions toward the research of silicosis and tuberculosis through the Picher clinic, and although it hired a visiting nurse whose services were available to the employees and their families, as an employers' association its primary concern was understandably not public health. Thus the lack of a strong labor organization committed to the rights and interests of workers left them voiceless and powerless to confront the numerous companies and jurisdictions whose actions and inaction impinged on their lives. Once again, therefore, the leadership of the International Union of Mine, Mill, and Smelter Workers turned to the Tri-State where adverse social and economic conditions had persuaded hundreds of workers that they must organize in order to reshape and improve the environment in which they lived.

2

"Strike Until You Whip Hell Out of This Bunch"

In the early thirties, the Tri-State District was fertile ground for an imaginative labor organizer. For years the seeds of discontent had been sown throughout the district, causing hundreds of miners and mill workers to be more disposed toward unionization than in the past. Diminishing opportunities for advancement, abominable housing for scores of families, chronic health problems of silicosis and tuberculosis that afflicted hundreds of workers, widespread unemployment, a gnawing insecurity about jobs among those fortunate to have work—all had been exacerbated by the onslaught of a nationwide depression. As a consequence, among the lead and zinc workers there developed a festering, generalized hostility, waiting to be mobilized and directed against whomever or whatever was thought to be responsible for the troubles of the district. Even before an organizer of the International Union of Mine, Mill, and Smelter Workers arrived in the fall of 1933, unemployed miners had begun to articulate their discontent and to focus on the Picher clinic as the cause of their troubles.

That they should do so was ironic, for the clinic had been founded to help erase a chronic, disabling disease that ravaged their ranks. When physicians arrived in the district in 1914 to conduct the first studies on silicosis, they found it necessary to organize the Joplin operators into the Southwestern Missouri Mine and Safety Association to facilitate the medical research. When the studies ended, the association died. In 1924, however, the district operators organized a new association, the Tri-State Zinc and Lead Ore Producers' Association, primarily to protect and ex-

tend their interests. Nevertheless, it was this association
that entered into the agreement with the United States Bureau of Mines and the Metropolitan Life Insurance Company to establish a medical clinic at Picher in 1927 to facilitate a five-year research program designed to improve
diagnostic techniques and to educate workers and operators about silicosis and its prevention. To assist the research, corporate members of the zinc and lead producers
required that their employees be examined at the clinic.
The families of workers were also eligible to receive free
physical examinations.[1]

The medical research, which uncovered hundreds of
cases of silicosis and tuberculosis in various stages, did not
endear either the clinic or the association to scores of Tri-
State workers. If either silicosis, tuberculosis, or silicosis
complicated by tuberculosis was found, the worker was denied further employment in the mines or smelters of the
association's members. Nonmember mines and mills would
sometimes hire these "unemployables," who then continued working until totally disabled. Furthermore, the
clinic's physical examination included tests for venereal
diseases. If the tests revealed syphilis or gonorrhea—diseases that often flourished in many mining camps where
prostitutes served lonely men—the worker was also denied
employment at member companies. Unlike silicosis, venereal disease was not an industrial malady; however, if left
untreated it could incapacitate or kill. As an assistant personnel manager for the Eagle Picher companies in the late
thirties, Glenn Hickman recalled that many men were refused employment when clinic tests revealed active syphilis
or gonorrhea. Based on his experience with employment
applications and clinic reports, Hickman remembered the
incident rate of venereal disease as high. But because Oklahoma, unlike Kansas, did not begin collecting county statistics on venereal disease until 1953, it is impossible to be
precise about its prevalence throughout the Tri-State for
the thirties. Furthermore, because some miners were aggressive in initiating compensation litigation for alleged injuries in the mines, Tri-State operators refused to employ

a worker whose examination showed, for example, a hernia or any abnormality of the spine. They rejected such men rather than incur the risk of future lawsuits for compensation claims.[2]

As a consequence of the clinical examinations, from 1927 until the Great Depression a backlog of partially disabled unemployables accumulated in the district. Meanwhile, a stream of healthy young men entered the mines, usually to work as unskilled shovelers who loaded ore buckets—the dustiest, most unhealthy job in the mine for contracting silicosis, only to leave short years later broken in health and unable to work. One author referred to the numbers afflicted with silicosis as the "hordes of unemployables," as a "vast army" without hope of work in the principal industry of the district.[3] Many men, who in the early stages of the disease retained sufficient strength to work in the mines, became embittered at being excluded from a livelihood. They blamed the clinic, which they perceived as a tool of the member companies, and they blamed the operators for their disabled condition. Hickman, in 1935 a ground boss at the Black Eagle Mine, recalled that to make the operators and the labor force aware of the "great health hazards" involved in mining,

> it was necessary for the clinic to detect through X-ray and weed out those miners already affected with silicosis, the precursor to tuberculosis. One of the tragedies of this development was that with loss of jobs there was no compensation because no legal liability existed where hardly any miner worked in a single mine or for a single employer long enough to establish total responsibility for contraction of the disease. Of course this led to dissatisfaction and was a contributing factor to the organization and early success of the International Union.[4]

Hickman also remembered that great dissatisfaction was generated among those workers with other medical problems such as hernias and back conditions who were denied employment because the operators feared possible compensation suits. "This was hard to take by those miners who were self-respecting and not malingerers," recalled

Hickman. "They knew there would be no false injury claims, but the employers did not know and would take no chances."[5] Before the Great Depression, therefore, the diagnostic work of the Picher clinic, which had been initiated to find a solution to silicosis and related occupational diseases affecting workers, had generated a reservoir of bitterness among those Tri-Staters forced into unemployment because of the clinic's adverse medical findings and the operators' fear of compensation suits.

As the depression deepened, an increasing number of healthy workmen joined the medical "misfits" in the ranks of the unemployed. Those men fortunate enough to retain their jobs labored on the edge of uncertainty, for their job security was nil. The price of ore concentrates—on which wages were based—dropped to new lows, while the erratic market demand for concentrates made sustained, high-level production impossible. One might be working today and laid off tomorrow. Despite such circumstances, jobs in the industry were highly prized and sought after because there were few alternative sources of employment even after the start of Roosevelt's New Deal. Exploiting the district's labor surplus and the desperate need for jobs, some ground bosses exacted a price for the opportunity to work. In interviews conducted in the 1950s with workmen of the district during the early thirties, William J. Cassidy found that in order to hold their jobs, "some of them" were forced to pay a kickback to the ground boss.[6] With wages in some mines as low as a dollar a day in 1932, such a practice produced increasing hardship and bitterness among the workers involved. How widespread the practice of kickbacks was remains uncertain, but before the 1933 organizational drive of the International Union of Mine, Mill, and Smelter Workers, it was another hateful grievance that inclined an undetermined number of workers toward unionization.

Under such circumstances in June 1933, Congress passed the National Industrial Recovery Act, which reactivated labor's organizing efforts in the Tri-State. The purpose of the law was to stimulate economic recovery by allowing business and industrial leaders a free hand in forming self-governing codes of fair competition for their industries without fear of prosecution under federal antitrust laws. Because of the increased power that naturally accrued to business as a result of legitimizing industrial self-governance, Congress provided workers with certain safeguards that were embodied in Section 7(a) of the law. Under this provision, Congress recognized the right of workers to organize and engage in collective bargaining. Labor leaders, interpreting Section 7(a) to mean federal encouragement to form unions and protection for them, rapidly moved to organize nonunion workers wherever found.

In the fall of 1933, the International Union sent Roy A. Brady, an intelligent and young outsider, into the Tri-State to organize the metal workers. A persuasive opportunist whose abilities won the grudging respect even of the operators, Brady skillfully exploited the workers' specific grievances and general discontent, nudging hundreds of them to accept unionism as the panacea for their problems. He organized anyone who would listen—miners, smeltermen, retail clerks, relief workers, women, and the unemployed. To the disaffected his arguments were powerful, convincing, and hopeful. He told them the National Industrial Recovery Act *required* that workers join unions. President Roosevelt wanted them to organize and engage in collective bargaining to assure general recovery and their own economic salvation. Organizing would improve their wages and give them more work hours. Working and living conditions would improve. The mine operators' Picher clinic would be closed. The workers could recover the wages lost when the work week was reduced to five days (estimated at as much as one million dollars), and the Act would bring about the enactment of effective mine safety laws. Failure to join the union, however, would result in exclusion from jobs when the International Union established the closed shop, and the union would prevent

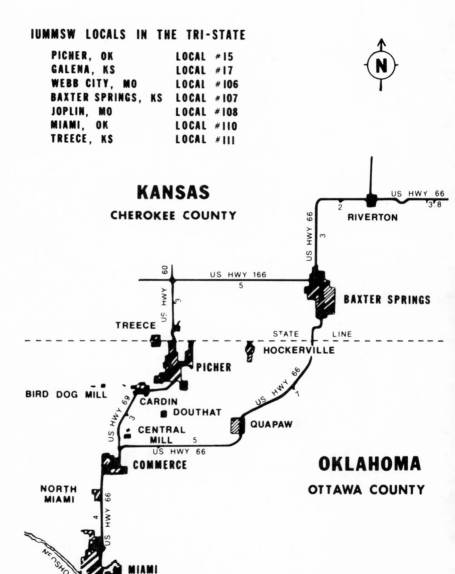

IUMMSW LOCALS IN THE TRI-STATE

PICHER, OK	LOCAL #15
GALENA, KS	LOCAL #17
WEBB CITY, MO	LOCAL #106
BAXTER SPRINGS, KS	LOCAL #107
JOPLIN, MO	LOCAL #108
MIAMI, OK	LOCAL #110
TREECE, KS	LOCAL #111

N

KANSAS
CHEROKEE COUNTY

US HWY 66
RIVERTON
2   3.8

US HWY 66
3

US HWY 166
60   5

US HWY 3

BAXTER SPRINGS

TREECE

STATE LINE

HOCKERVILLE

PICHER

US HWY 66
7

BIRD DOG MILL

US HWY 69
3

CARDIN
DOUTHAT

QUAPAW

CENTRAL
MILL   5
US HWY 66

COMMERCE

OKLAHOMA
OTTAWA COUNTY

NORTH
MIAMI

US HWY 66
4

NEOSHO RIVER

MIAMI

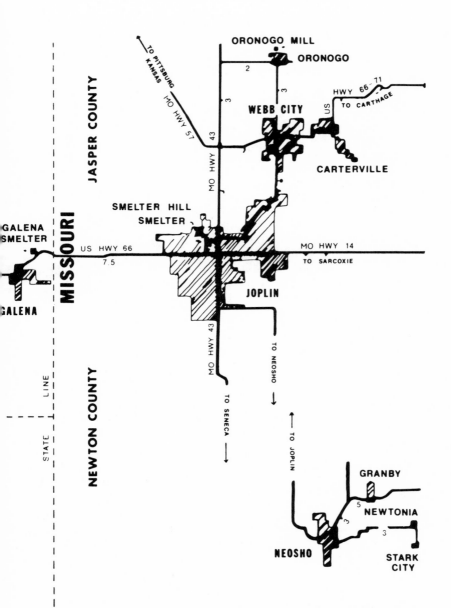

Tri-State Mining District with locations of union locals of the
International Union of Mine, Mill, and Smelter Workers. Map
adapted from William James Cassidy, "The Tri-State Zinc-Lead
Mining District," p. 4.

the operators, in collusion with local newspapers, from de-
ceiving the workers concerning the price of ore concentrates on which their wages were based.

Furthermore, according to one unfriendly observer,
Brady and his associates

> brought into the district as speakers, radical labor leaders, in-
> cluding some who many years ago helped deprive the miners
> of the Kansas coal fields of their jobs. Other outsiders of red
> stripe contributed their bit to inflaming the men—and their
> women, too—in the holy war of labor against capital. They
> wrote for the radical press of the country, and in some cases
> the material was gullibly printed by the more respectable
> press, depicting horrible working conditions in the mines,
> pitiful wages, and informing the world that the men lived only
> five years after starting to work in the mines and that they
> died by the hundreds of lead poisoning contracted there.[7]

By using such arguments and tactics, Brady played upon
the fears, the raw nerves, and the aspirations of hundreds
of Tri-Staters who, convinced, flocked to organize until
"there was a union for nearly everyone in the district."

After the outbreak of labor trouble in May 1935, however, the size of union membership in proportion to the
working labor force of the district became a disputed matter when the operators questioned the legitimacy of the
International Union's claim to represent the workers. In
these claims and counterclaims, precise figures were never
used, only vague estimates and impressions.[8] Addressing
the American Mining Congress in September 1935, M. D.
Harbaugh estimated that "at one time or another, a considerable proportion of the men actually employed in
the mines and mills did join the union and pay dues for
awhile."[9] Arrell M. Gibson, a historian of the Tri-State,
placed the International Union's membership at four thousand.[10] Malcolm A. Ross, a staff member of the National
Labor Relations Board's regional office in Kansas City, Missouri, who was familiar with the district's labor situation,
estimated union membership at five thousand.[11] C. A. Million, secretary of District 4 of the International Union,
claimed that "more than 51 percent of all mine, mill and

smelter workers in the Tri-State district" were members in May 1935.[12] Membership requirements, however, were not stringent because of the depression, and the operators were convinced that the "large ranks of the union were filled by the unemployed who were hoping that the promise of jobs would materialize."[13] Furthermore, within the union itself the exact membership status of unemployed members and others who were unable to pay their dues was uncertain. However viewed, the number of temporary or permanent workers who were members of the International Union was generally recognized as significant relative to the estimated forty-eight hundred men working in the mines and mills in May 1935.

For nearly two years Brady labored in the Tri-State, trying to build vigorous and assertive locals. When it seemed that the union was on the verge of demonstrable power, it suffered a serious blow, administered not by the mine operators but by Brady himself. For whatever reason, Brady, who had been a conspicuous figure at the union convention of 1934, endangered the future of his union in the district by absconding with organizational funds. Tried by Picher Local 15 for his indiscretion, Brady was ousted, an action concurred in by the executive board of the parent union.[14] Only the arrival of Thomas H. Brown, president of the union, salvaged the situation. By the spring of 1935, the union, although tarnished in reputation, was back in business in the Tri-State. Ably assisted by local leaders like Bert Carpenter, who had helped to organize Picher Local 15, and Sylvan Bruner, a sympathetic attorney, Brown helped to restore and organize six other locals. These were located at Miami (No. 110), Galena (No. 17), Treece (No. 111), Baxter Springs (No. 107), Webb City (No. 106), and Joplin (No. 108).

Surprisingly, Tri-State operators made little effort to counter the union's organizing efforts. Expecting the union's campaign to founder in the quagmire of the district's historical indifference or hostility toward unionism, they displayed little concern as the miners and millmen joined the union locals. With hundreds of unemployed men desperate for work, they were confident of their ability to retain the open shop. Concluding that the union did not immediately threaten their interests, they conceded their employees' legal right to form or join whatever organization they wished. Thus the operators met the organizing campaign with a strategy of superficial tolerance, but one that would prevent permanent union footholds in the district. This strategy was based on the strong conviction that the levers of power were firmly in their hands. Not until directly challenged would they use that power.

The union's initial challenge was to encourage its new members to initiate lawsuits for work-related injuries or illnesses. Attorneys Louis Wolf and Sylvan Bruner usually represented union members in these compensation cases. The larger companies viewed this stepped-up litigation as a form of harassment and, when possible, made out-of-court settlements as cheaply as possible to rid themselves of the nuisance. According to one observer, since 1919 the Eagle Picher companies had been self-insurers in compensation matters and had tried to reduce the number of damage suits by establishing a "well-organized department for treatment, ambulance transportation, hospitalization, investigation, legal defense and plain settlement of injury cases, along with an equally well-organized safety program for prevention of both accidental injury and disease."[15] For Eagle Picher the increase in union-sponsored compensation suits was but a form of harassment. Other companies, however, had not taken comparable steps to manage the litigation threat. Before the formation of the union locals, these companies had been financially protected by the reluctance of employees to resort to the courts to obtain compensation for injuries and illness. For example, Glenn Hickman, a ground boss in May, 1935, at the Black Eagle Mine, did not recall that injury claims had been a "burden" to his company, and he was "certain" that "there was no disease-related damage suits . . . , in spite of the fact that several of the crew members, some of them close friends, later died of silico-tuberculosis as a result of years of exposure to dust and to concomitant infection."[16] Even so, the union practice of encouraging compensation suits caused some operators to either discharge or threaten to fire any worker who joined the union.[17] When firings or intimidation occurred, the union charged discrimination.

The union's challenges to discriminating practices began as early as May 1934. In a letter of May 5 to the manager of Eagle Picher Lead Company's Joplin smelter, officials of Local 15 complained about discrimination against union members only to be informed that although the company would deal individually or collectively with its employees about such matters, it was determined to operate the smelter on an open-shop basis without third-party interference. It would not negotiate with the union about its charge of discrimination.[18] As early as February 1935, officials of the Eagle Picher Mining and Smelting Company, a subsidiary of Eagle Picher Lead Company, refused to discuss with a union committee the matter of union recognition and collective bargaining at its Galena smelter where an estimated 80 to 90 percent of the workers belonged to Local 17. Although expressing a willingness to meet with individual employees or their representatives, officials of Eagle Picher Mining and Smelting refused to negotiate with union delegates because they were not the "duly accredited" spokesmen for the smelter workers. Like its parent company, the subsidiary stood squarely behind the open shop.[19] Unable to crack the intransigence of Eagle Picher, whose companies dominated the district, union leaders were forced to reconsider their strategy of seeking piecemeal resolution of problems and union recognition in those mines and mills where they had substantial strength. That strategy had obviously failed.

At a joint conference of leaders from six local unions held in early March 1935, a new approach was devised that the rank and file subsequently approved. In a letter of March 13 to all the operators, the union formally proposed that there be created two negotiating committees—one representing the local unions, the other the operators—which would meet "for the purpose of reaching an agreement by collective bargaining; said agreement when arrived at to be

signed by parties of interest for a definite period of time."[20]
Possibly because of the manner in which the proposal was
presented (a letter written in pencil requesting a response
within a week), the operators ignored it. Furthermore, the
large number of companies with conflicting interests operating in the district made unlikely a quick and favorable
response. The operators also were confident that the majority of their employees were ignorant of the proposal.
Consequently, this new initiative, which reflected the union's
groping for a way to exercise its members' right of collective
bargaining provided under Section 7(a) of the National Industrial Recovery Act, conspicuously failed. As of April
1935, the Tri-State companies, such as Eagle Picher, maintained an official open-shop policy and refused to recognize
the union as the official spokesman of the workers.

Upon his arrival in April to direct the organizational
drive after the Brady fiasco, Thomas H. Brown found
the rank and file growing restless. After nearly two years
of organizational work in the district following the enactment of the Industrial Recovery Act, the union had gained
nothing for its members, not even the recognition of the
union as their bargaining agent in the Joplin and Galena
smelters where union strength was substantial. Nor had
the union mustered sufficient power to convince the operators that their interests and the welfare of the district
necessitated a response other than indifference or con-
tempt. The growing frustration of the membership over
the discrepancy between what the union had promised
and what it had delivered forced Brown to search for a
more effective method of dealing with the operators. One
had to be found or the district locals would disintegrate.

Devising such a strategy was difficult because more than
fifty widely scattered companies operated in the Tri-State.
It was for this reason that Brown, J. A. Long, president of
District 4, and local union leaders decided to approach the
ore producers' association, whose membership included
most of the mine, mill, and smelter companies. The Tri-
State Ore Producers' Association had long been recognized as the voice of the owners and operators. Union

leaders hoped, perhaps naively, that within the framework of Section 7(a) of the new law, the producers' association would recognize the union as the legitimate spokesman for all the workers and that representatives from the two organizations could then negotiate a collective bargaining agreement concerning wages, hours, and working conditions for the entire district. If successful, this strategy would simplify the recognition problem and make the union a partner of the association in determining working conditions throughout the Tri-State.[21]

The association, however, also ignored the union's request for a conference on the grounds that its function was to market ore concentrates, not to negotiate working conditions for its corporate members over which it had no authority. It could not recognize the union; it could not negotiate contracts; it could not dictate to its members. Each company was free to decide its own labor policy.[22] Thus Brown's expectation that the union and the association would respectively represent the workers and the operators was not realized. Once more union leaders found it necessary to search for a new approach to exercise their right to engage in collective bargaining.

They now turned to the United States Department of Labor's Conciliation Service, which sent W. H. Rodgers into the district. As reported in the *Citizen and Herald* (Baxter Springs, Kansas), Rodgers was no more successful than union leaders in persuading the operators to meet with representatives of the union. Unable to overcome the intransigence of the operators and convinced that his mission had failed, Rodgers returned to Washington without conferring with Brown and local labor leaders.[23]

The operators' hard stance transformed the issue from one of union recognition and collective bargaining to that of the union's survival in the district. Without discernible progress in bringing the operators to the bargaining table to negotiate the grievances they had been articulating for months, union leaders became increasingly concerned about the loss of credibility among the workers and about the possible disintegration of the locals that they had

worked so hard to establish. Having exhausted all reasonable means for exercising the right of collective bargaining
embodied in the new law, union president Brown was
forced to consider a strike against the mining and milling
companies. Consequently, during a conference with local
and District 4 leaders, he reviewed all their efforts to obtain recognition for the union and the implications of their
failure to acquire it. From the ensuing discussion, they
concluded that the operators would never voluntarily aban-
don the open shop and extend recognition to the union as
the exclusive bargaining agent of the mine and mill workers. To obtain that recognition would require more than
persuasive arguments or appeals to the law. Reluctantly,
therefore, Brown and his colleagues considered a shutdown of the district. Although the time was not propitious
for a successful strike, they decided to recommend it to the
membership as the only means of forcing the operators to
recognize the mine and mill workers' union and to enter
into collective bargaining with its officials.

During the last week in April 1935, Brown and his associates met with the locals and recounted their failures to
obtain union recognition. They explained why a shutdown
of the district was imperative if their union was to have a
voice in resolving the problems that plagued the Tri-State.
Following these talks, strike votes were taken. With approximately seven hundred members of the union participating, nearly six hundred (86 percent) endorsed the
recommendation to strike.[24] Unfortunately, however, less
than 15 percent of the 4,800 active workers in the mines
and mills voted on the strike question. Opponents of the
shutdown later pointed to this small percentage of the
total work force as evidence that the majority of Tri-State
workers had had no voice in the decision to strike, and
they charged that it was therefore the handiwork of a
minority that did not represent the sentiments of the majority. They also claimed that among those voting in the
union halls were the unemployed and the "unemployables," who had nothing to lose from shutting down the
mines and mills. Nevertheless, even if the union leaders

had been so inclined, there was no practical way to poll all the workers on the strike issue. Furthermore, in the absence of such a poll, the allegations of the operators and their supporters carried no more weight than the union's assertions to the contrary. Unquestionably, the charge of union and minority manipulation of the strike vote seriously undermined the integrity of the walkout.

The union leadership scheduled the strike for midnight of May 8, 1935. During the morning and early after-noon of that day, union leaders notified the officials of the Eagle Picher Lead Company, the Eagle Picher Mining and Smelting Company, the Commerce Mining and Royalty Company, and other large properties of the impending shutdown, allowing them sufficient time to close down operations in order to prevent damage to the mines, mills, and equipment. They offered to provide night watchmen to protect the properties from damage, and they agreed to allow the continued pumping of watered mines. That evening union officials met with their members and supporters in Joplin, Baxter Springs, Treece, Miami, Webb City, and Picher to instruct them how to set up and maintain peaceful picket lines around the mines and mills. A throng estimated at two thousand gathered at Picher to hear Brown and Long, while another crowd of nearly three hundred met at Joplin to hear C. A. Million, secretary of District 4, exhort Eagle Picher workers to walk out at midnight. Explaining why the shutdown was necessary and pleading that it be kept peaceful, they called for the support of all metal workers in the district.[25] From their actions and statements, it was clear that the union officials recognized that preventing violence and destruction of property was essential for success against the companies.

With unemployment so widespread, the wisdom of the strike was immediately questioned throughout the Tri-State. But Brown, Long, and others had reluctantly concluded that although the larger companies, such as the Eagle Picher companies and the Commerce Company (representing "approximately 75% of the production of the District") would deal with their employees as "employees,"[26] they would never negotiate with the union spokesmen. Under their open-shop policy, these companies had consistently rejected negotiating with union representatives about workers' problems. The smaller operations had fallen in line with this adamant antiunion stance. Consequently, in addressing the throng at Picher on the evening of May 8, Long emphasized that the operators' refusal to negotiate with union representatives was the major cause of the strike. He stated that the "operators [had] ignored all attempts of the union to negotiate for collective bargaining, and establishing industrial relations between employer and employee provided under [the] NRA [National Recovery Administration]." A strike had not been called until all reasonable means of obtaining union recognition had been exhausted. He insisted that recognition was a necessary first step toward collective bargaining, which was labor's right under the National Industrial Recovery Act. In addition, Long explained that the union was seeking "better working conditions, a shorter work week and adherence to American standards of a living wage."[27] Although a strike was regrettable, it had occurred because of the operators' obstinacy.

Some operators expressed surprise at the strike and in their public statements and private correspondence, they blamed it on the union's leadership and absolved themselves of any responsibility. They alleged that union leaders had failed to inform them about the size of their membership, failed to have their organization properly designated the exclusive bargaining agent of the workers, and failed to present any complaints from the miners and millmen concerning wages, hours, and working conditions. They insisted that "there was no controversy between employers and their employees, and there was no known violation of Section 7(a) of the NIRA."[28]

In addressing the annual convention of the Western Division of the American Mining Congress in Saint Louis on September 25, M. D. Harbaugh blamed the strike directly on the irresponsibility of union leaders when he stated:

> This [strike], an offspring of disordered minds dragging cred-
> ulous men into a maelstrom of trouble out of which they were
> somehow led to believe they would be delivered into the prom-
> ised land, left its victims, as usual, stripped by the storm. They
> were deserted by the leaders who got them into the mess, and
> who then advised them . . . "to stay out on strike until you
> whip hell out of this bunch."[29]

Harbaugh further charged that union leaders had called
the strike in order "to 'save face' after so many vain
promises to union members had begun to pall upon them.
Then, after the strike was in effect and proved to be a serious mistake, there was no face-saving move which could
be made by the union officials to call it off, and so on it
goes—*ad infinitum*."[30] Harbaugh's statement undoubtedly
represented the official view of the major operators whose
refusal to budge from their open-shop stance had precipi-
tated the strike.

The operators also described the strike as the work of an
oppressive minority. Writing to Governor Alfred M. Landon of Kansas on July 15, 1935, F. J. Cuddeback, a mining
engineer who opposed the strike, voiced the operators'
view when he stated that "this strike was obviously forced
upon the laborers and operators by a minority which in-
cludes union organizers, relief workers, mine workers of
the radical and lower element, a few misled miners who
have held on until it is difficult to back out, and many local
would be politicians who could gain power in no other
way."[31] Cuddeback was convinced that the strike had been
"caused directly by the New Deal relief and labor policies,"
which forced men and women in need of relief to join the
union in order to get it. Such policies and the "lies by
union leaders created a situation [in the district] in which
hundreds of men were literally forced to join [the union
and its strike] against their better judgment and in spite of
the evident radical leadership."[32]

In the opinion of the operators and their supporters like
Harbaugh and Cuddeback, labor relations in the district
had been ideal—even democratic—because management's

doors were always open to the workers. Furthermore, the mines and mills had been running; men had been working when jobs were unusually scarce; the strike under the circumstances was foolish, unjustified, and irresponsible. Consequently, they did not intend to surrender their control of the district, a control they considered benevolent, to the union, which they believed was directed by "radicals" and "reds." Their interests and those of the district were at stake and they were determined to defend them.[33]

Thus the stage was set in the Tri-State for another of the no-holds-barred clashes between capital and labor that marked the 1930s. As in so many instances, organized labor had been maneuvered into a position where, whether wise or not, the strike was its only means to gain rights guaranteed by law. As Malcolm Ross later wrote in *Death of a Yale Man*, the "economic circumstances had ripened the area [the Tri-State Mining District] for a knockdown-dragout fight, one in which the miners were willing to make sacrifices for a dimly envisaged heaven of more wages, better hours, fresher eggs, sturdier kids, better rooms, more cigarettes, the jingle of spendable cash."[34] Standing between the workers and these goals were the mining and milling companies whose officials saw no reason why the union should be permitted to intrude into their affairs and those of the district. They now became determined to do whatever was necessary to expel the union and retain control.

Warned of the impending strike, officials of the larger companies began shutting down operations several hours before midnight. The Eagle Picher companies reported that many of their employees, unaware of the strike, showed up as usual for the morning shift of May 9. They were, however, halted by a

> band of approximately two hundred armed men recruited by the [union] from the coal fields of Kansas, the pool halls of the Tri-State District, unemployed WPA workers and loafers generally, including only a small sprinkling of employees of [Eagle Picher] and other operators in the District. . . . [The] band went from place to place and plant to plant and mine to

mine throughout the Tri-State District and by force and threat prevented the men from going to work where plants had resumed operations by full crews, [and] forced such plants to suspend such operation under threats of physical violence.[35]

One such plant was Eagle Picher Mining and Smelting Company's recently opened Central Mill at Cardin, Oklahoma, which shut down when Ottawa County Sheriff Eli Dry was unable to disperse a band of strikers who had successfully blocked Oklahoma Highway 6 into the property. An estimated one thousand miners lined the road between Commerce and Cardin to enforce the strike, spreading their ranks for a mile along either side of the highway.[36] Another property was the Ballard Mill of the Saint Louis Smelting and Refining Company near Baxter Springs, Kansas, that closed when Cherokee County Sheriff Dave Hasenplaugh was unable to disperse a band of strikers at the entrance to the mill.

According to F. W. Gooch, an official of the Evans-Wallower Company who claimed not to have been notified of the strike:

> A large group of men (one hundred or more), more than 95% of whom were absolute strangers to me, visited our plants and ordered us to shut our plants down, stating there was a strike on. These men did not state who they represented, nor give any reason for closing our plants except that there was a strike. We had not been notified by any of our employees or by any organization that there was any kind of organization representing our employees, nor had any demand of any kind whatsoever been made to our company. To avoid any violence or trouble of any nature we did close our plants as per their orders.[37]

Gooch asserted that throughout May his company's plants remained closed, even though he had not received any demands from either employees or any organization claiming to represent them.

The union's tactics produced confusion among many operators who, like Gooch, claimed to have had no formal contact with the union and among operators whose men,

like the workers at some Eagle Picher properties, claimed
to be ignorant of the strike. Hearing that a strike had been
called, some operators closed their properties only to have
a large percentage of their work force, apparently unaware that a strike was in progress, report for the morning
shift on May 9. In some mines and mills where crews reported as usual, operations continued until a throng of
strikers arrived and demanded that they be shut down.
Thus roving bands of union members, alleged by some of
the operators to be nothing more than "armed mobs" of
outsiders and reliefers, halted operations throughout the
Tri-State District.

During the next three weeks, production reached the
lowest levels ever recorded in the district. When the strike
began, fifty-four mines, mills, and tailing plants were operating, employing approximately forty-eight hundred men.
Before the end of May 9, work stopped on all these properties except for several of the smallest located in Missouri.
It was the "first effective strike ever to be called in the Tri-
State," wrote the editor of the *Engineering and Mining Journal*.[38] Ernest Berry, vice-president of Baxter Springs Local
107, naturally gave credit to the union for shutting down
Tri-State operations for nearly thirty days. In conferring
with Eagle Picher officials on July 16, Berry stated that
picket lines had been so effective that the operators, superintendents, and other bosses had been forced to obtain
permits in order to gain access to their properties. Under
Berry's direction, these permits were issued from union
headquarters in Picher.[39] The operators also acknowledged the effectiveness of the strike. According to John
Campbell, personnel manager of Eagle Picher Mining and
Smelting Company:

> For a period of about three weeks from May 9 to May 27 there
> was a complete stoppage and shutdown of all trade and traffic
> [in ores and concentrates] in the District. Not a wheel at ours,
> not a car of ore moved out of there [the district] except one or
> two possibly from the smaller mines.
>
> The so-called strike of the International was the cause
> of that.[40]

Furthermore, a survey of the weekly sales reports of lead and zinc concentrates for the district, which appeared each week in the *Joplin Globe*, revealed the drastic reduction in production and sales during the first weeks of the strike. The *Globe* reported on May 19 that there had been "no purchase" of lead and zinc concentrates for the first time in the history of the Joplin district. All evidence pointed to a nearly total shutdown of mining and milling. The assumption was that the union's strike was solely responsible.

Nevertheless, factors other than the strike contributed to the cessation of operations, causing union leaders later to charge that the major companies had actually imposed a lockout of union members.[41] Reporting on the abortive efforts of the union to bring about negotiations for collective bargaining, the editor of the *Engineering and Mining Journal* suggested that the operators' refusal to negotiate had resulted from the overproduction of lead and zinc ores that occurred in the district since January 1. Ore bins at both the mines and smelters were reported to be full. A slowdown or a stoppage of production would therefore help to reduce this glut, assuming a continued sale of concentrates.[42] The price that the companies were receiving for lead and zinc concentrates at the time of the strike was, however, alarmingly low. On May 9 the Baxter Springs *Citizen and Herald* reported that the price had dropped to the point that some companies found it difficult to justify continued operations. The implication was that they had operated at a loss in order to provide, as a humanitarian gesture, employment to their personnel and to maintain skilled crews. Under such circumstances, a shutdown of the entire district would be welcomed by such companies.

In September 1935, Harbaugh implied that the operators had suffered little damage by the temporary shutdown in May. He stated: "In normal times, nearly every spring about strawberry picking time, or somewhat later, the mines reach a point of saturation of concentrate stocks, so they shut down for a couple of weeks or more for a sort of tonic both to the men, and to the industry. So the strike was well timed to effect the usual spring shutdown."[43] Although Harbaugh asserted that "under the circumstances this shutdown was hardly a tonic" for the workers, he did not deny that from the standpoint of the companies, with their "saturation of concentrate stocks," the work stoppage was a godsend.

The condition of the industry partly explains why the operators complied so quickly and easily to the union's notification of the impending strike and closed their properties. It explains why they failed to make an immediate effort to resume operations when nearly full crews reported for work on the morning of May 9. It also explains why law enforcement officials in both Ottawa and Cherokee counties were not more vigorous in dispersing the strikers who blocked the highways leading to the principal mines and mills, and why the operators rejected the continuing efforts of the union to negotiate a settlement. For the larger companies, the strike—if limited to the normal spring shutdown—was indeed an event that served their interests. Not only could they reduce inventories of concentrates and cut labor and operational costs for awhile, they could also discredit the International Union in the eyes of district residents by blaming it for the suffering and deprivation the work stoppage would surely produce. From the standpoint of the operators, the strike could not have been called at a more propitious time. It was for this reason that there was little immediate corporate response to the strike and little demand that it be quickly ended. Union leaders, concerned about their loss of credibility among the workers and worried that the local unions were in danger of collapsing, ignored the historical production cycles in the district and risked all on a strike that they hoped would be short and effective and result in union recognition. Their gamble played directly into the hands of the operators.

3

The Rise Of The Back-To-Work Movement

ALTHOUGH the economic paralysis gripping the Tri-State seemed to assure victory for the International Union of Mine, Mill, and Smelter Workers, the long-term outlook was unfavorable. Success hinged either on the union's ability to marshal sufficient resources to sustain the strikers, or upon the strikers' capacity to endure increased hardships until the endangered interests of the operators forced them to a settlement. Militating against either of these imperatives was the failure of union leaders to anticipate the enormous human costs that the strike entailed. Consequently, they failed to plan for managing and alleviating the widespread distress that swept the district in the wake of the shutdown. The union members were thus forced to rely upon their own meager resources and those of public agencies. Inept union leadership undermined the strike before it began.

At the beginning, union officials had advised their members to "quit and go on relief," but relief agencies already carried capacity loads and could not readily absorb the scores of men with families who immediately applied for assistance. The depression had already devastated the budgets of local governments. Although providing direct or work relief primarily preoccupied local officials, a fact reflected in the minutes of city councils, boards of county commissioners, and county courts, they lacked the financial resources to assist any but the most destitute of the new applicants. When the strike began, district newspapers immediately reported increased applications for public aid—for example, 35 to 40 at Joplin on May 8, with an-

other 300 expected, and 186 at Galena and 51 at Baxter
Springs on May 9. In Cherokee County, Kansas, the case-
load statistics of the Poor Commissioner chronicled the
start and end of the strike.

May 8, 1935	3,077	Strike begins
May 31, 1935	3,305	
June 15, 1935	3,427	
June 22, 1935	3,571	
June 30, 1935	3,227	
July 15, 1935	3,070	[Strike broken][1]

"Going on relief" to weather the strike proved difficult if
not impossible for many union members.

Nevertheless, their leaders had promised that the union
would not let its members starve, that the parent American
Federation of Labor (AFL) could be counted on to provide
assistance. Forty years later, one unidentified old-timer remembered a promise to send a "carload of groceries . . . ,
flour, beans, potatoes [and] lard" into the district.[2] But,
other than assistance from locals of the United Mine Workers (UMW) at Pittsburg, Kansas, the aid did not arrive.
The union's treasury was nearly depleted in 1935; it could
not possibly sustain a strike as large as that launched in the
Tri-State.[3] Nor could its impoverished locals provide substantial help to their members. In August 1935 when Ted
Schasteen attended the International's annual convention
in Salt Lake City as a delegate of Treece Local 111, its
officers forwarded a request to the convention "for a loan
of $25 on our note for six months for the purpose of fur-
nishing board and room for [Schasteen] and transportation home."[4] Fortunately for Schasteen, the convention
granted the request. Addressing the convention, Tony
McTeer, who represented Picher Local 15, described
"conditions in the Tri-State, especially Picher, Oklahoma,
where the relief was entirely inadequate and the miners
and their families were practically starving. . . . He stated
there were 1,800 families to be fed every day, and that
there was no money to feed them, and they could not get
anything like the relief needed."[5] None of the six locals

had the financial resources to maintain its struck members. Further complicating the situation was the abundance of unemployed men, who were a surplus labor force that saturated the district. Consequently, for the forty-eight hundred men idled by the strike, there were no readily available alternative employment or income opportunities, unless they qualified for public work relief as openings occurred. Under the circumstances, the strike would have to be won quickly. Otherwise, an increasing level of misery would force the strikers back to work.

Union leaders thus confronted a situation that daily became more critical, a fact the operators recognized and fully exploited. Although marginal companies were financially unable to endure an extended strike, the larger companies, such as Eagle Picher and its subsidiaries, could easily afford to hold out. Their officials realized that in the absence of substantial aid from the International Union or the AFL, privation and family considerations would soon drive the men back into the mines and mills. John Campbell, personnel manager of Eagle Picher Mining and Smelting Company, later described the compelling circumstances that forced Tri-State workers to think "work" instead of "strike":

> Conditions with labor, the workmen that were out of work, were becoming desperate. There is not much else in this community on which the working man can live except the mines, and that is practically the support of other industry and business in the district. And the men had been on reasonably low wages and, in fact very low wages up to the time of the strike on account of very low market prices for concentrates. And being down, being out of work a week or 2 weeks, brought most of them to destitution.[6]

Campbell correctly concluded that neither the union nor its locals had the financial resources to sustain the strike. He therefore waited patiently for the inevitable desperation among the workers to erode their commitment to the cause of organization and collective bargaining. The reliance of union leaders on overburdened public and private relief agencies to handle the scores of new requests for aid generated by the strike, and their failure to devise alternative strategies for coping with increased levels of need severely prejudiced their effort from the start. No other single factor was more important in producing a vigorous back-to-work movement.

From the start, opponents of the shutdown searched for ways to renew operations. On May 16, led by Tom L. Armer, a blacksmith from Treece who worked for the Commerce Mining and Royalty Company, a group of back-to-workers met to discuss the strike. Not much is known about Armer, but one of his contemporaries later described him as being "away out in front as a leader of the back-to-work movement." A courageous man, "who wanted more than anything to get back to work at a job where he could support his family," Armer was a "well-liked" but uninspiring leader. Nevertheless, he initiated the drive to break the strike.[7] Certain members of this group had already met informally with the larger operators and workers to determine their attitude toward a resumption of mining and milling. Their reports revealed that the operators, who had not resisted the work stoppage for reasons already noted, were ready to reopen their properties when large numbers of employees showed a willingness to return to work in the face of union opposition. The reports suggested that scores of men were willing—even eager—to return without changes in working conditions. Convinced that circumstances were right for breaking the strike, Armer's group scheduled a follow-up meeting for next day to explore further the matter of returning to work.

When the group met near Buffalo School west of Cardin, it found a crowd of several hundred men present, including many union members. News of the meeting, which had been intended as a planning session, had spread throughout the district. Armer reluctantly opened the proceedings to both advocates and opponents of the strike to present their case. An overwhelming majority rejected arguments that the strike was necessary to obtain union recognition, a living wage, and better working conditions. An estimated two hundred men signed petitions requesting the operators to reopen their properties and allow them to return to work.[8] Encouraged by this evidence of antistrike sentiment, Armer called another meeting for the next afternoon at the same place and requested that everyone wanting to work be there.

On May 18 nearly fifteen hundred men, including an estimated two hundred union members, gathered in a field near the Buffalo School. Once again they heard both sides of the strike issue presented by a variety of speakers, some not directly involved in the strike. When unionists like Jimmie Hall, a Picher miner who had worked hard to organize the union in the district, urged them to stand fast and stay off the job, shouts arose demanding to know how they and their families were to live without jobs. When Hall suggested that they go on relief until the assistance promised by the union arrived, the majority strongly rejected the idea as unacceptable. Speakers who opposed the strike, including such men as Judge F. D. Adams of Miami, several mine inspectors, and small operators, argued persuasively that the strike should end. More than nine hundred men agreed with them and signed the back-to-work petitions that Armer had circulated.

The meeting of May 18 was a major setback for the union, for it clearly exposed a growing groundswell of antistrike sentiment in search of leadership. The hostile role of mine inspectors, small operators, and prominent citizens such as Judge Adams also signaled trouble for the strike. With the opposition clearly growing, Armer scheduled another rally for the following day at the Miami fairgrounds, which could comfortably accommodate a larger crowd. The announced purpose of this meeting was to appoint a committee to meet with the operators and negotiate a settlement to end the strike.[9]

The fairgrounds rally attracted a crowd estimated at twenty-five hundred. As expected, Armer was selected to chair the session. Unlike the proceedings of previous meetings where some semblance of impartiality was maintained, Armer prevented union spokesmen from addressing the gathering, which included scores of union members. He explained that the meeting had been called for men who wanted to work, not for those who wished to remain on strike. Highly visible as leaders were several small operators and mine supervisors, such as Joe Nolan, a former sheriff of Picher and then an official of the Luck O.K. Mine, and Newt Keithley, a ground boss at Eagle Picher Mining and Smelting Company's Southside Mine. Armer announced that their intent was to form a new workers' organization, an alternative union to the Mine, Mill, and Smelter Workers. He stated that "this [new] organization of workmen of the Tri-State district is going to be permanent and it will be composed of men such as are at this meeting who will protect our interests from here on out." When Nolan later asked for a show of hands of the men willing to join up and return to work, the response was nearly unanimous. Approximately six hundred signed petitions requesting the operators to resume mining and milling, bringing the total since May 16 to 1,782. After further discussion, Armer appointed a committee composed of one worker from each of the companies represented at the meeting and charged it with planning a course of action. He then called another general meeting for the following afternoon at Baxter Springs where the committee would report its recommendations.[10]

The next morning Armer's committee met at the Pentecostal church at Cardin and, after much discussion, decided that a first step toward getting the men back to work was to meet with union officials and persuade them to call off the strike. Although violence had been minimal, committee members feared that unless this was done, a peaceful resumption of mining and milling was impossible. Consequently, they selected four men—Armer, Keithley, Nolan, and Ray Morris, a watchman for Eagle Picher Mining and Smelting Company—to contact union officials at their headquarters in Picher and request that the strike be called off. Upon arrival there, however, the mission failed because the union officials were absent. Armer and Nolan then drove to nearby Baxter Springs where an afternoon crowd estimated at two to three thousand had gathered at city park for the scheduled back-to-work rally.

The Baxter Springs meeting had a strong potential for violence. Union members, miffed and upset that their spokesmen had been prevented from addressing the fairgrounds crowd, came to the back-to-work rally in great numbers. Rumors circulated that the union intended to disrupt the meeting, rumors that seemed to be confirmed by the presence of important union officials and substantial numbers of their members. Expecting trouble, Armer requested police protection from municipal and county officials, but when it failed to promptly arrive, he attempted to initiate the proceedings. He was unsuccessful. Each time that he or Nolan tried to speak, union members near the speakers' stand loosed a chorus of hisses and boos that made it impossible for the crowd to hear. Unable to continue, Armer and Nolan left the platform, driven into silence by the hundreds of union members who opposed the back-to-work drive. Understandably, when Brown, president of the International, and Long, president of District 4, attempted to address the meeting, back-to-workers reciprocated with yelling, shouting, and booing, making it impossible for them to be heard. Union efforts to break up the back-to-work rally were successful; their efforts to capture it failed. Neither side was heard.[11] Nevertheless, the meetings at Miami and Baxter Springs revealed an accelerating back-to-work movement that was rapidly crystallizing into organizational form.

Union officials watched these developments with growing concern. If back-to-work leaders, with the support of the companies, formed a competing organization and attracted workers with promises of work, not only the strike but the union itself would be greatly endangered. Something had to be done to counter the movement and refocus public attention on the strike issues. On May 21 the union displayed its power with large demonstrations throughout the district that climaxed in a massive meeting at the Miami fairgrounds. Using the Oklahoma–Kansas state line between Picher and Treece as a staging area, more than a thousand union men and women assembled with American flags and union banners for a march through Picher and nearby Cardin. Afterwards, they reassembled outside Miami and, with flags and banners flying, marched two abreast through that city before crossing the Neosho River bridge en route to the fairgrounds. There, Brown, Long, and other union spokesmen exhorted nearly three thousand persons to reject the appeals of the back-to-workers and stand fast in support of the strike. Ira M. Finley, the principal speaker and editor of *Labor's Voice*, gave more explicit advice. He urged the workers to stay off the job "until you whip hell out of this bunch." In his opinion, victory was theirs unless they allowed themselves to be seduced into a return to work. The meeting ended with an appeal that everyone rally that evening at Picher.[12]

The evening rally attracted a crowd of nearly two thousand. Once more union spokesmen lashed out at those who wanted to end the strike before its goals had been achieved. They appealed to the workers to remain steadfast in their determination to change conditions in the Tri-State. As for the charge that the union represented only a minority of the workers, Brown informed the crowd that "the object of today's demonstration [was] to give a proper view of the situation in the Tri-State district. It [was] said that we do not represent 10 percent of the workers of the field but this demonstration [indicated] that our estimates of 90 percent are correct."[13] The Picher rally ended a full day of orderly demonstrations throughout the Tri-State, which union leaders hoped would turn back the surging back-to-work campaign. Unfortunately for the union, the demonstrations did not intimidate its opponents, who continued to organize and obtain signatures on antistrike petitions. Nor did evidence emerge in the days that followed that the rallies, the exhortations, the marches, and the flag and banner waving had stiffened the backbones of the rank and file.

For impoverished workers the prospect of a job was a powerful and seductive lure that pulled them into the back-to-work movement. Union demonstrations, stepped-up picketing, pleas for solidarity, loyalty to the strike cause—none obscured the reality that labor conditions were becoming daily more critical. The back-to-work alternative therefore attracted a growing number of idle men who desperately needed jobs and incomes. They could not allow their wives and children to starve for union promises of a better tomorrow. Under such circumstances, the mine operators and their agents easily assumed direction of the movement to break the strike, which had originated in the widespread distress of the workers.

On the morning of May 25, Armer and his committee of about thirty, which included a number of supervisory personnel from the Eagle Picher, Commerce, and other companies, convened for a strategy session at the John L. Mine of F. W. ("Mike") Evans on the open prairie near Quapaw. In contrast to the earlier meeting held at the Pentecostal church on May 20, when emphasis had been placed on persuading the union to call off the strike, the committee now determined that Armer's proposal for a "new" workers' organization should be immediately implemented.[14] With this decision the movement embraced two specific goals—getting the men back to work and replacing the independent union with a "union" more compatible to the interests of the companies and their supporters. At this meeting, Evans replaced Armer as the principal leader of the back-to-work campaign. With the support of the district operators, he transformed the movement and the organization it spawned into a vigorous assault on the International Union.

Evans, who had substantial property holdings, had been a well-known entrepreneur in the district since the twenties. After serving a term in the federal penitentiary at Vinita, Oklahoma, for producing and selling bootleg whiskey during prohibition (his still, located in an abandoned mine, was reported to be the largest ever raided by federal agents in Oklahoma), Evans became an economic force in Picher. He operated lead and zinc mines employing a large number of men; he owned the Connell Hotel (Picher's largest), a business building, a pool room, and a dance

Glenn A. Hickman, secretary-treasurer of the Blue Card Union and editor of the *Blue Card Record*. Courtesy of Glenn A. Hickman.

Joe Nolan, the "Pick-handle King." Courtesy of Glenn A. Hickman.

F. W. ("Mike") Evans, president of the Blue Card Union. Courtesy of *Blue Card Record*.

Left to right: F. W. ("Mike") Evans, president of the Blue Card Union; Joe Nolan, president of the Picher local of the Blue Card Union; and Kelsey Norman, attorney for the union. Courtesy of *Joplin (Missouri) Globe*.

hall. He was a partner in two businesses, a used-cable company and a Ford automobile agency, and he was an active member of the Tri-State Zinc and Lead Ore Producers' Association. Moreover, when the strike began, Evans operated the Craig lease, which he had obtained from the Eagle Picher Mining and Smelting Company, and which employed about thirty-five men. His financial interests were therefore immediately threatened because his lease required that ore from the property be shipped to Eagle Picher's great Central Mill, which the strike had closed. Consequently, although only one of Evans's workers had struck, he was forced to suspend operations until the Central Mill reopened.

A renowned gambler who was into "anything and everything that would make a 'buck,'" Evans was popular throughout the Tri-State, having, as one of his colleagues later recalled, "an uncountable number of friends from all walks, including all degrees of respectability in the communities" of the district. Short and pudgy, with thinning, sandy hair, Evans possessed qualities of leadership that pushed him to the forefront of the movement. Intelligent, articulate, persuasive, and experienced in managing men, he was tough and ruthless if need be. His self-confidence and bearing gave him an aura of authority that a contemporary described as "Napoleonic." Among his friends and subordinates he inspired intense loyalty. He did not hesitate to delegate authority to those who would use it as he directed. Evans's recognized toughness, his rapport with the workers, his leadership qualities, and his ability to endure the "heat and ferment of the occasion" made him an excellent choice to lead the back-to-work movement.[15]

Following the meeting, Evans and the committee adjourned to the Miami fairgrounds where several hundred supporters had gathered. There Evans formally presented the proposal for establishing the Tri-State Metal Mine and Smelter Workers Union, whose objective was to "break the strike, . . . get the men back to work," and replace the International as the workers' organization in the district.[16] These goals were inseparable and had to be achieved simultaneously, a task beyond Evans with his time-consuming enterprises and limited education. For the first time Glenn A. Hickman, a man whose talents proved essential in accomplishing the objectives of the movement, stepped to the forefront. He was destined to become secretary-treasurer of the new union and editor of its newspaper, the *Blue Card Record.*

Hickman's roots were deep in Tri-State mining. His miner father had died at fifty-two from the scourge of the district—silicosis complicated by tuberculosis—and one of two brothers had been forced from the mines after becoming silicotic. Like hundreds of miners after years of exposure to silica dust, Hickman himself eventually contracted a serious case of tuberculosis, the contagion that seeded the district. Furthermore, before the strike of 1935 he had joined the International Union, a move that he soon regretted. He later wrote: "I had been a good-faith member of the International Union . . . and had attended two meetings before deciding their goals and advocacies were not for me—not anything I could subscribe to. I'm sure I expressed myself in all company rather strongly to that effect." [17]

When the strike began, Hickman was a ground boss at the Black Eagle Mining Company (a position formerly held by his father and then a brother) with nine years of mining experience. He quickly concluded that the strike was irresponsible and detrimental to the interests of the workers and that the International was an "outlaw union" and "loaded with Communists," conclusions that undoubtedly influenced his later decision to join union opponents. [18] But, expecting a "long spell of unemployment," Hickman had returned to the family farm between Columbus and Baxter Springs where he busied himself in gardening. He later held that when he heard that there was to be a back-to-work meeting at the Miami fairgrounds on May 25,

> I went directly there and soon found myself involved with the enrollment and other work that was going on. There was not a single person later active in the BCU [Blue Card Union] that I had ever met before this day.
>
> My involvement, of course, brought me into contact with

those who later became leaders. I wound up with the enrollment records in my custody, and it must have been that on the
following day that I met Mike Evans, Kelsey Norman, Joe
Nolan and others who became officials in the BCU.[19]

A man of strong convictions and substantial abilities, Hickman provided much of the intellectual content of the
campaign against the union. At the May 25 meeting, he
emerged as a determined and fearless advocate of the
back-to-work movement. Inside the exhibition hall, surrounded by men desperate for jobs, he dictated to Evans's
bookkeeper a more comprehensive petition for circulation
to the crowd.

Unlike the others it supplanted, Hickman's petition did
more than merely express a desire to return to work. A
signer disavowed the strike, promised to protect the property of the companies that resumed operations, agreed to
join the proposed back-to-work organization, and, if a
member of the International was required to resign from
and sever all connections with it. A signer committed
himself foursquare to breaking the union's strike. Within
two days 3,125 disillusioned men readily signed the new
petition that back-to-workers were aggressively circulating
throughout the Tri-State.[20] Last-ditch efforts by the union
to halt the drive were futile. Large rallies at Picher addressed by prominent labor leaders Alexander Howat,
president of District 14, UMW, and G. Ed Warren, president of the Oklahoma State Federation of Labor, failed to
blunt the back-to-work campaign.[21]

Sensing a groundswell shift in the mood of the workers
away from the union, back-to-work leaders accelerated
their drive to reopen the mines and mills and to establish
the new union on a formal basis. On May 26 they held a
Sunday meeting at the Miami fairgrounds that was attended by an estimated twelve to fifteen hundred supporters. Backers of the International Union were carefully
screened out at the gates. With Evans presiding, various
spokesmen again discussed the necessity of creating an alternative union to break the strike. Actively participating

were supervisors from various companies whose officials supported the concept of a permanent Tri-State union because, as Hickman later recalled, the strike had forged an identity of interests between large numbers of idle men who desperately wanted to work and the companies; the former were losing wages and the latter were losing profits. From the beginning, therefore, the back-to-work movement and the Tri-State union it spawned had the "full support of the operators, and there was no doubt about it."[22]

This became evident in the election of a twelve-man executive committee to form the new organization. Seven of the twelve were minor supervisors from five mining companies of the district, and an eighth was a mine operator. Immediately after its formation, the committee met and chose nonmember Guy Blackmer as president. Blackmer, a family man who supervised the night watchmen at the Commerce Mining and Royalty Company, refused the position. Newt Keithley, a ground boss at Eagle Picher's Southside Mine, had recently had his "skull cracked by a ballpeen hammer wielded by one of the strikers," and Blackmer apparently thought the "honor not worth the risk."[23] When Kelsey Norman, a Joplin attorney, advised that these Sunday elections should be nullified and that all officers should be elected on a weekday to preclude any legal challenge to their election, another meeting was scheduled for the next day to organize and review organizational documents that Norman had been asked to frame.

Participants at an earlier meeting at the John L. Mine had recognized that a permanent counter-organization to the International Union necessitated articles of association and a constitution with bylaws. To provide these documents, Evans's group had turned to Norman, a well-known figure in Joplin's Democratic party politics whose most prominent legal work had been in damage and compensation cases on the side of plaintiffs. A highly successful lawyer who had moved to the district from Arkansas, he accepted the task of preparing the documents and thereafter became counsel for the Tri-State Metal Mine and Smelter Workers Union. Who recruited him, who paid him, how much, and how he was paid remain unanswered questions; however, circumstantial evidence strongly suggests that Evans recruited Norman into the movement. Norman's enthusiasm for the back-to-work cause led Hickman, a later friend and colleague, to conclude years afterwards that it was Norman's "sense of purpose and his effective oratory that got us off to an organizational start."[24] Norman's role far exceeded that of merely providing legal service, for he conspicuously devoted much of his time for many months to the new Tri-State union's attack on the International Union. His abilities blended with those of Evans and Hickman to power the movement forward. His service was invaluable.

Norman surfaced as a significant back-to-work leader on May 27 when nearly three thousand people gathered at the Miami fairgrounds to form a permanent organization based on articles of association and a constitution with by-laws, all of which he had prepared and had printed for distribution. The contents of these documents revealed that Norman had been substantially advised by individuals who wanted the new organization to be controlled by the district operators. He consulted eight or ten times with Evans—and possibly others—about the provisions of the documents; however, their meetings, advice, and recommendations were buried in the secrecy of attorney-client privilege.[25] Although one cannot confirm a "precisely plotted and planned" conspiracy to form a company union, circumstantial evidence suggests that Evans, Norman, and perhaps Hickman, together with about fifteen others, carefully orchestrated the preparations and the proceedings of the May 27 meeting to assure that the new organization would not be controlled by rank-and-file workers who might insist upon independent unionism and collective bargaining. They accomplished this objective by controlling the process of its formation and by determining the rules of its governance. Norman's documents served to legitimize their efforts.

Before attending the mass session at the Miami fairgrounds on May 27, Norman met with Evans, Hickman, and others (possibly members of Armer's committee that had earlier convened at Evans's John L. Mine) for their review, amendment, and approval of the documents. Twelve men, the same ones who had been elected to the aborted executive committee on the previous day, agreed to endorse the articles of association. Among the signers were six ground bosses (work-level supervisors generally with the power to hire and fire upon approval), one operator, one engineer, and four workers drawn from six companies of the district, each represented by at least one supervisor. Of the twelve, eight held supervisory positions and several were already in the forefront of the back-to-work movement.[26] Their endorsements marked the formal founding of the Tri-State Metal Mine and Smelter Workers Union because, among other things, the articles specified the name, the offices, the headquarters site, and the objectives of the organization. Thus, while the crowd assembled, back-to-work leaders set the stage for a formal public sanctioning of their handiwork.

They easily persuaded the fairground throng of idle workers that their interests and those of their employers would be best served by supporting the new organization. Opposition to the strike and the International Union had continued to gain momentum, predisposing work-hungry miners and millmen to accept any proposal that might speed up their return to work. Yet the necessity for popular approval may partly explain the moderate statement of objectives found in the articles of association. Nowhere were the breaking of the strike and the eradication of the International Union mentioned, although the new Tri-State Union, the visible expression of the back-to-work movement, had been established specifically for these purposes. Nor was there any mention of collective bargaining. Nevertheless, the anti-International character of the articles of association, though unstated, was well understood. For when Evans recommended that the articles be adopted, there was no challenge to the document nor to the process employed in its preparation. This easy acceptance accurately reflected the antistrike, anti-International consensus developing between the back-to-work leadership and growing numbers of Tri-State workers.

The unanimous rubber-stamping of the constitution and bylaws also revealed how deeply the crowd was committed to resuming operations. The articles of association had specified three officers for the new union (a president, a vice-president, and a secretary-treasurer) and stipulated that its business would be conducted under the rules set forth afterwards in the constitution.[27] This constitution provided that the executive committee would exercise "exclusive management" of the new union and that all its decisions would be by a majority vote, which would be "final and binding." It empowered the committee to negotiate contracts with district operators concerning wages, hours, and working conditions; to frame rules and regulations for governing the organization; to prescribe membership requirements; to expel members; to hear controversies; to issue charters for locals; to assess members for revenue; to punish the misconduct of "subordinate" bodies; and to do generally whatever was necessary for the welfare of the organization.

The eligibility requirements for membership on the committee were restrictive. To qualify one must have worked five years in the mines or mills of the district—the last three years immediately prior to election—as a "vice-principal," a term generally understood to mean a supervisor of some type, usually a ground boss or a superintendent. (The same requirements were stipulated for officers in the proposed locals of the organization. Thus workers were formally excluded from its controlling body and from positions of authority in its locals.) These qualifications, of course, made the organization anything but an independent labor union.[28] No consideration was given at the meeting to the matter of workers' control, and no concern was expressed over the lack of constitutional provisions providing for collective bargaining. Under the constitution, the Tri-State Metal Mine and Smelter Workers Union would be something less than a bona fide workers' organization. Nevertheless, upon Evans's recommendation the crowd adopted it, apparently oblivious to the implications of its control provisions.

Afterwards and without opposition, the meeting elected to the executive committee the same twelve men who had been elected on May 26 and who had endorsed the articles of association, placing in their hands the destiny of the new union. Paradoxically, and apparently in violation of constitutional provisions excluding them, four workers were among the twelve. Not surprisingly, in its first meeting on May 27, the committee elected Evans as president; Ray Morris, a watchman for the Eagle Picher Mining and Smelting Company, as vice-president; and Hickman as secretary-treasurer. Evans later stated that he had protested his election to head the organization on the grounds that he was an operator; however, the committee, two-thirds of which were low-level supervisors, overcame his reluctance and arguments.[29] Morris was probably elected for symbolic purposes, for he never played a significant role in the affairs of the organization. Hickman was undoubtedly elected secretary-treasurer because of his demonstrated commitment to the movement and his abilities. After assuming the post, he quit his job as ground boss for the Black-Eagle Mining Company, becoming the only full-time, paid officer of the new union. Hickman and Evans were excellent choices to direct the Tri-State Union in breaking the strike and replacing the International Union.

The organization created on May 27 gave definite form to the back-to-work movement, but whether it was the kind of organization that embodied the best interest of Tri-State workers remained an open question. Before a fairgrounds crowd of twenty-five hundred on May 19, Tom L. Armer had called for a permanent "organization of workers" that would "protect [their] interests from here on out." What had emerged was an organization that was formally based on documents that placed control in the hands of operators and/or their agents and excluded workers from positions of power and influence by restrictive qualifications. Consequently, two-thirds of the executive committee consisted of supervisory personnel; the president was a mine operator; the secretary-treasurer was a ground boss;[30] and a principal leader, although without formal office, was a lawyer. Rank-and-file worker participation in the governance of the organization was virtually nonexistent, the presence of Ray Morris as vice-president and three other workers on the executive committee notwithstanding. Under such circumstances, the likelihood was remote that the new union would represent bona fide workers' interests, especially in the absence of any reference to collective bargaining in the articles or the constitution. These documents, which assumed a harmony of interest between the workers and the operators, left no doubt that control of the union was a function of the latter. Such control, of course, precluded the possibility that it would ever become an instrument to force changes solely beneficial to Tri-State workers.

The role of the operators in launching the back-to-work movement and the new union is difficult to assess. Undoubtedly, these developments, as Hickman later stated, had the "full support of the operators, and there was no doubt about it."[31] Prior to May 27, however, their involvement was a shadowy, behind-the-scenes involvement that cannot be fully documented. But in the meetings that gave form and substance to the movement, mine and mill supervisors were always present and, in most cases, active participants. Furthermore, during the back-to-work petition drive, both before and after the meeting of May 27 that gave formal birth to the new union, some supervisors from companies such as Eagle Picher contacted striking workers at their homes throughout the district and tried to induce them to return to work. When persuasion and other enticements failed, they resorted to intimidation, threatening never to hire the worker again if he remained on strike.[32] Whether these activities signified merely the desire of supervisors to return to work, or whether they acted as agents for the operators remains an open question. Without their active leadership, however, it is unlikely that the new union would have been established so rapidly.

Supervisors also came to dominate the executive committee of the organization. This development seems more than coincidental, although no solid evidence was found to confirm that highly placed company officials, working through Evans, Hickman, and Norman, conspired to manipulate supervisory personnel onto the committee.[33] The early connection between the companies and the back-to-work leadership is therefore imprecise; however, the role of the supervisors is highly suggestive. Until May 27, the impetus for a return to work lay with the supervisors (e.g., ground bosses who had been severely hurt by the strike) and Evans, who may have exploited an opportunity to ingratiate himself with the larger companies for business purposes. It is highly probable that officials of the major companies informally encouraged their subordinates, while being careful to avoid any formal identification with a movement designed to destroy the International Union.

Several reasons explain the rush of Tri-State workers into the back-to-work movement. Before the start of the strike, there were hundreds of unemployed men unable to be placed in the mines and mills of the district. They were anxious to work under any circumstances, and they readily joined the movement. Furthermore, from the beginning hundreds of employed Tri-State workers opposed the International and its strike. Consequently, they welcomed the opportunity to enlist in the back-to-work movement and join the new Tri-State Union because its objectives were compatible with their wishes. The presence of lower supervisory personnel, who had the closest contact with the men on the job, in the forefront of the movement may also partially explain the rapid desertion of the strike and the International by growing numbers of Tri-Staters. If the strike was broken, ground bosses and superintendents who had pushed for a return to work would be positioned to discriminate against strikers and union members.

Most important in explaining the rapid change in attitude of many workers toward the strike and the International Union between May 8 and May 27 was the inability of union leaders to persuade them that the goals of union recognition and collective bargaining justified the increased sacrifices which, in the absence of external assistance, they had been called upon to make. Later statements of Tri-State workers indicated that they flocked into the movement hoping to avoid or alleviate the extreme suffering of their families. For this reason hundreds joined the new Tri-State Union, which was billed as a workers' organization or union, despite evidence clearly indicating that they would not control it. To them the question of control was immaterial. What was important was that the new union was organized around the idea of returning to work, which they wanted and needed. If work could be had by joining the new union, they were prepared to join.

The creation of the Tri-State Metal Mine and Smelter Workers Union was a turning point in the strike. Two organizations now competed for the loyalty of the workers, and each had demonstrated the power to rally huge crowds. The two unions, however, had entirely different and incompatible objectives. The International Union was determined to maintain the strike until it was recognized, and until wages were raised and working conditions were improved through collective bargaining. The new Tri-State Union was equally determined to break the strike and renew operations immediately with nothing changed. Behind each of these positions rallied hundreds of Tri-State workers whose individual circumstances dictated their choices. The presence of two competing organizations with opposite goals led by determined leaders increased the potential for violence in the district. It was not long in coming.

4

Pick Handles and Troops

THE STRIKE began peacefully. When it is recalled that many workers had reluctantly joined the locals of the International Union of Mine, Mill, and Smelter Workers only because the times were bad, that nearly forty-eight hundred men left jobs when hundreds more desperately searched for work of any kind, that scores involved in the strike opposed it because they feared unemployment, and that armed bands of International Union members reportedly swept over the district on May 9 to force the closing of mines and mills, the absence of immediate and frequent violence is surprising.

During the first two weeks when enthusiasm for the strike was greatest, only two reported incidents of violence occurred—one on May 9 when pickets attacked Herschel Northcutt, who insisted on working at the Ballard Mine after being ordered to quit, and the other on May 20 when Tom Wilkerson, an outspoken critic of the strike who operated the Grace Walker Tailing Mill, was severely beaten by unknown assailants while in Baxter Springs.[1] Several acts of intimidation also occurred when union pickets brandishing rocks and other weapons prevented the loading of ore at several small properties. Nevertheless, after conferring with superintendents and foremen of the mines in the district, W. W. Waters, who was the personal representative of Oklahoma Governor Ernest W. Marland, reported that violence attributable to the union was almost nil.[2] Because of the effectiveness of the shutdown and the absence of trouble, most picket lines were removed from the properties after May 10 and were not renewed until nearly two weeks later.[3] Brown's expressed hope for a peaceful strike seemed to have been fulfilled.

Unfortunately, the emergence of the back-to-work movement and the formation of the Tri-State Metal Mine and Smelter Workers Union, which challenged the existence of the International Union in the district, undermined the fragile peace. The objectives of the two organizations were diametrically opposed. The struggle to control industrial conditions and the means employed to effect that control generated enormous tension and eventually provoked violence. As in so many labor-management disputes of the past, its ripple effects gradually involved forces and institutions beyond the district.

Before the strike, the headquarters of District 4 of the union had been located in Joplin, Missouri, the largest city in the Tri-State Mining District. To direct the walkout more efficiently, J. A. Long, president of District 4, on May 9 moved his office to Picher, Oklahoma, which was then the center of mining and milling. As local leaders moved in and out of strike headquarters on Connell Avenue, Picher's principal street, union activities became immediately and highly visible. Not surprisingly, the first significant violence erupted on Connell Avenue. It apparently stemmed from the keen awareness of union leaders that the back-to-work movement was even then crystallizing into organizational form that endangered the union's drive to be recognized as the spokesman for Tri-State workers. It altered the heretofore peaceful character of the strike and opened the door to back-to-work retaliation against the union membership. As *The New Republic* later stated, the violence set off a sequence of events that made the strike "one of the bloodiest chapters in [American] labor history."[4]

On the morning of May 27, approximately one hundred union members gathered in front of the union's headquarters, milling about and discussing recent strike developments. Down the street clusters of their emotional supporters stood before the Connell Hotel, owned by Mike Evans who was inside with backers. That Evans had recently emerged as a prominent back-to-work leader was known to every unionist in the Tri-State. Not far away at the Miami fairgrounds, opponents of the strike were even then gathering to complete their organization of the new Tri-State Union. Evans was expected to attend that meeting and play a dominant role. Informed that angry strikers were in front of the hotel and threatening to prevent his departure for the fairgrounds, Evans telephoned Ottawa County Sheriff Eli Dry who, accompanied by a deputy and Picher's police chief, came and escorted him and six non-union men through a jeering, hostile mob to a pickup truck. As the vehicle moved off protected by the officers, someone threw a brick and the mob, now enlarged by additional union members attracted to the scene by the arrival of the police, spontaneously surged forward in an unsuccessful attempt to halt the truck. Although Sheriff Dry fired a warning shot into the air, he and his assistants were quickly overcome and severely beaten by individuals armed with pick handles and pieces of lead pipe. Following the melee, Dave McConnell, superintendent of the Oklahoma State Bureau of Investigation, arrived with state troopers and rescued the officers who had received severe scalp wounds. The men were taken to the Baptist Hospital in Miami for treatment. Dry's injuries required several days of hospitalization.[5] Thus, contrary to their leaders' instructions, frustrated union members initiated violence and set the stage for more. Their assault on Sheriff Dry was unusually damaging to the union's cause, for he thereafter committed himself and his office to supporting the back-to-work movement.

News of the violence in Picher swiftly reached the organizational meeting of back-to-workers then in progress at the Miami fairgrounds. There, many nonunion men, obviously anticipating trouble, were armed with "short pieces of steel and guns and clubs." Upon hearing of the violence in Picher, Joe Nolan, who emerged as a dominant figure in the movement to break the strike, made an impassioned speech, exhorting several hundred men to join him in returning to Picher and take back "something that belongs to us."[6] Nolan's impulsive offer to lead the back-to-work forces into Picher for a toe-to-toe confrontation with union members revealed a disintegration of restraint among strike opponents and a growing unwillingness to tolerate the International Union.

Nolan was superbly qualified for the role he now assumed as the mailed fist of the Tri-State Metal Mine and Smelter Workers Union. Like Glenn A. Hickman, with whom he became a fast friend and protector, Nolan had sprung from hard-rock miners who had migrated into the Tri-State from Missouri's eastern lead belt during World War I. A product of the mining camps, he was virtually uneducated. Yet he was a natural and powerful leader who operated the Luck O.K. Mine, which employed about twenty-five men. Before the strike, he had served as police chief of Picher. Hickman, who remembered Nolan "as [the] nearest I had to a friend among all the associates in the hierarchy of the Blue Card Union" (the name commonly used for the new Tri-State Union until formally named that in 1937), later recalled that he (Nolan) stood over six feet tall, weighed approximately 225 pounds, and was "actually devoid of fear." And while Nolan "had an easy tolerance of gambling, drinking, prostitution and similar mining-camp behaviorisms," Hickman also remembered him as "always popular, fair" and eager "to protect the respectable family life which did exist" in the mining camps of the district. Nolan enjoyed a "close personal relationship with Mike [Evans]" and was willing "to act unquestioningly on Mike's orders."[7] Nolan was thus the strong right arm of the most influential leader of the back-to-work movement. With such a background, Nolan's offer to lead antiunion forces in recapturing Picher was not surprising. The increased tension produced by the organization of the new union and the outbreak of violence catapulted him to the forefront of the movement to break the strike.

Led by Nolan, hundreds of men at the fairgrounds loaded into scores of cars and trucks and drove on Highway 69 through Cardin to Picher, stopping en route only to arm the unarmed with pick handles stored in a nearby school. From the Picher High School athletic field, Nolan organized his followers into a four-block-long column of four and led them to and then south down Connell Avenue. Brandishing pick handles and firing guns into the air, the marchers passed union headquarters and drove union supporters off the street to safety. Nolan, who was thereafter known as the "pick-handle king," then returned with his "pick-handle boys" to the schoolgrounds for an impromptu back-to-work rally. When union hecklers dared to interrupt the proceedings, a mob chased them into the union hall and challenged union members to "come out and fight." Only the intervention of McConnell and fifteen state troopers, whom Governor Marland had sent following the assault on Sheriff Dry earlier in the morning, prevented further violence. Firing tear-gas cannisters, state officers dispersed the mob and restored order. In the afternoon, Nolan's forces demonstrated again. Carrying pick handles and wearing blue ribbons to identify themselves, they once more threatened the International Union building, only to be thwarted a second time by McConnell and his troopers.[8]

The events in Picher on May 27, initiated by the impulsive acts of some union members, unleashed the latent energies of the back-to-work movement and provided it with a rallying symbol—the pick handle. As a tool of law and order, the pick handle had a long history in the Tri-State. According to Dolph Shaner, its use as such probably originated in Carterville, a mining camp near Webb City, Missouri. Tired of having the camp invaded by scores of rowdy drunks after the saloons closed in Webb City, a deacon in the Methodist Episcopal Church, South, formed a vigilante group and armed its members with hammer handles in order to avoid fatalities when they acted against the drunks. Hammer handles were commonly called "pick handles" and the Carterville group came to be called the "pick-handle police." After Nolan's demonstration in Picher, the pick handle became the symbol of the back-to-work movement and the new Tri-State

A back-to-work "pick-handle parade" down Connell Avenue in Picher, Oklahoma. Courtesy of *Kansas City (Missouri) Star*.

Back-to-work rally at Picher. Courtesy of *Kansas City (Missouri) Star*.

Union. It became "something like a badge" for opponents of the strike. Willingness to shoulder a pick handle, to march with it in antiunion demonstrations, and to use it against union members became a test of commitment to the back-to-work cause. "Pick-handle parades" subsequently were a major means of intimidating supporters of the union strike.[9]

The tumult in Picher had a profound effect on the outcome of the strike. At the beginning, Brown, Long, and other union officials had emphasized the necessity of keeping the stoppage peaceful in order to assure its success. They wanted to prevent violence and the destruction of property from being used to justify the introduction of outside forces capable of breaking the strike because as early as May 18, rumors had circulated that Governor Marland planned to send units of the Oklahoma National Guard into the district. Marland denied the rumor, however, stating that "I think everything is quiet up there [Ottawa County] and there will be no troops. There is no violence, no destruction of property—everything is well in hand."[10] Yet a change in the peaceful nature of the strike could easily alter the governor's position. Already Dave McConnell of the Oklahoma Bureau of Criminal Investigation and state troopers were on the scene. Although they had rescued union members and their headquarters from a mob on the afternoon of May 27, there was no assurance that the power of the state would thereafter be impartially applied to the contending forces in the district. Consequently, the outbreak of violence drastically reduced the likelihood that the strike would be successful because, as union leaders feared, the assault on the three law enforcement officers prompted a request from Ottawa County officials for state military intervention.

In their assessment of the breakdown of order and the circumstances that had provoked the disturbances in Picher, county authorities concluded that additional forces were essential to control the threatening situation. The Tri-State Union and the International Union now confronted each other—one determined to break the strike,

the other equally determined to maintain it—and the episode in Picher seemed but a harbinger of future clashes
beyond the power of local authorities and a few state
troopers to manage. Large numbers of armed, desperate
men struggled to control industrial conditions in the district, some who would not hesitate to vent their anger and
frustration upon law enforcement officers as the assault on
Sheriff Dry had indicated. In the absence of the hospitalized Dry, Undersheriff Jim Elliott requested Governor
Marland to order units of the Oklahoma National Guard
into the state's portion of the mining district. It is unknown
who participated in the decision to request the Guard, although it is unlikely that Elliott made the request without
consulting with others or without being himself requested to do so, perhaps by the operators. The governor rejected Elliott's petition because it had not come from Dry
and County Judge John M. Venable. Upon *their* request,
however, Marland promptly instructed Adjutant General
Charles Barrett to comply.

The Oklahoma National Guard was ready. During the
summer encampment of 1934 at Fort Sill, great emphasis
had been placed on teaching techniques for containing
"mobs, strikes, hunger marches and demonstrations." To
psychologically prepare the guardsmen for such duty,
some officers had ridiculed striking workers as "damned
cowardly rats," "yellow bellies," "bastards," "sons of
bitches," "socialists and communists," "a bunch of lousy
bums who claim to be hungry, . . . [and] just a lot of scum."
If it became necessary to take action against such persons,
the officers advised their men, they should show them no
mercy because they deserved none. With his men thus
prepared, Adjutant General Barrett responded quickly to
the governor's instructions. Before midnight of May 27,
two full companies of the Guard—Company A, a rifle
group from Wagoner, and Company M, a machine-gun
unit from Eufaula—were stationed in and about Picher.
Colonel Ewell Head, commander of the 120 guardsmen,
placed a machine-gun squad in front of Evans's Connell
Hotel (which next day became the headquarters of the Tri-

Governor Ernest W. Marland, who ordered the Oklahoma Na-
tional Guard into the Ottawa County portion of the Tri-State
Mining District. Courtesy of Oklahoma Historical Society,
Oklahoma City.

State Union), ordered squads of soldiers to patrol Connell Avenue, and dispatched military patrols throughout the Oklahoma portion of the district. By morning, the threat of open clashes between the new organization and the International Union had substantially subsided.[11]

Headquartered at the Miami fairgrounds until a flooding Neosho River forced a move to the American Legion Hall in Picher, the Oklahoma National Guard became the decisive element in breaking the strike. Governor Marland's ostensible purpose in sending the Guard into the district was to restore and preserve law and order. To accomplish that goal, Colonel Head and his forces further tipped the scales in the strike on the side of the operators and the new Tri-State Union. If nothing else, the Guard's presence persuaded those strikers who were wavering in their commitment that the time had come to desert the union and join the back-to-work movement. Head also left no doubt concerning where his sympathies lay in the industrial dispute, a fact that encouraged the Tri-Staters to commit acts that violated the integrity of the Guard's mission and accelerated the back-to-work movement.

Upon arrival in the district, Colonel Head publicly announced his intentions to maintain order and to protect lives and property. Assisted by McConnell, who remained in the area with a reduced force of state deputies, Head concluded that this could be done without further trouble. Yet he let it be known that if future outbreaks of violence occurred, he had on call five thousand men who could be ordered into the district.[12] On May 29 and 30, Head consulted with groups and organizations whose intent was to break the strike—ore buyers, operators, and the executive committee of the Tri-State Union.

After conferring with Colonel Head, district ore buyers announced their intentions to load ore. Head had assured them, they said, that units of the Guard would be available to protect life and property, although he would not interfere with "peaceful" picketing. On May 30 loading began, observed by union pickets who had unsuccessfully requested the buyers to respect the strike. Instead, the buyers requested that troops be sent and Colonel Head promptly ordered a truckload of guardsmen to the properties involved. Union pickets promptly left the scene and made no further appearances. Loading continued under the protection of the Guard. The buyers made no attempts to remove ore in the Kansas and Missouri portion of the district.[13] On May 30, Head conferred with the executive committee of the Tri-State Union concerning a resumption of mining and milling. Afterwards, Evans, who had now been chosen president of the new union, reported that Head had advised that the military had been sent to preserve law and order and that the companies were therefore free to reopen the mines and mills at any time, fully protected by the Guard.[14] Evans concluded that his organization's drive to get the men back to work, which would break the strike, was totally compatible with Colonel Head's concept of his mission.

Under the aegis of law and order, Head's forces were drawn into the camp of Evans's back-to-work movement which, in the early days of the military presence, gained increasing momentum. Although it is true that neither International nor Tri-State Union members were allowed to congregate in district towns and that demonstrations by unionists or nonunionists were prohibited, it is also true, whether officially intended or not, that the National Guard assisted the operators in reopening the Oklahoma portion of the Tri-State. In the beginning Head severely restricted the number of pickets that the union could place at individual and mills, tolerating only a few. The reduced number around the struck properties publicly signaled a decline in union strength and support for the strike and undoubtedly encouraged the back-to-work movement. Colonel Head also informed the operators that troops would be sent at their request to restrain or disperse pickets who might interfere with their efforts to resume operations.[15] And there were reports that some pickets, although guilty of nothing more than informing the public of their cause, were actually dispersed by the Guard. For example, *Harlow's Weekly* reported on June 8 that "national guardsmen dispersed union picket lines which were formed in the Picher district Monday as mining operations increased." As early as June 4, the *Miami Daily News-Record* reported that "patrolmen of the Tri-State Metal Mine and Smelter Workers Union" had joined squads of the National Guard when they positioned themselves at the mines and mills scheduled for reopening. While the troops remained, their mission complemented the work of the Tri-State Union.

Until the departure of the Guard on June 26, Colonel Head provided military protection upon request to all companies resuming operations in the Oklahoma portion of the district. With each start-up, the union's position became less tenable. When combined with the work of the new union against International Union members, which Head tolerated, the role of the National Guard became the decisive element in breaking the strike. On June 10 the *Joplin Globe* reported that half the mines and mills operating before the strike were back in production in Oklahoma and Kansas, where Governor Alfred M. Landon had also ordered the National Guard into Cherokee County. By June 13, Colonel Head had reduced his command to twenty-six men,[16] a clear indication that authorities expected little, if any, trouble from striking union members. This small contingent of troops was withdrawn on June 26, ending the military presence in the Oklahoma portion of the district.

Before June 6, most of the strike events were centered around Picher where the headquarters of the International Union, the new Tri-State Union, and the Oklahoma National Guard had been located. Across the state line in Cherokee County, Kansas, where only minor incidents had occurred between union and nonunion members, the shutdown remained totally effective. Although many Kansas workers had enlisted in the back-to-work movement of the Tri-State Union and participated in such activities as the "pick-handle parade" in Picher on May 27, these events had had no effect on the strike in the Kansas portion of the district. International Union pickets remained

at various struck properties. Nevertheless, responding to
the strike and the request of different operators, county
authorities had increased law enforcement personnel,
hiring extra deputies in order to provide guards for the
mines and mills of owners who requested protection.[17] Although the Kansas district remained peaceful, the disturbance in nearby Oklahoma and the drive to break the
strike suggested that the prevailing calm in Kansas would
soon end, thus setting the stage for state military intervention. Except for the strike-related unrest across the state
line, county and state officials in Kansas undoubtedly
would not have placed much importance upon a minor incident that they later used to justify ordering the Kansas
National Guard into Cherokee County.

Encouraged by the emergence of the Tri-State Metal
Mine and Smelter Workers Union and its aggressive drive
to break the strike and resume operations in Oklahoma,
F. H. Beck, owner of the Beck No. 3 Tailings Mill near Baxter Springs, reopened his mill on the morning of June 7.
This event attracted nearly fifty International Union pickets who watched during the morning as two trucks hauled
tailings from the nearby Ebenstein Mine, allegedly "threatening violence to the personnel of the mine and refusing
to disperse at the order of the undersheriff [Dick Helman]
and his deputy sheriff."[18] Around 3 P.M., the strikers positioned themselves across the road, stopped and attempted
to overturn the trucks, and physically threatened the drivers. In the confusion, an altercation occurred in which a
driver was slapped across the face. No other violence to
persons or property occurred, although miners working at
the Ebenstein Mine were harassed. With the flow of ore in-
terrupted, Beck's mill was forced to close. As evening fell,
an estimated two hundred pickets, fearing a renewal of
operations next morning, gathered near the mill. This incident, although minor in itself, initiated a sequence of
events that ultimately broke the strike in Kansas.

Fearful that the episode at Beck's mill was a harbinger of
future violence beyond their ability to control when operations resumed, and pressured by area businessmen to seek

state help, Cherokee County Attorney Corbin Shouse and Undersheriff Dick Helman requested that Governor Alfred M. Landon order units of the Kansas National Guard into the Kansas portion of the district. By telephone, telegram, and letter, they described the tense situation around the mill and pleaded for troops to control the pickets who were said to be armed with "rocks, clubs, shot guns and pistols" to prevent another start-up of operations. In a follow-up letter to their initial requests, which revealed their perceptions of events in the Tri-State, Shouse and Helman elaborated on the need for troops. Denying the claims of union leaders that picketing had been peaceful, they charged that pickets had threatened nonunion workers with "bodily harm and in a number of cases" had carried out their threats. Pointing to the new Tri-State Union with its membership of several thousand and its "avowed purpose of making it possible to those who wished to work to go back to their jobs," Shouse and Helman expressed concern that it and the International Union had become "practically . . . two armies" confronting each other. The situation had been made more dangerous in Kansas because "most of the trouble-makers [had] moved up into Cherokee County and [begun] agitating here" when the Oklahoma National Guard had been sent into the Oklahoma portion of the district. Shouse and Helman reported that before their request for troops, they "firmly" believed that the pickets were preparing to seize and destroy the Beck Mill. In their judgment, the Tri-State Union's determination to renew operations had produced a great potential for violence. Troops were necessary to help local officials prevent its outbreak.[19]

Claiming that Section 48-281 of the Revised Statutes of Kansas obligated him to honor such requests from local authorities,[20] Landon ordered Adjutant General Milton R. McLean to send troops into Cherokee County. This action roughly conformed to guidelines concerning the use of the Kansas National Guard that the governor, upon assuming office, had issued to the adjutant general, who had then distributed them broadside to all county sheriffs and mayors throughout Kansas. Missing from the guidelines, however, was any direct reference to the use of the military in either industrial disputes or situations of *potential* violence.[21]

Under the command of Colonel Charles H. Browne, Troops A and F of the 114th Cavalry from Iola and Pleasanton, Troop G of the 137th Infantry from Kansas City, and medical and supply detachments from Wichita and Kansas City, Kansas, moved into the strike area by truck, a total of 243 men arriving before daylight on June 8.[22] Establishing his headquarters at the Empire Hotel in Baxter Springs, Colonel Browne rapidly deployed his forces before dawn at the mines and mills near Treece and Baxter Springs that were expected to resume immediate operations. Protected by the National Guard, work began at several properties on the morning of June 8. As in Oklahoma, the only force capable of breaking the strike was now in place.

Whether the level of violence at the Beck Mill justified a military occupation of the Kansas Tri-State by the Guard remained debatable. On June 8, Labor Commissioner George Blakeley sent Harry Burr, a former official with the United Mine Workers, into the district as an observer. After conferring with county authorities, including Shouse and Helman, Burr reported by telegram:

> [They] stated that no violence had occurred at or near any mine and there had been no destruction of property. County Attorney and sheriffs deputies stated *their requests for Guard based on what might happen.* Toured the mining area with undersheriff [Helman]. Press reports of violence at Beck mine are not true. Small justification for local authorities' request for immediate presence of Guard. Armed forces from Oklahoma area coming across line to compel pickets to withdraw only danger that local officers might not handle. Such force was turned back at state line by undersheriff ten days ago.[23]

Unlike in Picher, Oklahoma, where a significant level of violence on May 27 had led to military intervention by the Oklahoma National Guard, no comparable level of violence existed in the Kansas Tri-State. The request for

Governor Alfred M. Landon, who twice or-
dered the Kansas National Guard into the
Cherokee County portion of the Tri-State
Mining District. Courtesy of Kansas State
Historical Society, Topeka.

General Charles H. Browne, who as a colonel commanded
Kansas troops ordered into Cherokee County during the metal
workers strike. Courtesy of Kansas State Historical Society,
Topeka.

and the sending of the troops resulted from the Tri-State Union's determination to resume operations in Kansas that was expected to spark violent outbreaks from the International Union. The mission of the Kansas Guard was, therefore, to preserve and not to restore order. Paradoxically, sporadic violence occurred in Kansas only after the call for troops had become known. Before the arrival of the Kansas National Guard, at 2 A.M. on June 8 southwest of Riverton, a dynamite blast destroyed two towers of the Empire District Electric Company, shutting off power to the mines, mills, and towns of the district. Unexploded dynamite charges were also found at other towers. Later that day, Ronald Burrell, a member of the new union, used a shotgun to wound Ted Schasteen, an International strike leader picketing the mines near Treece, in both legs and the right arm during an argument about the strike. On June 10, Bob Wells, a truck driver en route with a five-ton load of explosives from Carl Junction, Missouri, to a powder magazine west of Baxter Springs, was harassed by a carload of unidentified men. At Galena, however, he received a National Guard escort to his destination.[24]

Because there was no widespread violence to suppress, Colonel Browne deployed his troops at points where he anticipated violence upon renewal of operations—Treece, Baxter Springs, and Galena. Presumably to maintain the integrity of his mission, he ordered the citizens disarmed; he revoked constable commissions of company guards and seized their weapons if they left company property; he announced that labor meetings and picketing would be tolerated, but he prohibited street crowds and forbade publications that discredited state authorities or their actions. Operating from the Empire Hotel in Baxter Springs, he sent patrols throughout the district, which quickly demonstrated that, despite Browne's rhetoric of impartiality, the Kansas Guard was not an impartial force in the existing industrial dispute between the companies, the Tri-State Union, and the International Union.

On the morning of June 8, Browne's forces dispersed

nearly thirty pickets at the Beck Mill and nearly one hundred around the Webber Mill. These properties immediately resumed operation.[25] Throughout the next few days, mines and mills in the Kansas Tri-State gradually reopened under the protection and supervision of troops. Browne announced that guardsmen would be sent at the request of any operator who wished to resume work. The stated purpose, of course, was to protect lives and property.[26] International Union members in Kansas immediately realized, however, that regardless of Browne's statements of impartiality, the arrival of the Kansas National Guard meant death to their strike. Exploiting the presence of the troops, Evans and the Tri-State Union leaders pushed hard for a start-up of the mines and mills. Browne obliged by providing soldiers upon request to protect the properties, to escort loaded ore trucks from mines to mills, to patrol the district, and to keep union halls and meetings under surveillance.[27] As in Oklahoma, the National Guard played a crucial strike-breaking role.

Nevertheless, Browne was anxious to withdraw the Guard from the strike area. His troops had not encountered any significant violence to suppress. Only a few minor disturbances around Treece had been investigated; there had been no arrests since the troops arrived. Browne insisted that county authorities reassume jurisdiction as soon as possible because the situation was quiet. By June 13, he had reduced his forces by 10 percent and by June 18 a total of eighty-five guardsmen had been ordered home.[28] The colonel continued a rapid decrease of the men in the field.

Browne's reductions provoked a June 19 appeal to Landon from Shouse that a minimum of thirty guardsmen remain in the area. Admitting that there was "no open violence . . . except isolated cases of beating and intimidating throughout the district," Shouse insisted that a total withdrawal would encourage violence because only the "awe on the part of the general public of the National Guards in the district . . . is all that keeps the situation in hand we feel at the present time." He estimated that within two weeks the Tri-State would again be fully operating and that work would diminish the "strength and bitterness of the original trouble making organization [the International Union]" so that local authorities could control the situation. Shouse wanted all the mines and mills operating before a final removal of the Kansas Guard.[29] His sentiments were echoed by Mayor S. A. Douthit of Baxter Springs where Browne's forces were headquartered. In a letter to Landon, Douthit warned that

> to remove from the field at this time the entire force would mean bloodshed in a very few hours, while the presence of these guards for a couple of weeks yet or maybe a little longer will mean a successful ending of a bad situation, and I believe it would be better to keep a few of the guards here a while than to have the whole force back again immediately with possibly the loss of life. Just the presence of these boys in uniform sure has a lot to do with the calmness of the situation.[30]

In contrast to Douthit's gloomy prediction of violence, Ed Cassell, president of Treece Local 111, did not foresee "any trouble after the soldiers leave, because there [had been] no trouble or violence before they were called, not even a fist fight." Local union officials, he asserted, "[were] at a loss to understand why the national guard was called in the first place."[31]

Responding to the appeals of Shouse and Douthit, Landon called Shouse, County Sheriff Earl Neely, and the three Cherokee County commissioners to Topeka where, together with Browne, Adjutant General McLean, and Attorney General Clarence V. Beck, they discussed the replacement of the troops by a special force of civil officers. The Democrat commissioners had previously refused the sheriff's request for twenty-five extra deputies to replace the soldiers as they were withdrawn. According to Landon, they refused to hire the deputies "unless Eagle Picher Lead Company paid their salaries—which it was willing to do. I said no; that would make them company police."[32]

After being threatened by Landon, who was a Republican, with ouster proceedings, the commissioners acquiesced to hiring and placing the deputies on the county payroll.[33] With this agreement, Colonel Browne pulled out his remaining troops on June 27, one day after Colonel Head ended his military occupation of the Oklahoma portion of the Tri-State. For the first time since May 27, the entire district was free of troops.

As the military departed, more than forty of the fifty-four mines and mills operating when the strike began had reopened on a full or part-time basis. Several of the larger properties, such as the Eagle Picher Mining and Smelting Company's Galena smelter, which employed approximately three hundred men, remained shut down. If trouble did reoccur, it was likely to be at such mills where large numbers of unionists worked. Ironically, on June 27 as the last troops were being withdrawn from Cherokee County, Eagle Picher officials announced that the Galena smelter would reopen the next day. A petition to the company from forty "leading" Galena merchants may have influenced the decision to renew operations.[34]

From the standpoint of public order, the timing of the reopening could not have been worse. Landon was not pleased. He later wrote that:

> [W]hen it [the smelter] had opened the day the troops were leaving, I said to the attorney for the Eagle Pitcher [sic] who had come to see me, "Either your management is dumb or ignorant." He said, "I don't know, Governor, I'll ask the superintendent to come and see you." He came in, sat down in front of me, said, "I understand you think I am either dumb or ignorant." I said, "Yes, and I'll make up my mind when I get through our conversation which, if it is just plain dumbness, I might forgive you." Later on I became well acquainted with him. He was a pretty nice chap and it was just typical corporation management thinking especially evident in those days.[35]

Despite his reservation about the reopening, Landon did not interfere. Nevertheless, striking union members throughout the Tri-State determined to keep the huge smelter closed.

Located east of Galena and just north of Old Highway 66 near the Kansas–Missouri state line, the Eagle Picher smelter stood as a "great gray hulk surrounded by a maze of chat-covered roads and railroad tracks" on twenty acres of land. When in operation it ran twenty-four hours a day, processing daily nearly 200 tons of lead concentrate into 150 tons of pig lead. It employed nearly three hundred workers with a normal monthly payroll of approximately $20,000.[36] It was the loss of this payroll that undoubtedly prompted Galena's merchants to petition Eagle Picher to reopen the plant. The attempted start-up provoked the greatest violence to date in the strike and confirmed Mayor Douthit's dismal prediction of June 19.

During the night of June 27, several hundred armed pickets gathered across Highway 66 in front of the smelter. Officials of Eagle Picher later charged that hundreds of International Union members had boarded trucks in Treece and traveled to Galena, where they took up positions to block the reopening of the smelter. What happened there, they claimed, was not a spontaneous outbreak of violence by striking workers but was "planned, concerted, deliberate violence."[37] By morning an angry crowd, apparently drawn from throughout the district, lined each side of Highway 66, determined to keep the smelter closed. As strikebreakers from Missouri crossed the state line into Kansas, their automobiles were stoned, clubbed, shot at, overturned, and in one instance, burned. Windshields and windows were broken, fist fights erupted, and a riot ensued, causing a number of personal injuries. Although one person was shot, there were no fatalities as the strikers successfully prevented anyone from entering the smelter. In the afternoon, back-to-work miners returning to Missouri were also beset by the mob. Estimates of the numbers blocking Highway 66 varied, ranging from three hundred to nine hundred. Throughout the day, the strikers and their supporters prevailed until dispersed by a heavy rainfall about 7:30 P.M. Two hours later, however, they were back, concentrating now in front of the smelter rather than along the roadside.[38]

Nightfall failed to reduce the potential for violence. Inside the smelter were twenty-seven armed guards, including Luther Sons, a known criminal employed by Eagle Picher.[39] These men had entered the works during the night of June 26. Across Highway 66 in front of the smelter, an estimated two hundred pickets, some with weapons, had stationed themselves. About 9:30 P.M. a shot rang out, each side later denying responsibility. Heavy gunfire then erupted between the guards and the strikers but, miraculously, no one was injured in the exchange. For two hours or more the opposing forces fired on each other.[40] This episode, by far the most serious clash between the strikers and the back-to-workers, raised again the possibility of general violence throughout the Tri-State. Reports circulated that nonunion workers were arming and threatening to move against the strikers at Galena. And in Picher, 150 Tri-State Union members rallied in response to the new turmoil in the district.

In a telegram to Governor Landon, County Attorney Shouse and County Sheriff Neely appealed for one hundred men of the Kansas National Guard to restore order around Galena. Fred Farmer, mayor of Galena, was not asked to join in the request because he openly supported the strike.[41] Once again, Landon had to decide whether to inject troops into this continuing industrial dispute. He was reluctant to do so. Earlier he had concluded that much of the labor unrest in the district had been caused by obstinate operators and the new union, and he was noncommital about ordering a second military intervention. On June 28, the *Kansas City Star* quoted Landon as saying: "The operators organized company unions and placed a thoroughly disreputable man [Evans] at the head of them. No decent public officer can cooperate with him." This statement brought an immediate response from Evans's supporters who strongly defended him and his work with the new union.[42] Nevertheless, on June 28, when mobs rioted and closed Highway 66 and fired on the smelter, Landon again felt compelled to act. The level of violence at Galena far exceeded that at the Beck Mill in early June when he had ordered out the troops, and he again believed himself legally bound to honor the request of Shouse and Neely for assistance. He therefore ordered units of the National Guard back to Cherokee County.

In this second intervention, military rule was more severe than the first when no one was arrested. Commanded by Colonel Browne, approximately 225 guardsmen arrived early on the morning of June 29. Rushing to the smelter, they rescued the company guards and set up machine guns at strategic points. They occupied Galena. Browne then declared martial law and established a provost court in Galena to enforce it. He ordered the surrender of arms and, on June 29, the Guard seized 250 guns and a large collection of clubs, knives, pipes, and blackjacks. Most of these weapons were taken from Missourians en route on Highway 66 to work in Kansas and Oklahoma.[43] Browne placed restrictions on freedom of the press, speech, and assemblage; he ordered the arrest of anyone without visible means of support.[44] By July 18, as many as sixty men had been apprehended, tried, convicted, and sentenced up to sixty days by the Guard's provost court for rioting, perjury, or seditious speech.[45] Furthermore, Browne prodded local officers to enforce civil law more vigorously, causing them to step up their arrests for intoxication, improper license tags, violations of local tax laws, and so on.[46] Under his directions, they tightened law enforcement throughout the county, with striking workers being the principal victims.

In the meantime, Browne again performed a strike-breaking role. On the morning of July 9, he sent a "carload of guardsmen" to the Ballard Mine, which thirty or forty pickets had kept closed. Under military protection it reopened, causing all but a few of the pickets to disperse.[47] The Galena smelter, however, remained shut down, and

Machine-gun post of Oklahoma National Guard in Miami, Oklahoma. Courtesy of *Kansas City (Missouri) Star*.

A detachment of the 137th Infantry, Kansas National Guard, on strike duty in Cherokee County. Courtesy of *Kansas City (Missouri) Star*.

Military court of Kansas National Guard in session at Galena, Kansas, following smelter riot in June 1935. Colonel Charles H. Browne, commanding, sits second from left. Courtesy of *Kansas City (Missouri) Star.*

its labor force and monthly payroll were vital to the economic life of Galena. Consequently, nearly everyone was eager to have it reopen—the strikers, if an agreement with the Eagle Picher Company could be reached, and the merchants, with or without an agreement. On July 9, businessmen circulated a second petition requesting that Eagle Picher restart the smelter. Five hundred people endorsed it. In a surprise move before dawn on July 16, Browne's troops and a large force of special deputies quietly ushered approximately one hundred workers into the smelter and it reopened without incident.[48] Special deputies had been stationed on each side of Highway 66 in both Kansas and Missouri, indicating a well-coordinated, secretive plan involving officials in the two states. In Missouri, for example, more than a hundred armed and motorized special officers protected strikebreakers en route to Kansas and Oklahoma. Jasper County Prosecuting Attorney Charles R. Warden asked Governor Guy B. Parks to order out the

Missouri National Guard. He refused.[49] Ironically, no union
pickets or sympathizers showed up before the smelter during the day. Protected by military and county forces, the
smelter gradually returned to normal operations.

Desiring to withdraw the troops and yet to have the area
"protected," Landon and Browne insisted that a special
force of deputies be appointed and funded by Cherokee
County. Before ending the first intervention, Landon had
demanded that the county hire twenty-five deputies to
handle strike-related emergencies and public disorder.
But the county commissioners had failed to act promptly
and nothing had been done at the time of the Galena riot.
Prodded by Browne, the mayors of Columbus, Baxter
Springs, Treece, and Galena, the county commissioners,
the county sheriff, and the county attorney met on July 5
at Columbus where they finalized plans for a twenty-five-
man force to be trained by Browne's officers. To support it
and relieve the fears of county officials, Browne agreed to
continue martial law and the provost court until he had
withdrawn the last soldier. Within a week, new County
Sheriff Charles E. Simkin named the special deputies, who
came to be called the "civilian army" or the "civil army,"
and began twenty-four-hour patrols of the Kansas district.

On July 21, with this civilian force in place, Browne, who
had already withdrawn substantial numbers of his men, removed the remainder except for Major Ellis G. Christensen, who was left in command of the county until
August 7 when martial law was revoked. This unusual arrangement was effective. In a report dated July 28, 1935,
Christensen noted that "it is significant fact that not one
man on either side of the strike issue has been beaten up in
Kansas. Everyday from one to five are taken out and beat
up in Okla."[50] By early September conditions had so stabi-
lized that the county commissioners reduced the number
of special deputies to six, and in early October, they authorized Sheriff Simkin to discharge the remainder.[51]

To the south in the Oklahoma portion of the district, the
Galena riot produced reverberations. Under the protec-

tion of the Oklahoma National Guard and the repressive acts of the Tri-State Union, the companies had broken the strike, a fact reflected in the increased output of ores and concentrates during June and July. Several hundred International Union members, however, refused to accept defeat and continued to picket, visible evidence that the strike officially survived. Nevertheless, except for isolated clashes involving pickets, strikebreakers, and "squad car" crews,[52] Ottawa County was peaceful. Direct state intervention was limited to the presence of Owen J. Watts, an assistant attorney general, and four members of the State Bureau of Investigation. In response to the violence in Galena, however, Governor Marland ordered additional "operatives" and state highway patrolmen into the district for awhile,[53] and he sent Colonel Head to take command of law enforcement. He did not order in the Oklahoma National Guard.

Like Colonel Browne of Kansas, Head forced a reorganization of law enforcement in Ottawa County. He ordered Sheriff Dry to revoke hundreds of deputy commissions that had been issued before July 1. With the approval of the county attorney and the county commissioners, Dry then appointed seventy-five special deputies to serve under Deputy Sheriff Henry Blanton. (Dry also issued deputy commissions to company watchmen.) Operating in shifts, Blanton's deputies patroled the Oklahoma district around the clock. Special sleeping quarters were set up in Picher so that reinforcements would be immediately available.[54] When Major Christensen of the Kansas National Guard called on Colonel Head in Picher in late July, he found "almost as many deputies there as they have miners."[55]

With the creation of special deputy forces in Ottawa and Cherokee counties, the first phase of military intervention in the Tri-State ended. From the standpoint of the operators and the new union, the military presence had been a godsend; for the International Union, it had been a disaster. Behind the rubric of law and order, the National Guard of both Oklahoma and Kansas threw the power of the state behind the back-to-work movement, which was instrumental in breaking the strike. Protected by the military, the leaders of the new Tri-State Union and the operators struck blow after blow against the International Union and tightened their control over the district. In doing so, they set the stage for even greater violence in 1937.

The Tri-State Metal Mine And Smelter Workers Union And The Companies

ON May 28, the day after the formal organization of the Tri-State Metal Mine and Smelter Workers Union and the arrival of the troops, Mike Evans arranged for a temporary back-to-work headquarters at his Connell Hotel in Picher under the protection of the Oklahoma National Guard. Glenn Hickman, the custodian of the movement's enrollment records after becoming secretary-treasurer of the new union, temporarily moved into the hotel to facilitate the work of recruiting more workers to join the 3,125 who had already enlisted in the movement. According to Hickman, as "the custodian of the records, I was given a room by Mike, and worked, ate and slept for several days without leaving the building."[1] Operating from the Connell office, the newly organized union, ably assisted by the larger companies, rapidly came to dominate the district.

With the creation of the Tri-State Union and the military intervention of the Oklahoma and Kansas National Guard units, a shift of power occurred that favored the opponents of the International Union of Mine, Mill and Smelter Workers. Exploiting the presence of the troops, their mission of preserving law and order, and their assistance in reopening mines, mills, and smelters, Tri-State Union leaders launched a full-scale offensive against the locals of the International Union designed to destroy them and to reimpose company control over the district. This strategy forced the International Union into a desperate struggle for survival and severely limited its ability to direct a successful strike. In its assault on the International Union, the Tri-State Union established links with the major com-

panies of the district, particularly with the Eagle Picher
Lead Company, the Eagle Picher Mining and Smelting
Company, and the Commerce Mining and Royalty Company, and quickly became one of the boldest and best-led
company unions of the 1930s. According to Hickman: "I
have no doubt that members of the [Executive] Committee
had close communication with their respective superiors,
giving verbal reports and co-ordinating their views and
activities with their various company policy [*sic*] and
wishes."[2] The combined onslaught of the new union, the
companies, the National Guard units of both Kansas and
Oklahoma, and the prevailing adverse economic conditions sent the International locals reeling.

Before the formation of the Tri-State Union on May 27,
the direct involvement of the mining and milling companies in the back-to-work movement was difficult, if not
impossible, to confirm. Nevertheless, the highly visible
activities of supervisory personnel strongly suggested a
behind-the-scenes company encouragement and manipulation of the movement designed to break the strike and
return the men to work. The argument, later advanced
by an attorney for the Eagle Picher companies,[3] that the
workers naturally turned to their supervisors for leadership because they exercised the greatest influence in persuading the operators to reopen their properties was less
than convincing. Equally unconvincing was Hickman's explanation that the times and events, the ferment of the
movement, was primarily responsible for catapulting supervisors, such as himself, into dominant roles. Perhaps
more persuasive was the argument that the supervisors, as
hurt by the strike as everyone else in the district, forged to
the forefront of the back-to-work movement on their own
initiative, fully cognizant, however, that the operators fully
supported their efforts. Whatever the reasons for the involvement of supervisory personnel, their emergence as
the leaders of the new Tri-State Union was clearly more
than coincidental. However obscure the relationship between the companies and the back-to-work movement was
before the organization of the Tri-State Union, afterwards

that relationship became more clearly defined as the new organization rapidly assumed the characteristics of a company union.

The linkup between the Tri-State Union and the companies began early. In late May, Evans conferred with George Potter, vice-president of the Eagle Picher Mining and Smelting Company, and other operators concerning conditions in the district, the back-to-work movement, the suffering of the Tri-State's workers, and other matters. These discussions revealed a commonality of interests and purposes between the Tri-State Union and the companies, and they set the stage for major company involvement and support of the new union under a humanitarian guise. During his meetings with the operators, Evans professed to be greatly alarmed and concerned by the privation of Tri-State workers and their families, claiming that some people were actually starving. In the interests of relieving the destitution, according to Evans, "all the operators in the region or all the larger ones" agreed to contribute substantial sums of money to the new union.[4] This highly irregular procedure of giving funds to the Tri-State Union for distribution to suffering workers, thereby converting a strike-breaking organization into a relief agency, exposed an extraordinary naivete on the part of Evans and the operators. The sudden emergence of Evans as a humanitarian, the timing of the financial aid to the Tri-State Union, the decision of responsible company officials to funnel money through the union rather than to utilize the Red Cross and other established charities, and, above all, the subterfuge and unorthodox means employed in the transfer of money to the union and its subsequent use for non-humanitarian purposes—all suggested a smoke screen to hide the actual purpose of the funds. That purpose was, of course, to assist the Tri-State Union in eliminating the International Union from the district.

Working through Charles A. Neal, a mine-owning vice-president of the Security Bank and Trust Company of Miami, Potter arranged for the bank to grant immediate loans to the Tri-State Union upon the submission of its notes by either Evans or Hickman. No union collateral backed these notes, the only security being an oral agreement between Potter and Neal that Eagle Picher Mining and Smelting Company would immediately pay off the obligation upon notification. There was no written agreement to protect the bank against default by either the union or Eagle Picher. Nor did the bank receive any interest on the loans, nor compensation for its services, nor maintain any records of the transactions involving the union and itself. Neal gave W. P. Howard, a cashier at the bank, the responsibility of managing this unusual arrangement.[5]

From June 1 to July 8, 1935, Evans visited the Security Bank and Trust Company and, after presenting Howard with notes on the Tri-State Union for sums ranging from $1,000 to $5,000, received either cash, a cashier's check, or a deposit slip until the total reached $17,500. Although the checks received in payment of the notes by the Security Bank and Trust Company were drawn on Eagle Picher's account in the Commerce Trust Company of Kansas City, Missouri, Eagle Picher was not the sole source of the funds. Later, Howard indicated that although Eagle Picher repaid the loans, usually on the same day that they were made, Eagle Picher was "only acting as a collecting agency for other operators" who provided Eagle Picher with contributions to help pay off the notes of the Tri-State Union. Two years later, after becoming a vice-president of the Security Bank and Trust Company, Howard insisted that this highly unusual arrangement in which no records were kept occurred because the loans were for the "raising and distribution of relief, [and] this bank made no charge therefore." He portrayed the bank's role as a form of pulic service.[6] Thus under the rubric of humanitarian concern for the plight of the Tri-State workers, money from the operators flowed into the treasury of the new union at its inception, at a time when no dues were being collected on the membership and when organizational start-up expenses were heavy. No dues were imposed on Tri-State Union members until July. Not until then did the company contributions cease.

In later testimony before a National Labor Relations Board hearing, Evans repeatedly emphasized that the money the union received through the Security Bank and Trust Company was used exclusively to relieve the destitution among Tri-State workers without regard to their Tri-State Union or their International Union membership. Furthermore, he stated that in his discussion with Potter, Potter had stressed that the funds furnished by the companies must not be used for union activities. Howard also insisted at the hearing upon the humanitarian character of the arrangement described above. But, unbelievably, company officials did not demand any formal accounting of how the money was spent to confirm its humanitarian use. Evans stated at the hearing that he was not accountable to anyone and was not obligated to furnish written reports to anybody concerning the uses of the money. As he stated, "I don't remember that I accounted for it in any way."[7] The failure of the operators to require proof that the money was expended to help the destitute cast serious doubts upon their humanitarian intent, and it suggested instead that they placed a higher priority on the Tri-State Union's objectives of strike-breaking and union-busting than upon providing relief and assistance to Tri-State workers.

Under the cloak of charity and humanity, the larger mining and milling companies poured money into the new union during its formative period. On June 1 the Security Bank and Trust Company received a check for $5,000 from Eagle Picher Mining and Smelting Company to pay off a Tri-State Union note that Evans had presented to Howard on the same day. Using the proceeds from this and other notes, Evans and Hickman established a Tri-State Union account at the First State Bank of Picher where $14,000 was deposited between June 1 and July 1, 1935. From the start, officials of the Tri-State Union drew on this account to pay organizational expenses and other costs associated with breaking the strike and the International

Union in the district.[8] Because the Tri-State Union did not collect dues from its members until after July 1, it found the operators' money indispensable in establishing itself.

Because of the early financial links that Evans and Potter established between the Tri-State Union and the operators through the Security Bank and Trust Company, it is unlikely that the two men failed to consult with one another concerning the back-to-work movement before the formal organization of the Tri-State Union. Evans's business relationship with Eagle Picher Mining and Smelting Company produced frequent contacts between the two. In 1933, Evans had acquired the Craig lease from the company and, at the time of the strike, was supplying ore to the company's Central Mill. Furthermore, in May 1935 he acquired an additional lease (the John L.) and a shared interest in another lease (the Nesbitt) in 1936. During the years of 1935 to 1937, Evans sold ores valued at $350,000 from these leases to Eagle Picher, from which he received substantial profits under the leasing contracts. Because all the businesses in Picher had been constructed on land leased from the Eagle Picher companies, Evans—as one of the town's foremost entrepreneurs—was unusually vulnerable to the short-term cancellation provisions of the lease contracts.[9] To an unusual extent, Evans's fortunes and those of the Eagle Picher companies were irrevocably joined. In view of this close economic relationship, it would have been extraordinary had not Evans and Potter, a highly placed official of the mining and smelting company and the representative of the larger operators in the early funding of the Tri-State Union, conferred and discussed mutual strategy to break the International Union. That this occurred was further demonstrated by the cooperation that developed between the new union and the operators in breaking the strike and establishing the Tri-State Union as a dominant force in the Tri-State.

The aura of law and order that descended upon the Oklahoma portion of the district with the arrival of the Oklahoma National Guard on May 27 was deceptive. Fully supported by the larger operators and a sympathetic military presence, the leaders of the new Tri-State Union forged a powerful organization whose tactics and methods ranged from a sophisticated intimidation of the workers to outright violence and terror. Nevertheless, Ottawa County officials rallied to the anti–International Union nexus and, allegedly to protect lives and property from an expected onslaught by the International Union's members, they authorized an increase in the county law enforcement staff by deputizing men who soon fell under the effective control of Evans and the Tri-State Union's executive committee. County Sheriff Dry, reacting to the severe beating he had received at the hands of International Union members on May 27, informally surrendered his responsibilities of office to Evans's new union when he handed out deputy commissions to its members and engaged in activities of questionable legality.[10] Under Dry the sheriff's office became an arm of the Tri-State Union.

Other evidence indicated a rallying of anti–International Union forces behind the Tri-State Union and suggested that local, state, and company officials were expecting and quietly preparing to engage the union in industrial war if necessary to crush its locals. Turning to the Lake Erie Chemical Company and the Federal Laboratories, two companies the LaFollette Civil Liberties Committee had singled out as the major suppliers of tear and nausea gases, they purchased and stockpiled gas weapons similar to those being used by many corporations in the 1930s to break workers' demonstrations in support of strikes.

Between May 28 and July 23, 1935, when the Tri-State Union was engaged in its most violent acts against International Union members, eight companies of the district spent $2,304.56 for the tear and nausea gases, and state and local authorities spent $1,239.59 for such weapons. Evans himself made two purchases from the Federal Laboratories, one on June 19 for $54 and another on June 25 for $50. Whether these weapons were purchased for use by his companies or the use of the Tri-State Union is unknown. Most probably the weapons were readily available to the new union. Of equal significance to Evans's pur-

chases were those made by Sheriff Dry, who on July 3 and
9 ordered $182 and $99 in gas weapons from the Federal
Laboratories. (See tables 1 and 2.) Dry's supportive role in
the work of the Tri-State Union suggests that his purchases
were also available to the union for crushing the International locals. City officials of Joplin and Miami, officials of
the Oklahoma Bureau of Criminal Investigation, the Oklahoma Highway Department, and of Baxter Springs and
Cherokee County, who were all involved in the labor dispute in the Tri-State, made purchases of gas weapons from
the Lake Erie and Federal Laboratories companies. Both
employers and law enforcement officials clearly anticipated that the Tri-State Union's plan of breaking the strike
and the old union would provoke open warfare.

During the weeks following the birth of the Tri-State
Metal Mine and Smelter Workers Union, its leaders exploited the friendly presence of the Oklahoma and Kansas
National Guard units, the sympathetic support of Sheriff
Dry, and the strong support of the larger operators to
strike damaging blows against the International Union.
Vigilantism flourished. Shortly after May 27, the Tri-State
Union created a "squad car" force, an elaborately organized vigilante group allegedly formed to protect lives and
property by patrolling the district roads and mining properties. Sheriff Dry and Colonel Head of the Oklahoma National Guard, who knew of this group and collaborated
with it, approved its activities, most of which occurred during the military occupation in the Oklahoma portion of the
district. Directed by Evans and Fred Carpenter and composed of seventy-five to a hundred deputized unemployed
men who were placed on the Tri-State Union payroll, the
squad-car crews reconnoitered the Tri-State, usually at
night, to "secure" the district for the men wanting to return to work.

The squad-car operation allegedly served another purpose. According to Hickman, secretary-treasurer of the
new union, the utilization of men in the squad cars provided a form of "indirect relief" or work relief for the
unemployed Tri-State Union members. Consequently,

TABLE 1. *Purchase of Tear, Nauseating Gas, and Equipment by Mining, Smelting and Electric Companies in the Tri-State Mining District:*
May 28 to July 23, 1935[11]

Purchaser	Location	Date	Amount	Source
Commerce Mining & Royalty Co.	Miami, OK	5-28-35	$432.00	Federal Laboratories, Inc.
Commerce Mining & Royalty Co.	Miami, OK	6-3-35	296.00	Federal Laboratories, Inc.
Eagle Picher Lead Co.	Joplin, MO	6-12-35	121.26	Federal Laboratories, Inc.
Admiralty Zinc Co.	Miami, OK	6-12-35	71.50	Federal Laboratories, Inc.
F. W. Evans	Picher, OK	6-19-35	54.00	Federal Laboratories, Inc.
Empire District Electric Co.	Picher, OK	6-24-35	182.00	Federal Laboratories, Inc.
Peru-Laclede Syndicate	Picher, OK	6-24-35	62.00	Federal Laboratories, Inc.
F. W. Evans	Picher, OK	6-25-35	50.00	Federal Laboratories, Inc.
Woodchuck Mine	Picher, OK	6-27-35	30.00	Federal Laboratories, Inc.
Commerce Mining & Royalty Co.	Miami, OK	7-3-35	780.80	Federal Laboratories, Inc.
Peru-Laclede Syndicate	Picher, OK	7-9-35	55.00	Federal Laboratories, Inc.
Eagle Picher Mining and Smelting Co.	Galena, KS	7-23-35	170.00	Lake Erie Chemical Company

TABLE 2. *Purchase of Tear, Nauseating Gas and Equipment by State and Local Authorities of Missouri, Kansas, and Oklahoma: May 29 to July 12, 1935*

Purchaser	Location	Date	Amount	Source
City of Joplin	Joplin, MO	5-29-35	$54.97	Lake Erie Chemical Co.
City of Miami	Miami, OK	5-29-35	85.00	Federal Laboratories, Inc.
Sheriff, Ottawa County	Miami, OK	7-3-35	182.00	Federal Laboratories, Inc.
Sheriff, Ottawa County	Miami, OK	7-9-35	99.00	Federal Laboratories, Inc.
State Bureau of Criminal Identification & Investigation	Oklahoma City, OK	7-9-35	44.00	Federal Laboratories, Inc.
State Bureau of Criminal Identification & Investigation	Oklahoma City, OK	7-9-35	506.20	Federal Laboratories, Inc.
State Tax Commission	Oklahoma City, OK	7-9-35	81.92	Federal Laboratories, Inc.
State Highway Department	Oklahoma City, OK	7-9-35	81.00	Federal Laboratories, Inc.
Cherokee County	Columbus, KS	7-12-35	40.00	Federal Laboratories, Inc.
Baxter Springs	Baxter Springs, KS	7-12-35	65.50	Federal Laboratories, Inc.

much of the funds being channeled into the union by the operators through the Security Bank and Trust Company of Miami was used to underwrite this deputized enforcement arm of Evans's organization. If the operators' true intent was to relieve destitution among men thrown out of work by the International Union's strike, then nothing demonstrated more thoroughly than this use their poor judgment in arranging for large sums of money to be placed in Evans's hands without provisions for accountability. How much of the operators' $17,500 was spent to support the squad cars remains unknown. Hickman professed not to be certain of the exact amount because the original financial records of the Tri-State Union were allegedly stolen and burned. Nonetheless, he estimated that the sum ranged from $5,000 to $10,000.[12] Furthermore, Charles Windbigler, a bookkeeper for the new union from its founding until July 1, 1937, indicated that substantial payments to the squad-car members and to Evans for rental space in his Connell Hotel as headquarters of the union had been "charged to an account and wiped out by subscription," that is, by money from the operators.[13] Thus the squad-car crews symbolized the fusion of three elements of the antistrike nexus—the Tri-State Union, Ottawa County law enforcement, and the mining and milling companies.

Evans was responsible for launching the squad-car operation. On May 29, two days after the founding of the new organization, he asked Fred Carpenter, who also held a mining lease from the Eagle Picher Mining and Smelting Company, to coordinate, direct, and command this new group. Initially headquartered at the Connell Hotel, it was later moved to the old headquarters building of the Tri-State Zinc and Lead Ore Producers' Association. While in charge of the squad cars, Carpenter operated directly under the supervision of Sheriff Dry and, after the arrival of the Oklahoma National Guard, under Colonel Head. Dividing the district up into as many as eight zones for patrolling, Carpenter assigned one car, occasionally more, to each zone. Each car was operated by its owner who, with three other men, made up its crew. In selecting the personnel for this duty, Carpenter picked "qualified" men who had not been on relief. Each man received four dollars for an eight-hour shift on patrol, with the owner receiving extra compensation for the use of his car. Placed on the Tri-State Union's payroll, they were paid from the subscription fund donated by the operators.[14]

The activities of the squad-car crews raised serious questions about the relationships among the officials of the Tri-State Union, the Ottawa County sheriff's office, the Oklahoma National Guard, and the mining and milling companies of the district. In the weeks following May 27, the new organization rallied support with pick-handle parades, violence, and threats of violence, but its strongest arm in effecting a broad return to work was the fleet of squad cars that prowled over the district at night.[15]

The homes of union members were kept under surveillance. Ray Keller, a constable at Hockerville sympathetic to the International Union, recalled nights when squad cars were parked with headlights directed at his house for long periods of time. On other nights, crew members parked in front of his home and remained there for hours, causing him to flee into hiding. Keller recalled that "there wasn't no sleep them days."[16] Squad-car crews often stopped and searched automobiles suspected of carrying union members. Crew members devised a self-identifying system of signals for use at night that consisted of blinking the car lights a specified number of times with a designated response. If an oncoming driver failed to respond properly, his car was stopped, searched, and the occupants examined. In one incident, W. W. Waters, Governor Marland's labor representative in the district, failed to give the correct response and was stopped.[17]

Reports circulated of beatings and kidnappings on the public highways. If International Union members were found abroad at night, violence could result. On the evening of June 9, 1935, Dave McGregory was beaten by unknown assailants and left on the highway. Rescued by a squad-car crew, he was taken to the Connell Hotel where

Evans, Carpenter, Colonel Head, and others were present. McGregory later stated that Evans took him aside and informed him that Carpenter had sentenced him (McGregory) to jail, but if he agreed to join the Tri-State Union, he would be given a deputy commission and a gun and be released. When McGregory refused Evans's offer, Sheriff Dry temporarily jailed him at Miami. No charges were ever filed.[18] In early June 1935, a squad-car crew armed with rifles, shotguns, and pump guns aroused Ray Keller in the middle of the night and with the command, "Get in [the car], you son-of-a-bitch," took him to Tri-State Union headquarters at the Connell Hotel, which was being protected by Oklahoma National Guard patrols. Taken to a back room, he was interrogated by Carpenter about the incident at the Beck Mill. When he demanded to see the sheriff, he was taken out of the hotel and saved from a beating only by the timely arrival of deputies from Cherokee County.[19]

Pickets were subjected to the full wrath of the squad-car crews. While picketing, sixty-six-year-old John O'Dell was thrashed by five members of a squad car—two of whom were known criminals—leaving him with a broken arm and a badly damaged face. Among his assailants were Sylvester Walters and Roy Jamison who were identified by W. W. Waters as "rather top notch criminals." Dee T. Watters, a member of the Oklahoma Bureau of Criminal Investigation, also identified Walters as "Missouri Criminal No. 1." These two men served as Evans's personal bodyguards; they were on the Tri-State Union payroll and paid from funds contributed by the operators.[20] Herman Swearinger recalled that armed men from several squad cars beat him as he picketed a struck mine.[21] And Charles T. Meek reported being beaten by members of a squad car led by Blackie Branstetter.[22] Often the heavily armed squad-car crews merely intimidated the strikers. Clayton Johnson remembered such an incident at the Lawyers Mine of the Mid-Continent Lead and Zinc Company in Kansas where Joe Nolan arrived with four cars loaded with more than a dozen men. Nolan informed the pickets that

they would have to do their picketing across the state line
in Oklahoma nearer the entrance to the mine.[23] Unarmed
pickets were easily intimidated. W. W. Waters, who claimed
to have constantly patroled the district during the weeks of
the strike, later reported that he had never seen pickets
bearing arms and never seen them attack members of the
Tri-State Union.[24] This was in sharp contrast to the squad-
car crews of the Tri-State Union.

Parelee Meek, a waitress at the Connell Restaurant where
the crews ate, remembered that they were armed with clubs,
blackjacks, German Lugers, and other weapons when eat-
ing meals paid for by the union. On one occasion, Blackie
Branstetter warned Mrs. Meek that she should keep her
husband, an International Union member, off the picket
line because next day Branstetter's crew intended to beat
up on union pickets.[25] The shooting of Ted Schasteen,
president of Treece Local 111, by Ronald Burrell who had
been on the Tri-State Union's payroll, was further evidence
that membership in a local of the International Union was
dangerous. On June 8, 1935, while Schasteen put air into
automobile tires, Burrell shot the union leader, hitting him
in both legs and the right arm. Upon complaining to authorities, Schasteen was arrested and jailed before being
taken to the hospital for treatment. He subsequently was
jailed for ten days before being released on bond.[26] Various
International Union members were forcibly taken to the
Tri-State Union's headquarters at the Connell Hotel, where
they were interrogated by Evans and Carpenter in the
presence of local law enforcement officials. This procedure was to harass, intimidate, and force International
members to renounce their union membership, for few of
the men were ever remanded to the authorities for prosecution on any charge.[27]

Sheriff Dry joined in this harassment and violence. After
arresting one striking member, Dry informed his prisoner
during interrogation that he would be immediately released upon renouncing his membership in the union.
And during this same period, Dry and Puss Blanton, a former deputized member of the squad-car force, confronted

a group of two hundred strikers, with women and children present, who were listening to an elderly man named Roper discuss their constitutional rights in a vacant lot in Hockerville. Backed by twelve to fifteen men from several squad cars, Dry ordered the crowd to disperse. When Roper instructed his audience to remain, Dry commanded Blanton to hurl a tear gas cannister into the crowd. The escaping gas caused a mild panic. According to Dewey Knight, Allie Thompson, and Myrtle Price, all of whom were at the meeting, the escaping gas caused temporary blindness, choking, and nosebleeds among persons in the crowd.[28]

Throughout June and early July, the Connell Hotel throbbed with activity as heavily armed squad-car members, wearing their weapons in full view, left for and returned from patrol duty. While sitting in the Connell's lobby, Owen J. Watts, assistant state attorney general for Oklahoma, observed these armed crews and suggested to Tri-State Union officials that the number of weapons be reduced.[29] Watts's presence was further evidence that highly placed state officials knew of and tolerated, perhaps sanctioned, the work of the new union. Yet, occasionally the presence of these officials ameliorated somewhat the violence directed at the strikers. For example, while in an automobile with three associates near the entrance to Picher No. 12 Mine, W. W. Waters observed five pickets position themselves across the road near the mine. Eight men quickly emerged and a fight ensued. Waters and his colleagues intervened and arrested all thirteen persons involved in the fracas. Five pistols were seized from the eight men from the mine; no weapons were found on the five pickets.[30] Waters's intervention undoubtedly prevented bloodshed.

In April 1975, an unidentified miner from Quapaw, Oklahoma, recalled the violence of the times when he stated:

But you must remember that the companies had a lot at stake, too. And they had a "system" for use in any argument. Their men would cruise around and just get out and beat the hell out of any AFL picket. [The International Union was an affiliate of the AFL before becoming a charter member of the CIO.] Even the militia couldn't do much with that, and they were recalled after awhile.[31]

Ironically, most of the violence directed against striking International members occurred in June and July when the Oklahoma National Guard and an enlarged deputy force were highly visible throughout the district and when the "law and order" efforts of the Tri-State Union were therefore totally unjustified. This fact, together with the supervision that Sheriff Dry and Colonel Head exercised over Carpenter's direction of the squad cars, suggested an unspoken alliance among officials of the companies, the new union, the sheriff's office, and the Oklahoma National Guard to crush the International locals and return the men to work.

Evans speedily formalized the developing connection between the companies and the Tri-State Union. In doing so he enjoyed singular success. On May 29 the executive committee met with the leading operators, who agreed to renew production if assured that there would be no future strikes in the district. The committee provided that assurance, thereby confirming the new union as a no-strike organization.[32] Following this meeting, Evans obtained formal recognition of the Tri-State Union as the collective bargaining agent for the men actually working in the mines and mills.

The operators, who had rejected recognition of the International Union because of their commitment to the principle of the open shop, now signed identical contracts with the new union that provided for the preferential hiring of its members. Although reserving a company's right to continue to employ nonmembers, the contract stipulated that

we [company officials] hereby agree to meet with any representative or committee from your union [Tri-State Union], bearing proper credentials, to discuss any matters whatsoever pertaining to employment or working conditions, and *to recog-*

nize and meet with your representative to the exclusion of all organizations; and will endeavor to adjust matters which they may bring before us.[33]

The contract also expressed appreciation to the leaders of the new union for their "organizing the actual workers in the Tri-State field for the purpose of dealing with the employers."[34] Under the circumstances it established a closed shop, which practically eliminated the possibility that International Union members could find work in the district. John Campbell, who was in charge of personnel matters in the Eagle Picher mines and mills, acknowledged that Eagle Picher's agreement with the Tri-State Union, which Evans and George Potter had signed on June 8, was a "closed shop or preferential contract."[35] The clear intent was to force members of the International Union from the district by denying them employment opportunities.

The readiness of the companies to enter into contractual arrangements with the Tri-State Union confirmed this intent and further exposed the true character of Evans's organization. By June 6 twenty companies had signed up with the new union.[36] On August 2 the *Metal Mine & Smelter Worker*, then the official organ of the Tri-State Union, reported that "mining companies representing 95 per cent of the Tri-State Production [*sic*] [and] composing all the principal operators of the District" had contracted to hire the members of the union. Twelve days later it reported that 95 percent of the operators had agreed to employ Tri-State Union members "exclusively—which agreement is binding and obligatory for the life of the Tri-State Union."[37] The leadership of the union clearly perceived that the arrangement with the companies provided for a closed shop. Certainly this was Evans's perception. In an extraordinary move on June 4, Evans as the representative of the Tri-State Union negotiated a contract with *himself* as the operator of the Craig lease where he employed about thirty-five men.[38] Evans certainly did not allow International Union members among his work crews. The other operators, who had signed contracts identical to Evans's, clearly did not anticipate genuine collective bargaining by the Tri-State Union in behalf of its members. The contractual linkage, therefore, made a farce of collective bargaining and was visible evidence of the union's subservience to the companies and not to Tri-State workers.

Under such circumstances, workers flocked to join the Tri-State Union as news circulated about the reopenings based on contracts that excluded members of the International. When the Admiralty Zinc Company announced on June 5 a renewal of operations, its officials indicated that each worker was "required to show the blue [membership] card" of the Tri-State Union.[39] The operators of the Evans-Wallower Company also invalidated its old employment cards and required workers to obtain blue cards before returning to work.[40] To work in the mines and mills one had to belong to the new union, now becoming generally known as the Blue Card Union because its membership card was blue. Tri-State workers joined it in record numbers, surrendering their International Union cards for the chance to work.[41] On June 10, Evans reported the membership at 4,281 and increasing.[42]

The extant records of the Tri-State Union, for example, the minutes of the executive committee and the meetings of the locals, reveal the extensive control of supervisory personnel and the minor influence of the rank and file. They also demonstrate the persuasive influence of the major mining and milling companies in determining the policies of the union to protect and extend their interests. Furthermore, the records show that the Tri-State Union, although allegedly acting in the name of the workers, was a creature of the companies, which fully supported its efforts to drive the International Union locals from the district. In short, the records show the Tri-State Union to have been a company union. Nowhere was this fact more clearly demonstrated than in the matter of membership where the companies and the union acted in concert.

Under Section 69 of the new union's constitution, any white male of eighteen who had worked in the mines or mills of the Tri-State was immediately eligible for membership. As for others, they were subject to whatever additional "rules, conditions, and limitations" that the executive committee might impose in the future. It was soon evident that no one worked unless a member of the new union, because of the contractual arrangement noted above, and that obtaining membership in it was extremely difficult, if not impossible, for those identified as International Union activists.

The steps to membership in the new union were designed to eliminate any applicant sympathetic to the International Union and to prevent his employment in the district. This task was made easier by Section 73 of the Tri-State Union's constitution, which provided that any candidate be rejected if he received "three blackballs" or opposing ballots. The established procedure required the resignation of the applicant from the International (if a member) and the surrender of his membership card, the approval of the applicant by a former supervisor or employer in the district, the publication of the applicant's name in the *Metal Mine & Smelter Worker* (later the *Blue Card Record*), the applicant's appearance before a local association for questioning and a vote of acceptance, and a final approval or rejection by the new union's executive committee.[43] This involved procedure screened out "undesirables" and empowered the executive committee, two-thirds of whom were initially supervisors, to determine who would work in the mines and mills. The procedure became the basis for a district-wide "card system" representing a pool of acceptable labor, and it made the Tri-State Union a hiring hall for the operators. Without this union membership, one did not work unless hired by an unusually independent-minded employer.

Generally, the first order of business at meetings of the executive committee and the three local associations established in Picher, Joplin, and Galena was the matter of membership. Applicants were rejected for several reasons, but the foremost cause concerned their relationship with the International Union. An example was Forrest Taylor. According to the minutes of the executive committee for

Ground and mill crew of Bird Dog Mine, Commerce Mining and Royalty Company, during strike of 1935. Note back-to-work sign in center. Courtesy of Dobson Memorial Center, Miami, Oklahoma.

October 30, 1935, "Forrest Taylor, who had just arrived from Arizona, and had made application for membership in the Tri-State Union made the mistake of remarking to clerk in the office that he preferred the Int. Union to ours. He was brought before the committee where he reiterated his statement. The committee immediately voted to refund his dollar and send him on his way."[44] At this same meeting, a resolution passed that required former International members to surrender their membership cards or formal withdrawal slips to the new union. Earlier on October 23, the executive committee had rejected Harry Vanslyke because he had acquired four strike stamps in his International strike book.[45] Even after surrendering their cards and being accepted into the new union (usually after an investigation and delays ranging up to three months), former International members were never really trusted as having severed all connections with the union. Evans, for example, reprimanded Willard Keller at a meeting on January 21, 1936, because of his "past International Union activities, and admonished [him] to be very careful with

whom he associated in the future." He further advised Keller that he should "attend [Tri-State Union] meetings and make himself otherwise very active in the Blue Card Union."[46] Only in this manner could the stigma of past International membership be erased.

Further evidence of the close, directive link between the major companies and the new union was the unanimous passage of Evans's proposal of January 14, 1936, that "all applicants for membership in the Union shall be recommended either by their former employer or by some member of the Executive Committee."[47] Thereafter ground bosses and superintendents played a significant role in determining who would be allowed to join, hence to work, either by formal or informal intervention into the committee's membership deliberations. A supervisor's recommendation to reject an applicant usually had nothing to do with his lack of competence as a worker but instead concerned any relationship with the International Union, regardless of how tenuous. On March 10, 1936, Oscar Bailey, a ground boss at Eagle Picher Mining and Smelting Company's Tom Brown and Grace B. mines, appeared before the committee and recommended that Van Treece be rejected for membership in the union because he was residing with a "radical international."[48] When Joe Pruitt, a ground boss at Eagle Picher's Bendelari Mine, resigned in June from the executive committee, at Evans's suggestion its members unanimously voted in Bailey to replace Pruitt.[49]

Evans used his influence with the major companies to whip the smaller operators into line, to make them persuade or coerce their workers into joining the Tri-State Union when they were reluctant to do so. At a meeting of the executive committee on June 9, 1936, Evans reported that Jim and Sam Smith, operators of the Baxter Chat Company, had requested that he help them to sell ore. Evans refused the request "until every man on Baxter Chat Co. took out a blue card." The Smiths agreed to this condition.[50] This hardnosed attitude toward membership and work prevailed also in the local associations of the Tri-State Union. On June 3, 1936, a report in the Cherokee (Galena) local that Howard Geisler, a nonmember, was working at the Muncie Mine stirred up "extensive discussion . . . by the entire assembly," which ended only when an officer stated that the matter was "being worked on." Although Geisler's employer refused to discharge him because he was a "valuable man" and because the company had no contract with the new union, the matter was resolved when Geisler expressed support for it and agreed to join.[51]

The larger companies exerted direct as well as indirect pressure upon their employees who balked at joining the new union. On August 27, 1935, Leonard Vaughn, general manager of Eagle Picher Lead Company's Joplin plant, instructed John Sheppard, acting director of research, to recruit the twenty-six chemists in his department into the company union. Vaughn explained that the chemists had to join in order to maintain the organization and to eliminate possible violence against them by union members at the gates of the plant.[52] Vaughn's instructions to Sheppard, who was reluctant to force his professionally trained chemists into any kind of union, set off a sequence of events and an exchange of correspondence among company officials that clearly revealed Eagle Picher's strong commitment to the new union and its objectives.

Following his meeting with Vaughn, Sheppard distributed membership application forms to the chemists, pointing out to them that Vaughn had stated that the Tri-State Union was a "union not inimical to the policy of our company."[53] But next day Sheppard fired off a letter and telegram to J. R. MacGregor, a vice-president of Eagle Picher Lead Company at the home office in Cincinnati, Ohio, who was responsible for research, complaining that Vaughn had issued a "somewhat veiled, intimidation that every employee of the Research Department was going to be required to take out membership in the union and [that] I was to make it plain to all research employees that membership [was] obligatory." In Sheppard's view, the chemists would join the union if "they were told they must do so to keep their jobs." He insisted, however, that they did not wish to join.[54] He also forwarded a petition of August 28, addressed to himself and signed by all twenty-six chemists, that confirmed his assessment. It outlined the reasons for their opposition to membership, one of which showed a clear perception concerning the minor role of union members. *"We object to the internal organization of the Union on the grounds that too many dictatorial powers are delegated to the President* [Evans] *and the Executive Committee, and that practically no power or privileges—other than the paying of dues— are vested in the individual members."*[55] The petition requested that the chemists not be required to join the union.[56] Sheppard's letter, the petition, and a telegram asking whether membership was a condition of employment made it clear that members of the Research Department wanted no part of the new union.

MacGregor went to Joplin and conferred with Eagle Picher's local management. While there he reprimanded Sheppard for keeping records of the transactions concerning the issue of membership.[57] Afterwards, he addressed letters to the chemists advising them that Eagle Picher did not require their membership in any organization and that such membership was voluntary.[58] The matter thus appeared closed. The leadership of the Tri-State Union refused to let the matter drop, however. Kelsey Norman again approached Sheppard and asked that he and Evans be allowed to address the chemists about membership. And again Sheppard turned the matter over to MacGregor on September 17, asking by letter whether Norman's request should be granted.[59]

While awaiting a response from MacGregor, Sheppard confronted George W. Potter, the vice-president of Eagle Picher Mining and Smelting Company, who had made the arrangement with Evans and Charles A. Neal for the transfer of money from the companies to the Tri-State Union through the Security Bank and Trust Company of Miami. Calling Sheppard to his office, Potter told him that Eagle Picher wanted the chemists to join the union, that it was Sheppard's duty to have them join without records of his having done so, and that other Eagle Picher employees could not be kept in the organization as long as the chemists stayed out.[60] Questioning Potter's authority over Eagle Picher Lead Company matters, Sheppard telephoned MacGregor, who informed him that Potter was in "entire charge of all matters involving employment [in] our entire district."[61] Told that Norman should be allowed to address the chemists, Sheppard made immediate arrangements. On September 25 during the middle of a work day, the chemists assembled in a company laboratory to hear Norman, accompanied by Glenn Hickman, explain why they should join the Tri-State Union. No wages were deducted as a result of this meeting, although it lasted between two and three hours.

In defiance of a previous reprimand about keeping records of transactions concerning the membership issue, Sheppard's stenographer took extensive notes of Norman's remarks. Norman left no doubt that the Tri-State Union had the full cooperation of the Eagle Picher companies. Although the companies did not "demand" membership, they did not employ anyone who refused to join. Norman

indicated that the lead company was "intensively interested in keeping this organization going" and "would be
highly pleased" if the chemists would join and assist in
keeping the International Union out. Their membership
was extremely important to show solidarity and to end the
grumbling among the production workers about their
failure to join. "Eagle-Picher wants everyone to join this
Union," he said. "If you don't want to join it is your privilege, but I am sure that as a mark of loyalty, showing you
are behind your company, you will join."[62]

The questions that followed Norman's remarks showed
that his listeners were not impressed. They remained concerned about the effect of membership on their professional lives, the dues they would pay and how these would
be spent, their lack of influence on the union, and the
character of Evans, whom they considered to be something of a reprobate. Norman's answers to their questions
were unsatisfactory, and they remained unconvinced that
membership in the union was in their best interest. Nonetheless, after Norman's remarks and with Potter's directions in mind, Sheppard instructed each of his department
heads to inform the chemists that they would have to join
the union. They joined.[63] In forcing its professional employees to become members of the Tri-State Union in order to prevent production workers from dropping out,
Eagle Picher Lead Company clearly required membership
of all its employees as a matter of policy. Other operators
did the same. For his obstructionist role, Sheppard was
later replaced as acting director of research at the Joplin
plant.

By the end of 1935, the major companies, using the Tri-
State Union as their agent, had regained control of the
workplace in the district. So sensitive to the interests of the
operators were the members of the union's executive committee that on October 30, 1935, they decided that a previously voted stipend to themselves of five dollars per week,
retroactive to May 27, should not be paid "until Pres.
Evans had conferred with their various bosses to deter-

mine their reaction to such a move."[64] So supportive of the union were the operators that until November 12, 1935, the executive committee met on company time with no wages lost by its members. The time of the meeting was changed only because the "Committee felt that this [meeting on company time] was unfair to their employers," not because the operators complained.[65] Under such company influence, the Tri-State Union throughout 1936 and 1937 continued its growth and worked diligently to uproot the vestiges of the International Union of Mine, Mill, and Smelter Workers.

6

"Purged Of The Horrible Stench"

THE campaign of the Tri-State Metal Mine and Smelter Workers Union and the operators against the International Union of Mine, Mill, and Smelter Workers was not restricted to the workplace. From the beginning Evans and his supporters realized that merely destroying the International Union's locals would not eradicate the sentiment for a bona fide workers' organization held by substantial numbers of Tri-Staters. This latent support for independent unionism was a threat to the new order being imposed and it therefore had to be assailed. Countering this danger and arousing public hostility against the International Union without, at the same time, undermining the Tri-State Union posed a delicate problem because the new organization had consistently portrayed itself as a "union." Somehow *all* Tri-Staters had to be convinced that the International Union was destructive of the workers' interests, but that the Tri-State Union, although a "company union," was indispensable to their welfare. Somehow all positive images of the old union and independent unionism had to be erased from public consciousness.

The Tri-State Union's constitution and bylaws, presented to the Miami fairgrounds throng on May 27, provided a means to accomplish this objective. Clearly anticipating that the Tri-State Union would encounter a public relations problem, Evans and Norman incorporated Section 12, which provided for an official publication called the *Tri-State Metal Mine & Smelter Worker* (later renamed the *Blue Card Record*). It also provided for an editor-manager to have "full charge" of editorial policy and all business matters, "subject only to the supervision of the President of the Union" and to the requirement that the publication always be in "harmony with the general policies of the Union as such are outlined by the President." The editor-manager was also designated "legislative representative" and charged with the responsibilities of a lobbyist. The inclusion of Section 12 strongly suggested that Evans and Norman had joined with George Potter, vice-president of the Eagle Picher Mining and Smelting Company, and Charles A. Neal, vice-president of the Miami Security Bank and Trust Company, and others in a cabal to wreck the International Union in the Tri-State District. The section was evidence that the Tri-State Union leaders had received prior assurance from some source of substantial financial backing of the kind discussed in chapter 5.[1]

Nearly fifty years later, the question of how the Tri-State Union's official organ was initially financed remains obscure. It appeared that the first issue of August 2, 1935, which contained no advertising, was subsidized from the funds donated to the new union through the Eagle Picher Mining and Smelting Company and the Security Bank and Trust Company because Charles Windbigler, bookkeeper for the union, claimed not to know how the first issue was financed. Evans later emphatically stated that none of the companies, particularly Eagle Picher, received free advertising in later issues as compensation for their $17,500 in contributions.[2] At a meeting on August 5, 1935, the executive committee turned the newspaper over to B. B. Brumfield of the Tri-State Publishing Company, located directly across the street from the union hall. Brumfield was to "gather the news and print it without cost to us [the Tri-State Union]" in return for "all advertising space to make whatever profit from it that he could."[3] Within a short time, however, the *Metal Mine & Smelter Worker* was being financed from the general revenue fund derived from membership dues and the sale of advertising.[4] This fact, however, did not mean less company support for the newspaper. On the contrary, for more than two years after publication of the first issue, between forty-five hundred and five thousand copies were printed weekly and distributed inside the mines and mills of the Tri-State. Furthermore, the companies permitted Tri-State Union agents to collect dues within the gates and they heavily subsidized the publication with advertising.[5]

As determined by the executive committee, the *Metal Mine & Smelter Worker* consisted of eight pages of "news devoted wholly to affairs of the Union and mine employees."[6] According to Glenn A. Hickman, who became one of its two editors, its purpose was "generally [that] of any house organ—to unify in the promotion of a point-of-view."[7] Widely circulated and read, it hammered home the message that the International Union was foreign and destructive to the interests of the district and therefore must go. Its editorial policy constantly attacked organized labor, its leaders, and its purposes, while fully backing the work of the Tri-State Union in the district.

John Garretson, a member of the executive committee and an employee of the Commerce Mining and Royalty Company, was the first editor of the *Metal Mine & Smelter Worker*. On November 12, 1935, however, Hickman, already the secretary-treasurer of the Tri-State Union and a highly influential member of the executive committee, replaced Garretson as editor and held the position until the publication ceased. Hickman's commitment to the cause of the new union was unquestioned. He later confessed that had it been necessary to do so in the "interest of the men," he would have published untruths or certainly colored the truth in their behalf.[8] Evans and the executive committee had earlier recognized his loyalty and ability when they made him secretary-treasurer at forty-five dollars per week, twenty more than he had earned as a ground boss at the Black Eagle Mining Company. That he accepted his new post without additional compensation reflected his firm belief in the rightness of the Tri-State Union cause and his hostility to the International Union. In explaining how he became editor of the *Metal Mine & Smelter Worker*, Hickman modestly stated:

How I came to be editor of the paper is as much a mystery to me as how I became secretary of the union. I suspect it was for the same reason, mainly that I saw where I could be useful and took over the work that I thought needed to be done. . . . With the paper I thought I could do what needed to be done better than anyone else around and began doing it. The acknowledgment and title were a natural development of what was taking place. I get a little sick of the assumption that everything was so precisely plotted and planned.[9]

Whatever the reason for his selection, the choice was a good one for the union. From the depth of his convictions, Hickman produced impassioned and strident editorials that undergirded other forms of assault on the International Union. Like Garretson before him, Hickman pulled no punches despite the personal danger that his tough stance produced.

Under his intelligent and vigorous guidance, the newspaper boldly expressed the policies of the Tri-State Union as interpreted by Hickman. According to Hickman:

I don't think that I can saddle anyone else with the responsibility for the editorial policy of the *Blue Card Record* [the name given to the *Metal Mine & Smelter Worker* after June 6, 1936]. Kelsey [Norman] contributed a few pieces in the beginning, but when he went anti-Semitic with one of them and brought the B'nai B'rith and the Anti-Defamation League down on me, it made me as angry as it did them, and after that I took full charge.[10]

Although subject to Evans's supervision, there was much that appeared in the publication about which Evans was ignorant. Aided by Frank B. Hills, an elderly newspaperman who was made associate editor to sell advertising and to assist in composition and photography, Hickman wrote all the material except the "correspondence solicited from the members, their wives and families."[11]

When the Tri-State strike began, the great split in the national labor movement had not yet occurred. The International Union was affiliated with the American Federation of Labor and this connection led to a scurrilous assault on William Green, president of the AFL, and other labor leaders. The tone of the attacks was revealed dramatically in Evans's address to the throng celebrating the first anniversary of the founding of the Tri-State Union at the Miami fairgrounds. Evans charged that "all the major troubles of [the] entire country [were] directly chargeable to the leaders of labor unions who stir up labor trouble at the expense of the poor. If labor racketeers [had] ever done anything but impoverish their followers and bankrupt their employers," he asserted, "they've certainly kept it a carefully guarded secret." [12] Evans's comments reflected the drumbeat of criticism against organized labor that already marked the young union's official publication.

Claiming that the "A.F. of L. [was] infested with reds and communists" and that what the country needed was a "few more 'minute men' like those who formed the Tri-State Union," the *Metal Mine & Smelter Worker* charged on August 17, 1935, that "William Green and his dirty bloodsucking leeches . . . would have their poor misguided following believe that they have the interest of the working man at heart. In reality they have the interest of only one small minority at heart, namely the racketeers who run the A.F. of L." [13] After the labor movement had split and the International Union affiliated with the Committee for Industrial Organization (CIO), the attacks on national labor leaders sharpened. John L. Lewis, president of the CIO, was reviled.

> He [Lewis] cares nothing for human misery and privation; this is closely evidenced by the beastlike conditions of those communities which pay him tribute. Like a black tumble bug, he grows fat on filth; knowing that where there is filth there is ignorance and where there is ignorance there are possibilities of grafting. And so he works with all his might; first to hamstring prosperity, and second to reelect his tools. [14]

On April 30, 1937, the *Blue Card Record* continued its tirade when it stated that

> like the dog in the manger, that couldn't eat hay and wouldn't let the cow eat it, John Lewis has tried every way possible to

prevent the working class of people from reaping the benefit of prosperity, while on the other hand, he has made asses out of every simple-minded chump in the United States who would listen to his hooey, including himself. He really likes himself. If you don't believe it, just ask him.[15]

Following its affiliation with the CIO, the International Union under Reid Robinson attempted a comeback in the Tri-State District, sending in organizers during the spring of 1937. The *Blue Card Record* responded by directing a new flow of venom against Robinson and the CIO. Noting that the workers were already organized and engaged in collective bargaining, the editor wrote:

> We will not continue good naturedly to let "outsiders" such as garment and auto workers come into this community and agitate satisfied workers. . . . If the C.I.O. continues to try to tear up the Blue Card Union they are in for some of the toughest opposition they have ever had the misfortune to encounter. Ninety-five per cent of the men in this district like the Blue Card Union and don't propose to have any other union. . . .
>
> Unfortunately for Mr. Robinson, it takes men to make a labor union. He doesn't have them and he can't get them by hiding his men inside buildings and shooting into peaceful parades—committing, in other words, cold-blooded murder. Could the brother or father of a man who had been killed at the hands of these heathens be expected to forgive, join up and call the murderers "brother"?
>
> We think not. What do you think, Mr. Robinson? You damned fizzling false-alarm.[16]

In an earlier editorial, Robinson and his organizers had been castigated as "outside profiteering blatherskites," "wild-eyed fanatics" uninterested in work, and "fire-eating, profiteering agitators."[17]

Local leaders of the International Union were not spared. Calling them the "ragged remnant of the cesspool of communistic propagandists" and the "abscess [sic] of corruption in the breasts of hired agitators who live off unrest and unemployment," the *Metal Mine & Smelter Worker* charged that "when everybody is working and happy these buzzards move in, spewing their vomit in new and untried territories." Ernest Berry, a local International Union leader, was denounced by asking: "How does he dare breathe the air that has wafted to the ear of Heaven the wails of starving babes munching the dry breasts of undernourished mothers, all because a senseless strike sponsored and prolonged by Berry robbed their fathers and husbands of an honest living?"[18]

The wrath of the editor occasionally fell directly on those International Union members who refused to accept the new order imposed by the Tri-State Union, and it revealed how the latter's leadership viewed such workers.

Long-headed persons who have hunted the skunk know he really stinks most after giving him the death blow and that's what happened when the "pickhandlers," growing tired of their foul presence, decided to exterminate these night prowling varmints. . . . The gates closed . . . and any person who hangs around their den will soon find himself stinking and be cast out where Blue Card people circulate. . . . Since this district is purged of the horrible stench, white folks can go about their business of personal gain.[19]

On May 14, 1937, a piece entitled "Sapsuckers," an unusually harsh assault on International Union members, was published in the *Blue Card Record*. Among other things it stated:

The wind changed the other day and some of the district C.I.O. buzzards smelled their own breadth [*sic*] and gagged again, then puqued [*sic*] up another pack of lies on Evans, Nolan, Hickman, and Norman, which they published on a sheet issue[d] for the entertainment of their toilet-sitting members who are still hiding out in Picher privies from the pick-handle paraders.[20]

And in an adjoining column, an article entitled the "C.I.O. Boys Bow to Boss [Ernest] Berry" lambasted International Union holdouts who refused to join the new union.

You [CIOers] are "simple Simons" because the long ears of a Jack Ass would be a compliment to your long skinny faces. You are "Sapsuckers" for paying tribute to the Ted Schasteens and Tony McTeers [local International Union leaders] in the district who live off the grimy dimes you grovel in the dirt of a PWA or WPA relief job to get. You are "Wobblies" because your empty bellies can't "front" for your spineless backbones, so you wobble along on your way to eternity by way of the Poor Farm and the Potters Field, misguided, mistaken mis-fits![21]

Under the Tri-State Union's constitution and bylaws, editorial policy had to be in "harmony with the general policies of the Union." It was. For example, the new union opposed strikes and in an early editorial, that opposition was clearly expressed.

This Union is opposed to strikes, which always result in lawlessness, as a means of getting results. We know of no strike that has resulted beneficially either to the workers or to the community. . . . Your dollar [monthly dues] is more than well spent and we assure you that there will be no more strikes here. . . . Pay your dollar and pull with us, you will always be on the winning side.[22]

Not only did the union newspaper oppose strikes, it stood squarely behind the policy that one must belong to the Tri-State Union to work in the district. Pointing out that the new union had become "one of the most exclusive organizations in the district," it declared that fact to be "understandable."

They flatly refused to work side by side with men who but a short while back threatened, abused, rocked, and even shot at them.
From any way you look at it, the plight of these diehards is desperate. They are refused admission to the Union, they find practically every mine and smelter closed to them. They are faced with the alternative of getting into another line of work or leaving the district.[23]

And on March 23, 1937, the *Blue Card Record* alerted members of the Tri-State Union to a "danger from within," suggesting that the "trash" of the International Union was infiltrating the Tri-State Union and that the system devised for excluding International sympathizers should be fully supported. "It is up to us to keep these men out. And it is no easy job. . . . Now, we don't want that kind of men in the blue card union and we don't propose to have them. One way they can be stopped from making applications is for foremen of the district to refuse to recommend them.[24] A warning went out on May 7, 1937, that some mine operators had been "very incautious about working Internationalites and Non-Blue Card members. For the protection of our members working at these few properties and for the welfare of the community as a whole, this chiseling and cheating must stop."[25] There was no doubt that the editor strongly supported the executive committee's stance on employment in the district.

Although support for the activities of the squad-car crews was not so stridently stated, it was nevertheless clear that a resort to violence was acceptable. In an editorial of March 5, 1937, the *Blue Card Record* asserted that: "We know the spirit of May 27, 1935 is still alive—that there are many more now than there were then willing to show the pick-handle if necessary to protect their jobs. That the way to keep it alive is to keep it free from the cancerous corruption of reddecked radicals. And this we most emphatically are going to do."[26] In referring to a story about an incident on a Works Progress Administration location in Joplin by an "H.H.P.," the *Blue Card Record* on April 9, 1937, was more explicit. Its editorial stated: "We are positive that if there ever comes a time when we have to kick the rumps of some of these damned pole-cats parading around the streets of Picher, or sitting down on other peoples' property with their CIO buttons showing, H.H.P. is the type of Blue Carder who won't mind a little stink if he can just have the pleasure of busting the stink bag."[27]

Hickman left no doubt concerning his position and that of the *Blue Card Record* when he commented to a reporter of the *Miami Daily News-Record* on September 5, 1937, that the Tri-State Union would employ "every means of its command, whether it be by strong language or strong arms, in the prevention of a hostile or rival organization's infringing on its assigned territory."

Upon becoming editor, Hickman worked with Norman in creating a "network of correspondents" composed of

Tri-State Union members, their wives, and families. Hickman later doubted that the editorials in the *Blue Card Record* were as influential as the pieces from his contributors. "We paid nothing for the correspondence but the response was great," he later wrote. "It was an opportunity to get published most anything that the aspiring author cared to write."[28] Like the rest of the published material, however, the contributions favored the new union's position. For example, back-to-work leaders were praised; the men who refused to work were ridiculed.

But even before Hickman became editor, such pieces were being submitted. One unidentified "poet" of the Tri-State Union published the following in the *Metal Mine & Smelter Worker* on October 5, 1935.

> *The head of this Union, his name is Mike.*
> *He and Joe Nolan were in the lead of the Parade with*
> *Pick Handles when we broke the strike.*
> *Mike said let the yellow bellys [sic] stay on relief,*
> *And drink their dried milk and eat corned beef.*
> *Because our little union is doing just fine,*
> *Let the rest of the strikers stay on the soup line.*
> *They are losing their cars and selling their hogs,*
> *For the International Union has gone to the Dogs.*[29]

The poetry was bad, but its message was clear—the strikers were undesirables and were getting what they deserved. Another "poet" lamented the strikers' lack of concern for their families with these verses:

> *At the creamery where I get clabber,*
> *How the boys laugh and jabber—*
> *He is just a union man's boy across the way.*
> *You don't know how I feel*
> *When they call you a big Heel,*
> *Please daddy, get you a Blue Card today.*[30]

Malcolm Ross, a staff member of the National Labor Relations Board in Kansas City, Missouri, who had access to all the back files of the *Blue Card Record* while working on his *Death of a Yale Man*, concluded that it did not contain a "generous line" concerning International Union members or their strike.[31]

The *Blue Card Record* revived the latent hostility toward organized labor, which historically had prevailed among workers in the Tri-State, and directed it against the International Union. Its widespread circulation, its scurrilous attacks on local, district, and national labor leaders, its ridicule of workers who refused to acknowledge defeat of the strike, and its unyielding stance created a dangerous climate for those men who stubbornly clung to the International Union. As a result, many of that union's members left the district. Perhaps the greatest achievement of the *Blue Card Record* was to persuade or to intimidate hundreds of workers into accepting the idea of company unionism through the Tri-State Union as an imperative alternative to the International Union and independent unionism. In convincing reticent Tri-Staters that their best interest was now served by membership in the Tri-State Union, the *Blue Card Record* risked educating the workers to the benefits possible from organizations under their own control. Moreover, events at the national level later forced the Tri-State Union to affiliate with the AFL, a necessary but embarrassing move that caused consternation among its members who had taken the anti-AFL attacks seriously.[32]

To entrench itself in the Tri-State, the Tri-State Union resorted to other less strident means than the *Blue Card Record* to woo the workers and to legitimize its claim to speak for them. Regardless of the means employed to attack the International Union, the mining and milling companies continued to offer their full support. The extent of that support was revealed in the anniversary picnics of 1936 and 1937, which celebrated the founding of the company union and which were entirely underwritten by companies in the district. The supporters of the Tri-State Union had ample reason to celebrate, for its membership, which had climbed to approximately five thousand by May 1936, increased daily as more men enrolled in order to work.

On April 28, 1936, Evans reported to his executive committee that three unidentified "major operators" had agreed to "bear the expense" of a picnic to mark the first year of the Tri-State Union. Following discussion, the committee endorsed the project and instructed Evans to work out the arrangements with the operators.[33] As plans progressed, more than forty companies and businesses rallied to support the first celebration, scheduled for May 27.[34]

Although the first picnic was indeed a celebration of the success of the new union, it was also intended to demonstrate the power and influence of the union, to infuse its supporters with a stronger sense of solidarity, and to provide its leaders with a friendly forum of thousands for further attacks on the International Union. Advance publicity emphasized that only holders of the Tri-State Union's blue membership card and their families were to be admitted to the Miami fairgrounds where the event was scheduled. The *Miami Daily News-Record* of May 24, 1936, stated bluntly that the first "celebration [was] for Blue Card holders and their families only." Others would not be admitted and if found on the grounds would be expelled. The blue card also provided transportation from outlying towns on special trains of the Frisco and the Northeast Oklahoma Railroad companies. For those who missed the specials, both the railroads and businesses offered reduced round-trip fares throughout the day. The blue membership card also provided access to free food, refreshment, and entertainment. Money was unnecessary. The Tri-State Union members only had to furnish their drinking cups.[35]

To feed an anticipated crowd of fifteen to twenty thousand, mammoth preparations were made. Seventeen Aberdeen-Angus steers and twenty hogs were slaughtered and barbecued. An estimated fifty thousand buns and thousands of gallons of ice cream, coffee, and lemonade were purchased. To entertain the crowd, a full program was planned. For the boys, there were bicycle and three-legged races and greased pig and marble contests. For the girls, there were rope jumping and jacks contests and a fifty-yard sprint. For the women, there were potato carrying, rolling-pin throw, and nail-driving contests; and for the men, shoveling and drilling contests. For couples, there were square dance and waltz competitions. Prizes totaling nearly $350 were awarded in these events, the money supplied by the district merchants. In addition, there were three boxing matches, swimming at the Miami municipal pool, rides on the ferris wheel, the merry-go-round, and the glider, and an anniversary ball with music by Eddie White's Blue Carders.

Mining and milling ceased for the day. Throughout the district businesses closed to celebrate the occasion, and in Picher only the post office remained open. The picnic was indeed an unprecedented extravaganza, the trains alone bringing in nearly five thousand members and their families to the picnic grounds. Before this friendly and appreciative throng, Evans delivered a "state of the union" address, and Norman gave a speech that flayed the International Union and organized labor, while praising the progress of the Tri-State Union.

Blaming labor racketeers for all the nation's trouble, Evans compared the new union's success in the Tri-State in keeping more than five thousand of its members working for 342 days during the past year to the failure of Alexander Howat's UMW locals in the Pittsburg and Columbus (Kansas) field directly to the north where two thousand coal miners had worked about a third as many days. Evans called the UMW the "biggest and strongest racketeer-ruled labor organization in the United States" and declared that the Tri-State Union's membership would not tolerate Howat's kind of unionism.

> Those who want the kind of stuff Howat handles can have it, but they've got to get it somewhere else. We don't want it here. We are not threatening, mind you. All we want is the right to peacefully earn a living for ourselves and family. We want to work with our picks and pick who we work with, but if we are forced to do this with our pickhandles, thank God, we've still got the courage to do it.[36]

Evans left no doubt that despite the union's motto of "victory without violence," if necessary to preserve its victory in the Tri-State, the use of violence would not be rejected.

Norman's remarks, appropriately called "Keep the Blue Flag Flying," was a more brazen assault on organized labor. Norman asked his listeners to compare the Tri-State

Union with unions led by racketeers who used "violence and terrorism" to acquire their "ill-gotten gains," leaders who had "no bonds of decency to check their careers of crime to gain their private ends. Murder and sabotage fol-low[ed] in their wake while we practice[d] and preach[ed] that the prosperity of the worker can best be promoted and maintained by peaceful bargaining and mutual respect and confidence."[37] Charging that a "weak-kneed Congress and a willing President" had given William Green, John L. Lewis, and David Dubinsky whatever they wanted, that "national lawmakers [had permitted] themselves to be-come as clay in the hands of such putrid potters," Norman alleged that the true objectives of these "self-appointed prophets of the poor," "these labor racketeers," "these double-crossing crooks," was to create a labor party and use force and violence to place the nation under Commu-nist rule. He called for resistance.

Except for one major difference, the program and pro-cedural arrangements for the second anniversary celebra-tion of May 1937 were the same as the first one, the ex-penses again being assumed by the mining and milling companies of the district. The only difference from 1936 stemmed from the changed context in which the new cele-bration occurred. For a number of reasons, Tri-State Union leaders, who had constantly lambasted the AFL, William Green, and organized labor in general, had found it neces-sary to seek affiliation with the hated AFL. On April 12, 1937, the United States Supreme Court in *N.L.R.B.* v. *Jones & Laughlin Steel Corporation* had upheld the constitution-ality of the National Labor Relations Act of 1935. With the law now unquestionably applicable to the Tri-State labor troubles, it was likely that an earlier injunction preventing National Labor Relations Board hearings on the Inter-national Union's charges of unfair labor practices filed against the Eagle Picher companies would be struck down. In a radical move to prevent the Tri-State Union from being exposed as a company union at the expected hear-ings, its leaders had sought an immediate affiliation with the AFL, its old enemy. They found the much villified

The Metal Mine & Smelter Worker, the official voice of the company-backed Blue Card Union. Courtesy of *The Metal Mine & Smelter Worker*.

Green, whose union was then in a major struggle with the new CIO, ready and willing to have a marriage of convenience.[38] Thus the second celebration found Evans, Norman, Hickman, and other leaders hobnobbing on stage with G. Ed Warren, president of the Oklahoma State Federation of Labor, who had ably orchestrated the affiliation attempt. Norman and Evans, instead of lashing out at "labor racketeers" as they had done in 1936, explained in their remarks to the crowd why the Tri-State Union now found it expedient to seek the protection of the AFL.

Requested to address the picnic throng, Warren assured his listeners that the AFL convention in October would formally confirm its executive council's decision to accept their organization. And in a telegram read to the crowd, Green called upon Tri-State Union members to renew their "loyalty and devotion to the principles and policies of the A. F. of L.," preserve "our democratic form of government," and protect "American institutions against every onslaught . . . made upon them by subversive forces [the International Union and the CIO]." Eager to enlist the Tri-State Union in its battle with the emerging CIO, Green

F. W. ("Mike") Evans, *far right*, addresses crowd at first anniversary picnic of the Blue Card Union at Miami fairgrounds. Courtesy of *Metal Mine & Smelter Worker*.

found it wise to ignore the attacks of the past two years and promised the AFL's "full measure of co-operation and support."[39] The second anniversary celebration, therefore, was used to inform an estimated twenty thousand blue carders and their families of the reasons for affiliating with a national organization heretofore condemned as destructive of their interests and to undercut any opposition to the move.

The anniversary celebrations were tremendous successes for the Tri-State Union. In providing additional evidence of the value of that union's membership, the joyous respites fostered a happy feeling of belonging, a sense of community among thousands of blue carders and their families that caused them to identify more closely with their organization. Furthermore, there was evidence of a significant rallying of district businessmen into the ever-expanding coalition against the International Union. The Tri-State Union had ample reason to exult over the concrete and symbolic results of the celebrations, events that helped to dispel all doubts about its victorious domination of the district. But for the impoverished, die-hard Interna-

The *Blue Card Record*, successor to the *Metal Mine & Smelter Worker*. Courtesy of *Blue Card Record*.

tional Union faithful who remained barred from work in the mines and mills, exclusion from the festivities and the food dramatically confirmed anew their outcast status and the stinging defeat administered by the Tri-State Union, the companies, and their supporters. Consequently, the hard-core ranks of the International Union were further diminished.

Although the celebrations dramatized the Tri-State Union's power and influence over the district, the executive committee remained concerned about the International Union's refusal to concede defeat and end the strike. Consequently, Evans and his associates recruited additional parties into the anti-International coalition to enhance its strength. A targeted group was the local businessmen who, as noted above, provided the prize money for events in the anniversary celebrations. Persuading substantial numbers of them to join the company union had been an actively pursued goal since October 1935.

Meeting on October 30, 1935, the executive committee formally accepted a resolution that provided that the Tri-State Union print "membership cards for the [member] merchants, suitable for hanging in their windows; so that merchants who have joined with the Tri-State Union may be distinguished from those who have not."[40] That same evening Evans attended a meeting of the Cherokee Subordinate Association, Tri-State Union (Galena, Kansas), which inducted Leo B. McCartney of the McCartney Drug Store into the organization. Evans informed the local of the executive committee's decision to print special display membership cards for the merchants who joined. In response, the local appointed a three-man committee to call upon Galena's businessmen with a special invitation to join the union.[41]

When the Galena local met on November 6, the committee's report on its effort to enlist the businessmen consumed most of the meeting. Some merchants had objected to their having to pay for the printing of the special display card. Others deferred a commitment until they had "talked the situation over with other members of the firm." Apply-

ing gentle pressure to overcome their reluctance, the local voted to give its "full support to those merchants who are now members of our organization." In support of that decision a blackboard was placed in the hall where the names of the merchant members were prominently displayed. Glen Forrest Deem of the Deem Grocery and Market was inducted into membership.[42]

A further discussion concerning the merchants occurred on November 20 when it was revealed that some of them had questioned whether they should join a mine and smelter workers' union. They doubted that they would be full members, that is, allowed to vote and influence the management of the union. Their concern was similar to that expressed by the Eagle Picher Lead Company's chemists who objected to being members of a working man's organization. To eliminate this objection, the Galena local voted that "any Business man belonging to this organization would be entitled to the same privileges, benefits or assessments as any other members."[43] Equality was offered and recruitment pushed. Similar efforts were made in the other Tri-State Union locals.

Although the number of merchants who joined the locals cannot be precisely determined, circumstantial evidence suggests that a substantial percentage joined when thousands of Tri-State workers flocked into the organization supported by the major mining and milling companies. Under the circumstances, not to have joined would have been financially disastrous, particularly after

Grandstand scene of crowds attending the second anniversary picnic of the Blue Card Union at Miami fairgrounds. Courtesy of *Blue Card Record.*

the union actively sought their membership, publicly identified those who joined, and called on its members to patronize only member merchants and those who advertised in the *Blue Card Record.* Like the mining and milling companies, they subsidized the anniversary picnics and closed their businesses for the occasions. Their involvement broadened the membership base and strengthened the Tri-State Union's hybrid character, and it raised additional doubts that it was the exclusive and legitimate voice of the Tri-State workers.

As previously stated, the union functioned as a hiring hall, joining with employers to control access to mining and milling jobs by requiring Tri-State Union membership. Although membership did not guarantee a job, without it employment was unlikely. This fact tremendously eroded the loyalty of International Union members to their union and accelerated their movement into the Tri-State Union. Once in, the Tri-Stater found other reasons to value his new membership and to forget the old union. When jobs could not be found in the mines and mills, the Tri-State Union made possible other kinds of work and assistance to some of its totally supportive and loyal members.

The squad-car operation employed seventy-five to a hundred out-of-work men for about six to eight weeks. Hickman viewed their use in this fashion as a form of "indirect relief," an activity that produced income of $4 for an eight-hour shift for selected members of the union.[44] Squad-car crews often benefited while on duty by being fed at the Connell Cafe at the union's expense.[45] In order to facilitate the collection of dues from the members, the executive committee appointed collectors in each of the larger mines and mills of the district. These men were paid a percentage commission on the amount collected, which provided sorely needed income for some.[46] Like any organization, the Tri-State Union frequently needed maintenance work and odd jobs done. A variety of small jobs were given to unemployed members, ranging from scraping off a ball park, hauling water, building seats for the anniversary celebrations, and serving as night watchmen for the union hall.[47] And to handle the organizational work, a permanent staff was necessary, which included Hickman at $45 per week, C. L. Windbigler (bookkeeper) at $40 per week, and Thelma Forshee (clerk-typist) at $20 per week.[48] As soon as the matter had been cleared with their supervisors, members of the executive committee also received compensation for their work, each receiving $2.50 for each session attended, retroactive to the beginning,[49] and the vice-president receiving $15 per week for his services.[50] Evans was not directly compensated for his work as president.

In addition to controlling access to jobs, the Tri-State Union served as a lender of small loans for many of its members who needed financial aid in meeting emergencies. On September 18, 1935, the executive committee assigned to Evans the responsibility for handling all loan applications;[51] however, it continued to exercise final approval or rejection of the applications. The reasons for union members requesting loans varied. Ben F. Whitcomb applied for $16 to visit a sick relative;[52] John Hodges requested "enough money" to pay for a hernia operation;[53] members asked for loans "to pay back dues";[54] Macel Peak sought a loan because of illness;[55] and William E. Butler requested money for medicine.[56] For most of the loans, however, the reasons were not noted in the minutes of the executive committee meetings or locals. For example, on October 30, 1935, small loans totaling $225.50 were made

to eleven applicants—the smallest being $8, the largest
$50—with no reasons stated. Five applications were re-
jected at the same session.[57] On January 14, 1936, the committee approved loans totaling $454.65 to eight persons;[58]
on January 21, it made loans totaling $289 to an unspec-
ified number of applicants.[59] A "Balance Sheet" of September 30, 1935, for the union indicated that $4,113.70
had been loaned to its members since June 1, all repaid except $1,993.[60] The practice of extending small loans con-
tinued until July 10, 1936, when it was formally discon-
tinued,[61] bringing to a close a service that aided financially
beleaguered members. Even so, unofficial loans continued
to be made from time to time to Tri-State Union members.[62]

The close relationship between the union and the companies made the loans relatively safe when made to working
members whose wages secured the debts. But knowledge of
the availability of credit, although limited, undoubtedly attracted increasing numbers of workers who, because of the
hard times, needed this service. Furthermore, the loans
developed loyalty to the Tri-State Union, for like the anniversary celebrations, acquiring them enhanced the recip-
ient's sense of community as well as created an obligation
to the organization. The small loan service also proved
effective in further devastating the International Union's
locals, whose financial resources were exhausted when the
strike began. Tri-State workers easily contrasted the af-
fluence of the new union with the poverty of the old one
and embraced the former, which offered help in their hard
times.

The Tri-State Union reached out in other ways to claim
the loyalty of its members. A death in the family might
bring flowers; one's church might receive a small donation;
one's family might receive a Christmas basket; one's doctor
or hospital bill might be paid; or, as in the case of Evans,
one might receive sixty-five dollars per month for office
rent.[63] The benefits to the rank and file, however, were not
without reciprocal obligations. Members were expected to
behave in the union's halls; a failure to do so could lead to

suspension.[64] And when a shortage occurred in the account of Clifton Wylie, a dues collector at the Mary M.
Beck Mine, the executive committee promptly dismissed
him despite remittance of the alleged shortage.[65]

Officials of the Tri-State Union also exerted political pressure on the members to support candidates for office who
had backed their onslaught on the International Union.
When Jess Osborn complained to the executive committee
that former International Union members were receiving
preference in acquiring jobs, he was rebuffed for having
voiced opposition to the reelection of Eli Dry as sheriff
of Ottawa County.[66] The implications of the Osborn case
was clear to the membership, that is, total support of the
Tri-State Union was expected, or else. Although Evans
claimed that his organization was politically neutral, he did
not hesitate to remind his listeners at the anniversary celebration in 1936 that there were candidates up for reelection in Ottawa County who had "risked their lives, their
political careers, their all" when "we were beset with riots,
pickets and trouble makers in our darkest hours." He
stated that "we owe [them] a debt of gratitude. . . . I'm sure
you know what I mean, and I personally will consider it a
favor if you folks in Ottawa County will support these men
in the coming campaign." For those voters who did not
know the candidates to whom he referred, he suggested
that they stop by the union's headquarters where their
names would be given. "Keep our friends in office," Evans
advised the throng, and "they will keep peace for you."[67]
Evans's message was clear: support the incumbents who
backed the Tri-State Union with the powers of their office.

The campaign of the Tri-State Union and its supporters
to reduce the International Union to impotence was multi-
dimensional, persuasive, and effective. Exploiting by seductive and coercive means the despair and desperation of
Tri-State workers, officials eroded support for the International Union until only its die-hard adherents survived.
Yet their refusal to desert their union enormously complicated their lives. Denied opportunities to work in the

mines and mills and unable to find employment on work relief projects, many were forced to seek a livelihood elsewhere. Their departure was encouraged by Evans and others whose goal was the destruction of all the International Union's locals. For only then would the district be "purged of the horrible stench."

7

"Heads . . . Bouncing off the Cudgels"

TAPPING the large pool of surplus laborers in the district, the operators easily renewed mining and milling without resorting to imported strikebreakers. For the several hundred unemployed members of the International Union of Mine, Mill, and Smelter Workers who rejected membership in the Tri-State Metal Mine and Smelter Workers Union and stubbornly continued the strike despite the resumption of operations, life became increasingly desperate as the stranglehold of the anti–International Union coalition tightened. Because of their numbers and the heavy caseloads already carried by the relief agencies, their exclusion from the mines and mills was an unmitigated disaster for them and their families. Cyrus Slater, a field examiner for the National Labor Relations Board, reported in September 1937 that:

> Many of the former members of the International Union who were blackballed were unable to return to the mines and have drifted to other parts of the country, particularly California. Those who remain are doing so under extreme hardship and they can only endure for a short period of time. These men are not only blackballed from employment in the mines here, but they cannot obtain employment in mines in other parts of the country because their former employers refuse to give them recommendations. Neither can they get employment in other activities in the community, such as with the merchants, building construction companies, electrical construction companies, telephone companies, etc. The only means of livelihood left for the men in this community who are blackballed from getting a Blue Card is to take a sublease on some old

worn out mine and do individual "gouging." In the entire area, there are only a few small mines and mills, out of the fifty to sixty operating, that do not require Blue Card union membership [as] a condition of employment.[1]

Further complicating their situation was the financial inability of either the locals or the parent International Union organization to alleviate their hardship by channeling necessities into the district. Their expectation that the American Federation of Labor (AFL) and its national affiliates would rally to their cause with substantial aid was not realized. Thrown upon their own resources, many of the holdouts therefore left the district to search for work; others changed occupations, or resorted to "gouging," or accepted jobs from a few small operators who valued skill over union affiliation.

Compelled to leave their homes and families, the International Union's faithful scattered over the western states, roaming to the Rocky Mountain hard-rock mining camps, to California, and to anywhere else that rumors indicated jobs could be found. When unable to find work in mining and milling, they took whatever jobs were available. Some of them became occupational nomads, moving from one temporary job to another. Raymond Spurlock, who had worked sporadically for the Eagle Picher Mining and Smelting Company before the strike, found temporary employment as a pick-and-shovel man in the Evergreen Cemetery at Los Angeles, California. When that job expired, he worked part-time for the Berg Metals Corporation, then a short stint for the Forest Lawn Cemetery, and finally for three months at the Atolia Mining Company at Atolia, California.[2] James R. Rhodes, who had been a regular employee of the Eagle Picher Mining and Smelting Company, found five months of work in the American Smelting and Refining Company smelter at Selby, California. Afterwards, he worked three months for the Columbia Steel Company at Pittsburg, California.[3] Milton McIntire, who was an Eagle Picher Company truck driver before the strike, worked seven weeks as a common laborer for the Silica Sand Company at Brentwood, California, then for five weeks as a laborer for the American Smelting and Refining Company at Selby, California. Later McIntire moved to Monrovia, California, where he worked for the West Construction Company for nine months.[4]

In their search for employment, migrant International Union members like Spurlock, Rhodes, and McIntire became gravediggers, salesmen, truck drivers, watchmen, landscapers, mechanics, carpenters, roustabouts, common laborers, and farmers.[5] Their pursuit of jobs took them far from the Tri-State and its labor unrest.

For a variety of reasons, the jobs acquired by itinerant International Union members were rarely permanent. James O. Bryant's job with the Albertoli Mining Company of California ended after four weeks "when the ore 'petered out'."[6] Calvin Davis, who found work with the Frisco Railroad for ten months, was victim of a "reduction in force." Another job with J. A. Crain and Company as a truck driver ended after six weeks when the firm shut down.[7] Fred Foster's job with the Foster Lumber Company in Indiana terminated after a year when he broke his arm.[8] Cecil G. Harreld worked for the Continental Reclamation Company of Texas as a night watchman for seven months until the company became insolvent.[9] H. N. Hilburn's job with the Hecla Mine at Burke, Idaho, was terminated in order to "make room for a family man."[10] Burton (Ben) Kearney lost his job with a mining company in New Mexico because the "vein played out."[11] Blacklists, injuries, company failure, unhealthy work environment, exhausted ore, closed stores, ill health, mine shutdowns, irregular work— all produced a rapid turnover of jobs among the wandering International Union diehards.[12] Furthermore, most of these temporary jobs paid extremely low wages.

Such circumstances were particularly grueling for the men who left their wives, children, and other dependent relatives behind in the district and who sent part of their meager earnings home. Adrift from their moorings and separated from loved ones, they paid a heavy price for their adamant support of the International Union and its strike, which their absence from the district ironically helped to undermine. Some of the men, finding that the depression had riddled the job market nationwide, began to trickle back into the Tri-State District early in 1936. Some, like Harry Franklin James,[13] could not tolerate the separation from their wives and children and returned. Others, like James C. Thompson and Fay F. Stone,[14] came back after sustaining injuries that ended their jobs. A few, like Roy Bond,[15] returned because they had heard that the strike was about to be settled. Most of them, however, returned because their earnings were too inadequate to support themselves and their dependents who remained in the district. Upon their return, they confronted the old dilemma: in order to work in the mines and mills they had to join the Tri-State Union. Many of them surrendered their International Union cards and became "blue carders." Others held firm, surviving as best they could. A few of the men who left the district never returned.

The departure of die-hard International Union members from the Tri-State undoubtedly damaged the strike cause, for they constituted not only the hard core of the membership but also the most spirited element. For example, Ted Schasteen, the International Union activist who had worked regularly for the Eagle Picher Mining and Smelting Company before the strike, sought and found temporary work with the Utah Construction Company in Bingham, Utah, in 1937.[16] Driven by necessity to seek employment outside the district, he left, only to return as did many others. Nevertheless, their absence eased the work of the Tri-State Union in breaking the strike and reasserting the operators' control over the district.

The expectation of some wandering International Union members that the strike would be settled quickly was never realized. From the very start of the strike, both state and federal officials attempted to negotiate an end to the dispute. In Missouri the *Kansas City Star* of May 9, 1935, reported that W. H. Rodgers, a conciliator representing the United States Department of Labor, had tried to arrange a conference between the operators and an International

Union committee for May 8 to discuss union recognition
and a strike settlement. He failed when the operators rejected the proposed meeting. W. A. Pat Murphy, commissioner of labor for Oklahoma, and George O. Pratt, director of the National Labor Relations Board's regional office
in Kansas City, Missouri, scheduled a meeting in Picher for
May 17 to hear strikers' complaints concerning alleged violations of the zinc code. When Murphy was delayed, Pratt
spent the day talking to various operators and strikers concerning the shutdown, but he left without issuing a statement about his findings. Murphy's visit the next day did
not result in any movement toward a settlement.[17]

During early June, Finley B. Bell, another conciliator
dispatched to the district by the Department of Labor,
conferred with Colonels Head and Browne, George F.
Blakeley, labor commissioner of Kansas, and representatives of the twelve largest producers to discuss a settlement of the strike. The International Union was not represented at this meeting. With mining and milling resuming
under military protection, with workers deserting the International Union and flocking into the Tri-State Union,
and with the strikers beginning to scatter from the district
in search of work, the operators refused to consider an immediate settlement. They rejected any solution that would
allow the survival of the locals of the International Union.
Following the conference, Bell stated that "this strike could
[have been] settled in twelve hours if the operators would
[have] agree[d] to put all the men back to work. I suggested that they recognize neither union [the International nor the Tri-State] but put men of both [unions] back
to work."[18] However, the operators took a position that
precluded a settlement when they refused to employ anyone not a member of the Tri-State Union.

Immediately after the conference with Bell, George
Potter, vice-president of the Eagle Picher Mining and
Smelting Company and general manager of its mines,
announced the signing of a contract with Evans and the
Tri-State Union on June 8 which provided that insofar as
possible "ONLY members of your [Evans's] organization"

would be employed by his company.[19] Thus the company joined a growing list of companies that signed identical agreements with the new union. Because Eagle Picher was the largest producer in the district, Potter's announcement meant that nothing short of the International Union's destruction there was acceptable to the operators.

Following the Galena riot of June 28, 1935, Blakeley participated in another conference on July 19 at which Colonels Head and Browne and representatives of Oklahoma Governor Marland and a large number of the companies were present. They searched for an acceptable solution to the strike, although once again International Union leaders were not present. Blakeley later reported that:

> After hours of discussion no satisfactory basis for a settlement could be worked out, owing to the attitude of the operators, a majority of whom had already signed contracts with the new or "company union" and therefore refused to recognize or deal with the organization representing the men on strike. The discussion brought out many facts not generally known to the public, one of which was that the military authorities were having no trouble with the strikers and that disorders occurring were caused by members of the new organization or those in the employ of the mining companies.[20]

To Blakeley, officials of the mining and milling companies were clearly responsible for obstructing a settlement and for the turmoil that had sporadically erupted in the district throughout June into July.

Other initiatives were taken to end the strike but failed when public officials quickly came to accept the success of the Tri-State Union and its back-to-work movement. On July 12, Governor Landon of Kansas met with an unidentified group of labor leaders to consider the situation in the Tri-State District. Afterwards, Roy Wisdom, vice-president of the Kansas State Federation of Labor, reported that Landon was willing to meet with Governor Marland and Governor Lloyd C. Stark of Missouri, the presidents of the three state federations of labor, and representatives of the operators and the strikers to work out a settlement of the Tri-State dispute. This scheme collapsed when Marland informed Landon that such a meeting would be unproductive. Landon agreed with Marland after studying a survey prepared by his labor department which showed that 85 percent of the men working on May 8 in the district had returned to the mines and mills.[21] He reluctantly accepted the results of the anti–International Union coalition as a conclusive settlement of the strike.

During late July, the Department of Labor sent a third conciliator, William F. White, to investigate conditions in the district. For several days he met with International Union leaders and the operators and tried to arrange an official ending of the strike. White was also unsuccessful. His presence, however, disturbed some officials who were satisfied with the back-to-work settlement already imposed by the Tri-State Union and the operators. Major Ellis G. Christensen, who had been left in charge of Cherokee County during a period of extended martial law in July and August following the Galena riot of June 28, reported to Colonel Browne that he had "heard indirectly that Conciliator W. F. White told the men to continue picketing as a symbol that they were on strike. Tried to put him on record as to what he would advise in this situation but 'Nothing doing'."[22] Although White had been sent to resolve the labor dispute between the International Union and the operators, Major Christensen viewed his presence as a threat to the new order. He later wrote that White was an agitator who was the only person to give him trouble during his final tour of duty in the Tri-State.[23] In Christensen's opinion, there was nothing to conciliate. The strike was over.

This was exactly the position taken by the operators, who consistently undermined the efforts of conciliators like Rodgers, Bell, and White to resolve the dispute. When addressing the Metal Mine Convention in the fall of 1935, M. D. Harbaugh, secretary of the Tri-State Zinc and Lead Ore Producers' Association, succinctly explained the stand of the operators concerning the conciliation attempts of the Department of Labor. Harbaugh claimed that there was no controversy between the operators and their employees, that there were no known violations of Section 7(a) of the National Industrial Recovery Act that necessitated outside conciliation, and that, therefore, there was "nothing to conciliate." He further stated that the operators "with the help of their men who wanted to work, [had] settled the strike, insofar as they were concerned, by reopening their properties as soon as they could under police protection, and reemploying most of their former employees."[24] Harbaugh's statement was an open admission that the operators had never made a bona fide effort to end the strike. Their obstructionist tactics were designed to support the efforts of the Tri-State Union to destroy International Union locals in the district under the rubric of a back-to-work movement. His statement was further evidence of the linkage between the corporate members of the producers' association and the new union.

In late August 1936, Kansas Commissioner of Labor Blakeley requested that Tony McTeer, who was emerging as a prominent strike leader, and other officers of the International Union's locals meet to discuss conditions in the Tri-State. When Blakeley asked them to state their demands for negotiating a settlement with the operators, they called for a "full recognition of our organization for collective bargaining," "the check off [of union dues]," and a "seniority clause retroactive prior to May 8, 1935" to be included in the settlement.[25] Following this meeting, in early September 1936, International Union officials endorsed a plan, suggested by Blakeley, which called for the three state commissioners of labor to act as mediators to end the strike. Blakeley (Kansas) and Murphy (Oklahoma) were willing to participate, but when McTeer contacted Mrs. Edna Cruzen (Missouri), she refused. Cruzen informed McTeer that after a "careful" investigation, she had found that "the mines and mills [were] running and no strike exist[ed] in the state of Missouri." She declined therefore to become involved in mediating a labor dispute that did not exist.[26] The events occurring in Oklahoma and Kansas obviously did not concern her. The overlapping state jurisdictions in the Tri-State were clearly an obstacle to a negotiated settlement of the strike.

Thus, throughout 1935 and 1936, the attempts to bring the strike to an end failed. Although there were several contributing causes of this failure, the principal one was the intransigent refusal of the operators to cooperate in peacefully resolving the dispute. Having launched their own successful campaign to "settle" the strike, they saw no reason to encourage or participate in any formal solution that remotely recognized the International Union as a legitimate voice of the workers. Their objective was to destroy the original union, not to recognize and preserve it. As much as anything, their hard-headed resistance to independent unionism and their insistence on dominating the Tri-State District through the new union were responsible for a new International Union drive to organize the workers in the spring of 1937. This new challenge to the operators' control provoked the greatest violence of the strike.

Although a combination of forces had broken the strike within weeks after its start on May 8, 1935, it remained officially in progress in the spring of 1937 when Reid Robinson, who had replaced Thomas Brown as president of the union, challenged the Tri-State Union's supremacy in the district. Under Brown the International Union had become a charter member of John L. Lewis's Committee for Industrial Organization (CIO). But Robinson, who was even more committed to the principle of industrial unionism than Brown, initiated a new drive to organize the Tri-Staters as part of the CIO's goal to unionize all mass-production workers under the protection of the National Labor Relations Act of 1935.[27] The International's affiliation with the CIO, whose organizing efforts elsewhere had produced sit-down strikes and violence, was well known in the district, making the union even less acceptable to the coalition formed to defeat the International Union in the district. After several weeks of quiet, behind-the-scenes work, Robinson went public by announcing an open meeting to be held in Picher, the stronghold of the Tri-State

Union, on Sunday, April 11. The announcement provoked outbursts of violence in the district, which led to some serious personal injuries, one death, and the destruction of union halls and other property.

There were harbingers of the impending violence. On April 10, several International Union members attempted to distribute circulars to smelter workers leaving the south entrance of Eagle Picher Lead Company's Joplin plant. The handouts denounced "company unions" (a clear reference to the Tri-State Union), called upon the district miners and millmen to join the CIO, and announced the meeting at Picher. When presented with the circulars, approximately seventy-five of the departing workers—all reported to be members of the Tri-State Union—became infuriated. An altercation erupted that forced some of the distributors to flee, while others, unable to escape, were beaten. Although no serious injuries resulted from the skirmish outside the plant, the circulars were seized and burned.[28] A symbolic rejection of the CIO, this episode was the spontaneous beginning of a new assault directed at those workers who doggedly refused to accept the new order of the Tri-State Union and the operators.

News of the CIO's planned meeting prompted strong countermeasures from the Tri-State Union. On Saturday, April 10, at Picher, Evans assembled nearly four hundred foremen and ground bosses, all members of the Tri-State Union, and instructed them to rally their men early the next day in Picher to stop the CIO's meeting that had been set for two o'clock in the afternoon. He announced that the men on the Sunday shift would be excused from work and expected to participate. Evans told the supervisors to inform all the men that there would be plenty to eat and drink and that a failure to attend the Tri-State Union rally could cost them their jobs. He also instructed them to order their workers living in or near Picher to assemble that evening to prepare for next day's confrontation with supporters of Robinson's CIO. His strategy was to occupy and command the streets with hundreds of Tri-State Union members armed with pick handles because, whatever the

Reid Robinson, president of the International Union of Mine, Mill, and Smelter Workers during the April 1937 riots in Picher, Treece, and Galena. Courtesy of Western Historical Collections, University of Colorado, Boulder.

cost, the CIO's organizing campaign had to be stopped before it gained momentum.

With the obvious approval of the operators, the supervisors carried out Evans's instructions. Ray O'Dell, a ground boss for Eagle Picher's Mary N. Beck Mine, released his men early on April 10 in order to address approximately a hundred of them outside the mine office. Climbing onto a truck to be visible to all, he stated:

> There is, I suppose you fellows all know, . . . to be a meeting in Picher tomorrow. It is that damn thing, we thought we had it whipped, coming back on us. How many of you fellows

here have bought something that you want to pay for? There is going to be a meeting at the Blue Card hall tonight, and I want all of you men that live around here close to be there. . . . There will probably be plenty of tooth picks [pick handles] there, if anybody wants one.[29]

With such encouragement, toward evening scores of Tri-State Union members began gathering in Picher.

At the evening meeting, Evans, Nolan, and Norman addressed the crowd, stirring the men's emotions with inflammatory language and stressing again that Robinson and his supporters must be stopped if Tri-State Union members were to remain employed. Daniel House, a field examiner for the National Labor Relations Board who spent a week in the Tri-State investigating conditions there, later reported concerning this meeting:

They [Evans, Nolan, and Norman] told them they would be supplied with pick handles, which they should use if necessary to stop the [CIO] meeting. Nolan said that machine guns would be supplied if necessary. Foremen throughout the camp had told their men to attend this Blue Card Meeting or lose their jobs. At this meeting the men were promised that if they were arrested for anything they would be gotten out, as the chief of police [Al Maness] who was present at the meeting, was on the side of the Blue Card Union.[30]

The remarks of the Tri-State Union leaders exposed a clear predisposition to use violence to end the threat posed by Robinson. Claiming to represent 90 to 95 percent of the Tri-State workers, they were determined that under no circumstances was the International Union, now affiliated with Lewis's CIO, to be allowed a new foothold in the district.

That same evening Ray Keller, a constable at nearby Hockerville and a member of the International, was in Picher and he observed much public consumption of alcohol in violation of Oklahoma's prohibition law. When he visited the police station, he found a half-dozen pick handles in Chief of Police Al Maness's office and one of three other men was armed with the weapon. Concerned about the prevalence of drinking and pick handles, Keller telephoned Ottawa County Sheriff Walter Young and requested that he intervene to prevent the situation from getting out of hand. Young rejected the request, stating that he had been in Picher, had found the town quiet and peaceful, and saw no reason to intervene.[31]

Also alarmed by the events in Picher, Robinson met with Sheriff Young at the county courthouse in Miami on the evening of April 10 and asked for assurance that his scheduled rally the next day would receive police protection. Discounting the possibility of trouble and claiming that he would be out of town on official business, Young refused to promise that his deputies would attend the rally at Picher's city park. He also refused to place credence in the reports that a pick-handle parade was planned to disrupt the meeting. Obtaining no assurance of protection, Robinson and Tony McTeer then conferred with Ottawa County Attorney William Poteet, who claimed to have no authority to act until a crime had been committed. He promised, however, to keep Young in the county because, contrary to Young's statement, he was not scheduled to leave on official business.[32]

April 11 was a tumultuous day in the Tri-State District. Although all signs pointed to violence, Robinson forged ahead with plans for his organizing rally. Early Sunday morning, Tri-State Union members flooded into Picher, determined to block the rally scheduled for two o'clock. True to his promise, Evans supplied plenty of free whiskey, food, and pick handles at the union's hall. Cyrus Slater, a field examiner for the National Labor Relations Board, who, like House, later investigated conditions, estimated that "approximately 1,000 new pick and sledge-hammer handles" were distributed.[33] In 1975, an unidentified old-timer recalled that "the Blue Cards had a lot of liquor coming into the area. One man, a Blue Card company sympathizer, drove down main street in a flatbed truck loaded with boxes of pickhandles." He also remembered that "most of them were drunk and edging for a fight and picking up handles and swinging them at anyone."[34]

Tony McTeer, a Tri-State union leader. Courtesy of Western Historical Collections, University of Colorado, Boulder.

When "liquored up," some Tri-State Union members refused to wait for Robinson's meeting to vent their anger at the International's organizing threat. Early in the morning, a raucous group piled into automobiles and drove to nearby Hockerville where they seized and flogged Constable Keller and then ordered him to leave town. He remained. Keller was an International Union member and a CIO sympathizer who had earlier tried to persuade Sheriff Young to intervene. Before eleven o'clock, a similar group raided the International Union's Local 15 hall in Picher, one of three such raids on the hall that day. When the attack occurred, Hugh Arnold, secretary of the local, his daughter, and Edward O. Edwards were in a rear apartment of the hall. Arnold and Edwards later reported that plate glass windows were broken, tables and benches were overturned, filing cabinets were broken into and records scattered, and day sheets and index cards of the membership were stolen or destroyed.[35]

Pandemonium reigned on Picher's streets. Evans's men, hourly reinforced by an increasing number of cohorts ordered into town by their supervisors, formed into squads. Often reeking with alcohol, they carried their pick handles, clubs, and revolvers up and down Connell Avenue, yelling and cursing, waving and thumping their pick handles on the sidewalks and buildings, and attacking anyone who dared to wear the yellow CIO button. Bill DeWitt, a pick-handler who worked for the Eagle Picher Mining and Smelting Company, grabbed a CIO button from Clifford Doak, who with his wife and four others had driven to Picher for the International Union rally. Waving the button in the air, DeWitt shouted, "Here is one of the C.I.O. pins. There is the son-of-a-bitch I got it off." Shaking a pick handle in Doak's face, DeWitt dared him to "start something." Observing the incident from his car in front of the police station, Chief of Police Maness watched and laughed without intervening. DeWitt's pack followed Doak to his car where Roscoe Gather struck him in the face with brass knuckles. There followed a pick-handle assault on Doak's party during which Lester Wakefield was knocked unconscious.[36]

Street fighting erupted when Tri-State Union men, operating in packs, challenged any known International-CIO sympathizer. Pick handles were freely used in these brawls, the men having been promised immunity if they were arrested.[37] After being beaten with pick handles by Bert Craig, Floyd Fox, Jim Goble, Bill Cassell, and Lavoice Miller, Harry Blasor, an International Union member, then had his ribs cracked when he was kicked in the back. He was hospitalized. The *Blue Card Record* best described the turmoil and violence when it editorially gloated on April 16:

> Sunday morning early hundreds of miners, practically all of them armed with pick handles, were parading the Picher

streets and it wasn't long before C.I.O. sympathizers' heads were bouncing off the cudgels on account of their utterances or wearing of association buttons.

Squads of shock troops from the various mines milled about in the crowds, each with its captain in charge and the cry of "Hey Rube," would bring hundreds together in jiffy time. The situation was tingling tense throughout the entire day, but everyone seemed to enjoy it like a picnic. . . .

Every ambulance of the city was held in readiness and the siren shriek became so common that it was considered a rule instead of the exception. Both the Picher and the American hospitals were kept busy patching up the injured.[38]

Fifteen men required hospitalization after being beaten with pick handles. Long before the scheduled International Union rally, the streets of Picher belonged to Evans and his followers. Having driven out the enemy, they exulted in their victory by milling about, pounding the streets and sidewalks with their pick handles, and parking their cars in the space where Robinson was to have spoken.

Under the circumstances, Robinson had no choice but to cancel his meeting. Returning to Picher from Joplin about eleven o'clock, he found the city filled with hundreds of men armed with pick handles being sporadically used against his people. Telephoning Sheriff Young's office, he again asked for and was refused police protection, a deputy sheriff claiming that pick handles were not dangerous weapons. Robinson continued to call every thirty minutes until one-thirty with the same result—refusal.[39] Law enforcement officials were conspicuous by their absence. On April 13, the *Joplin Globe* reported that "throughout the Picher demonstration no county or city authorities were in evidence on the streets."[40] Dee T. Watters, an operative from the Oklahoma State Bureau of Criminal Investigation, arrived in Picher about three o'clock and did not observe any police in the streets or in the city hall.[41] Robinson saw Sheriff Young only in the very late afternoon after all the damage had been done. That law enforcement officials failed to curb the flagrant violence, to restore order, and to protect the freedom of union members to assemble peacefully was clearly more than coincidental. Without police protection, not to have canceled the rally would have been irresponsible.

Greater violence was yet to come. A rumor that a CIO meeting was under way in Treece, located about two miles north of Picher across the Kansas state line, was deliberately released from Tri-State Union headquarters and swept through the blue card host, which now numbered in the thousands. Directed from a sound car by Nolan, the "pick-handle king," scores of the unruly men loaded into cars and trucks and sped to Treece where, of course, there was no meeting. After an impromptu pick-handle parade down the town's main street, they methodically wrecked Local 111's hall after stealing union records and breaking up the furnishings. When they left, all union records were gone.[42] Like the Picher union hall, Local 111's hall was unoccupied when raided. But International Union members drawn to the scene were brutally beaten. "Boots" Irvin, a ground boss at the Mid-Continent Mine and a leader of the mob, awarded a dollar for each CIO button ripped off a union member.[43] As in Picher, law enforcement officers failed to intervene to stop the beatings and the destruction of property.

In both Picher and Treece, pick-handle law reigned supreme, resulting in two wrecked union halls and scores of intimidated or injured union members. Evans and his associates, however, were not satisfied with the damage done to the enemy. There was still the International local at Galena where the spirit of independent unionism had been most difficult to bridle. It was, as Evans later stated, "the hottest spot in the district for us."[44] If the organizing campaign of Robinson was to be stopped, the wrath and power of the Tri-State Union must be demonstrated in Galena. With thousands of their followers armed with pick handles and other weapons and susceptible to the meanest suggestion, Evans and his associates determined to display their strength there, to end forever any speculation about their ability to hold the district for the Tri-State Union.

Once more in Picher, Evans and his associates launched an inflammatory rumor that a CIO meeting was in progress at Galena, thus setting the stage for the most serious outbreak of violence. Once again emotions ran amuck, the crowd becoming greatly agitated and prone to irrational action. When Tri-State Union street leaders, later identified by George O. Pratt, regional director of the National Labor Relations Board, as minor supervisors of the mining companies, urged over a sound car a "march" to break up the rumored meeting, hundreds of volunteers stepped forward eager to participate. To assure maximum participation in this second uncontested invasion of Kansas, an appeal for supporters was broadcast over WMBH, a radio station in Joplin. Loading into an estimated one hundred cars and trucks, nearly five hundred men, armed with pick handles and other weapons, started to Galena, located about eighteen miles northeast on old Highway 66. According to Pratt, Ottawa County Sheriff Young, perhaps anxious to divert the troublesome mob elsewhere, escorted the long motorcade to the Kansas state line where authorities there made no attempt to challenge its movement north.[45]

Upon arrival in Galena, the men assembled at the Tri-State Union hall where they were informed that no CIO meeting was being held at the International Union's headquarters, which was about four blocks north on Main Street. Someone then suggested that there should be a pick-handle parade. The men formed into irregular lines in the sunny late afternoon and, brandishing their pick handles, began a noisy march up Main Street toward the Local 17 hall. A few women and boys joined the moving ranks of men, who were reported to be in a festive mood.

In sharp contrast, however, the mood among Galena's Local 17 members was anything but festive. They knew of the recent events in Picher and Treece—the beatings and the wrecking of union halls. As the pick-handle parade approached, fifteen union men who had been standing outside their headquarters moved inside the building. If necessary, they were determined to defend their lives and property. There would not be an easy, cheap victory in Galena for their opponents. Laughing and talking, the pick-handlers advanced on Main Street, unaware that within their midst were men who intended to attack the hall and unaware of the danger that lay in wait for them if an attack occurred.

When the front ranks of the marchers reached the building, a man reported to be Lavoice Miller dashed to its front and began smashing plate glass windows with a pick handle. From within, the occupants responded immediately with a burst of pistol and shotgun fire directed against the marchers, causing them to break and scatter. This initial burst was followed by a wildly erratic exchange of gunfire, with "considerable shooting done by various persons on and upon the streets and alleys . . . of Galena."[46] Several marchers hurled smoke bombs against the building, hoping to smoke the gunmen out. The exploding bombs temporarily covered the front area with a cloud of white smoke. Panic erupted on the street. Patrons in a theater across from the hall fled through a rear exit. Fearful of being shot, Sunday strollers and marchers huddled against buildings. A group of marchers raced back to Galena's Tri-State Union hall for guns; others telephoned Picher for reinforcement, pleading for guns and dynamite to use against the hall. Still others risked their lives to remove the wounded who lay sprawled on the street.

Within moments the firing ceased. Only then did the enormity of the incident become evident, for eight men and a teenage boy had been shot, several receiving serious wounds that required hospitalization. Eleven days later, Lavoice Miller, who had apparently initiated the riot by breaking the plate glass windows of the hall, died of complications stemming from his wounds. Fortunately, there was no retaliatory assault on the union hall, reducing the threat of further bloodshed by giving its then unknown occupants time to escape through a back door.[47]

When Cherokee County Sheriff Fred Simkin, who had been investigating the riot in Treece, arrived in Galena around six o'clock, he found Main Street quiet. Upon entering the union hall, however, he discovered two men looting the local's records. After arresting them, he padlocked the building and went to the Tri-State Union hall where he seized seven shotguns and ammunition from a number of men from Picher. He ordered them to leave town and locked the hall. Mayor E. B. Morgan, away in Joplin at the time of the riot, returned to patrol the streets with deputies.[48] Thus the Galena riot ended, a riot that climaxed two years of labor unrest in the Tri-State.[49]

Unlike the violent period of 1935, local authorities did not request state civil or military intervention. For nearly two years in Ottawa County, law enforcement officials had openly consorted with the Tri-State Union and the companies in reimposing their control over the district. On April 10 when Evans, Nolan, and Norman had promised immunity from prosecution to the men who broke the law in disrupting the CIO meeting next day, Picher's Chief of Police Al Maness was present.[50] Furthermore, local authorities had refused to provide police protection to Robinson and his union's members in Picher, even after repeated requests and occurrences that seemed to demand it. As reported in the *Joplin Globe*, the police were conspicuously absent when the Tri-State Union unleashed its mobs to assault and intimidate International Union members. Moreover, rarely had a potential mob en route to commit mayhem received a police escort, even part of the way. The events in Picher, Treece, and Galena, particularly the events in Picher, could not have occurred without the connivance of municipal and county law enforcement officials. On April 14, Mayor Morgan wrote to Governor Walter A. Huxman of Kansas that "my information is that the Ottawa County officers made but little if any effort to control the situation down there."[51]

State officials reacted cautiously to the disturbances in the Oklahoma portion of the Tri-State. Two "operatives" were sent with instructions to work closely with local authorities who, unfortunately, had supported the instigators of the violence. According to Adjutant General Charles F. Barrett, "We [were] in no position to act officially until local officials ask[ed] for aid."[52] Of course, with the Tri-State Union once more firmly in control, they did not want state intervention. Shortly after the Picher riot, Ralph Chambers, a banker, led a group representing fifty-four unidentified Picher firms to meet with Governor Marland in Oklahoma City. Many of these businesses were undoubtedly corporate members of the Tri-State Union. Claiming that the violence had been caused by "outside agitators who wanted to replace the Blue Card Union with a C.I.O. union," Chambers asked that the governor not intervene in the district because the people whom he represented could manage the situation themselves. Said Chambers:

> Our population up there [in Ottawa County] is less than 1 percent foreign. We feel like we can take care of any situation that may arise. Of course, some of the fellows got a little too much to drink last Sunday and did some things that perhaps ought not to have been done. They just prevented the opposition from meeting. It was the same tactic the C.I.O. union tried to pull on the local boys two years ago during the strike. We just turned the tables.[53]

Chambers and his group were persuasive. Marland did not intervene, although the level of violence far exceeded that of 1935 when the Oklahoma National Guard had been ordered into the district. Unlike 1935, however, the violence of 1937 had been directed against union members, now of the CIO, whose influence in local and state affairs was nil. The governor's inaction further legitimized the methods employed by the Tri-State Union to control the district.

Local authorities in Cherokee County also failed to request the Kansas National Guard to quell the new outbreaks of violence in Treece and Galena. Because of a recent mayoral election in Galena, confusion existed there concerning who was in charge when the riot occurred. Incumbent E. B. Morgan had not run for reelection, but when A. J. O'Connor, a "straw boss on a W.P.A. project," was elected, Morgan immediately surrendered the office and left town. Returning on April 11, he learned of the riot and found that O'Connor had refused to take the office of mayor prematurely. Morgan hastily took charge, only to discover that his police force was strangely missing. Although County Sheriff Simkin was called, he was away investigating the earlier riot at Treece and did not reach Galena until late afternoon.[54]

Governor Huxman, Landon's successor, was reluctant to act. On the night of April 11, neither he nor Adjutant General M. R. McLean had received an official notification of the Galena riot. Consequently, he claimed an inability to intervene unless called upon by the local authorities.[55] Nevertheless, Attorney General Clarence V. Beck sent J. S. Parker, an assistant attorney general, to investigate. About April 15, Parker reported that "unless [the] C.I.O. insists on calling a mass meeting over in Kansas, I am quite confident we will have no further difficulty at present. If they do call a mass meeting in Kansas, and it is near the Oklahoma line and in the vicinity of Picher, I doubt very much if anything short of a young army will avoid acts of violence on the part of the two rival unions."[56] Parker advised that he had persuaded all but one unidentified International Union leader to refrain from meeting near the state line, at least until the wounded Tri-State Union members were out of the hospital.[57]

Parker recommended to Beck that Cherokee County Attorney Joe Henbest "initiate wholesale prosecutions against all individuals taking part in the rioting, or at least individuals who actually and violently participated therein."[58] He believed that such action would have a positive effect on future events in the district. Henbest followed that recommendation, charging ten International Union members with the murder of Lavoice Miller and charging twenty-five members of the Tri-State Union with malicious destruction of union property.[59] The county later appointed a special prosecutor for these cases. Most of the charges were eventually dropped. The murder charges were dismissed because there was "insufficient evidence available . . . to justify prosecution."[60] In an ironic twist, Kelsey Norman, legal counsel for the Tri-State Union and a principal instigator in the events of April 11, accompanied Leo

Armstrong, the special prosecutor, to request of the court an order of dismissal.[61] Other than Parker's investigation of the Galena riot and the legal actions taken in compliance with his recommendation to the attorney general, the state failed to respond. No requests for troops were made and none was sent.

Using force and violence, the Tri-State Union successfully warded off Robinson's effort to recapture the mine and mill workers of the Tri-State for the International Union and the CIO. It was now abundantly clear that Evans and his supporters were so entrenched and his followers so desperately fearful of losing their jobs that there was little chance of organizing the district without substantial federal assistance. As long as the rights to organize and to bargain collectively, rights guaranteed in the National Labor Relations Act, were flagrantly violated with impunity, the Tri-State Union reigned supreme. Even as International Union members' "heads were bouncing off the cudgels," however, the Supreme Court was preparing to render a decision that offered hope to Robinson's several hundred diehards who refused to knuckle under to Evans's "company" union.

8

"We Are Yet Blue Carders"

BLUE-CARD power reached its zenith on April 11, 1937. Nevertheless, the violent response to Reid Robinson's scheduled rally at Picher exposed a continuing concern among Mike Evans and his supporters, who had engineered and orchestrated the violence, that the pesky holdout members of the International Union of Mine, Mill, and Smelter Workers clearly endangered the new order. Their concern was justified. While the Tri-State Metal Mine and Smelter Workers Union and the companies were suppressing all challenges to their control of the district, national developments were occurring that eventually broke their absolute domination.

Under President Franklin D. Roosevelt's New Deal, the federal government intruded more frequently into industrial relations. Labor's right to organize and to engage in collective bargaining had been federally recognized in Section 7(a) of the National Industrial Recovery Act of 1933. The United States Supreme Court's decision in *Schechter Poultry Corporation* v. *United States* in 1935, however, struck down the Act because it unconstitutionally delegated legislative authority to the president to establish codes of fair competition and, in the case at hand, exceeded federal authority over intrastate commerce.[1] The Roosevelt administration thereupon moved to salvage the labor provisions of the Industrial Recovery Act by incorporating them into the National Labor Relations Act of 1935.

The Labor Relations Act recognized labor's right to organize and engage in collective bargaining and it designated specific actions of employers as "unfair" labor practices. Among such acts were interfering with the rights of employees as defined in the Act (for example, the right of self-organization), controlling and/or interfering with the formation of a labor union or providing it with financial support, discriminating against a worker to encourage or discourage his membership in a labor union, discriminating against an employee who filed complaints with the National Labor Relations Board, and refusing to bargain collectively with the freely chosen representatives of workers. To administer and enforce the law, which became effective on July 5, 1935—approximately one month into the strike of the International Union in the Tri-State District—Congress established the National Labor Relations Board.[2]

Before passage of the Labor Relations Act, International Union members in the Tri-State were helpless before the combined assault of the Tri-State Union, the companies, and local and state authorities. Now the law offered hope of federal intervention on their behalf by allowing them to file complaints of unfair labor practices against the mining and milling companies with the National Labor Relations Board. If its investigation confirmed a violation of statutory rights, the Board was empowered to issue cease and desist orders against the violators that were enforceable in the federal courts. Attorneys for the Tri-State Union and the companies, however, had not been particularly concerned about the Labor Relations Act because they had early concluded that the Supreme Court would never uphold its constitutionality. Furthermore, because the law had been enacted on July 5, 1935, well after the start of the strike, they had also concluded that applying its provisions to a preexisting labor dispute would be legally difficult if not impossible.

In a special meeting of the Tri-State Union, Kelsey Norman, attorney for the organization, advised its members that the Act would not affect operations in the Tri-State District because the law applied only to businesses engaged in interstate commerce. Although mining and milling there sprawled over four counties in three states and although some companies, like Eagle Picher, were outwardly interstate operations, Norman stated that, in his opinion, the industry was intrastate. He therefore advised that there was no basis for the National Labor Relations Board to assume jurisdiction over industrial relations in the district, even if the labor law was upheld as constitutional and even if striking International Union members filed complaints against the operators under its provisions.[3] Following the advice of counsel, officials of the Tri-State Union and the companies continued practices after July 5 that clearly violated provisions of the Act. Like many employers throughout the nation, they were confident that the Supreme Court would rule that the Labor Relations Act was an unconstitutional intrusion into labor-management relations.

Early federal court tests of the law enhanced their confidence. In the first tests, federal Judge Merrill E. Otis of Kansas City, Missouri, granted an injunction on December 21, 1935, to the owners of a flour mill in Aurora, Missouri, which prevented the National Labor Relations Board from holding scheduled hearings on charges that the mill owners had refused to bargain collectively with their organized employees. Otis accepted the owners' arguments that the hearings would cause irreparable damage to their flour-milling business. But apart from being the first court test of the Act, what made Judge Otis's action so significant was his commentary concerning the constitutionality of the law, commentary widely publicized in Tri-State newspapers such as the *Miami Daily News-Record*.[4] Judge Otis held that the law was blatantly invalid because "nothing [was] more firmly . . . established in constitutional law" than the principle that manufacturing was not commerce. "There [was] no way," he ruled, "in which any of the specified unfair labor practices in any business, whether mill or mine or factory or store, conceivably can directly affect commerce." Judge Otis further observed that the National Labor Relations Act treated the worker "as an incompetent," making him a "ward of the United States, to be cared for by his guardian even as if he were a member of an uncivilized tribe of Indians or a recently emancipated slave." The judge rejected a federal involvement in labor-management relations that guaranteed workers the right to organize and engage in collective bargaining. The upholding of the Otis injunction by the Eighth Circuit Court of Appeals undoubtedly reassured Norman that his advice to the Tri-State Union officials had been sound and defensible, and local attorneys for the mining and milling companies, like A. C. Wallace, were surely gratified by Judge Otis's reasoning and conclusions. They had every reason to be. In a letter of August 23, 1936 to Tony McTeer, George O. Pratt, director of the National Labor Relations Board's Region 17, noted the negative impact of the ruling when he wrote: "The business of this Board has slowed down considerably, particularly since the recent decision of the Circuit Court of Appeals in St. Paul, upholding the decision of Judge Otis in the Majestic Flour Mill case, Aurora, Missouri."[5] All matters were on hold until a ruling on the act by the Supreme Court.

Although discouraged by these lower court rulings on the Labor Relations Act, local leaders of the International Union clung to the hope that the Supreme Court would uphold the law. On March 25, 1936, Tony McTeer, Ted Schasteen, Richard W. Murray, and Ernest B. Berry, officers of Locals 15, 111, 17, and 107, filed complaints of unfair labor practices against the Eagle Picher Mining and Smelting Company—and on April 23 against the parent Eagle Picher Lead Company—with the Region 17 office in Kansas City, Missouri. They alleged that the companies had schemed to create, dominate, and control the Tri-State Union in order to prevent their employees from engaging in collective bargaining; that the companies had forced supervisors to participate in the new union; that the Eagle Picher companies had contributed financial and other support to the Tri-State Union; that the companies had compelled their employees to join the Tri-State Union as a condition of employment; and that the Eagle Picher companies had actively discouraged membership in the International Union.[6] Although the International Union's local leaders filed similar complaints against most of the larger companies in the district, Pratt elected to focus on the Eagle Picher companies because they controlled approximately half the district's production. Success against them would nudge the other Tri-State companies into compliance with the law. Pratt set a hearing on the complaints for May 25.

Three days before the hearing, A. C. Wallace, attorney for Eagle Picher, petitioned the Federal District Court (Northern District, Oklahoma) for an immediate restraining order to block the proceedings. Obviously influenced by the Otis decision, Wallace denied the constitutionality of the Labor Relations Act and asserted that the hearings would cause the companies irreparable damage. He claimed that the companies were not involved in interstate commerce, and he denied that they had committed unfair labor practices as defined by the law or as described in the complaint.[7] The next day Judge Franklin E. Kennamer issued a restraining order to George Pratt; Thomas H. Brown, then president of the International Union; Daniel Lyons, designated trial examiner for the hearings; and Louis N. Wolf, attorney for the plaintiffs, that blocked the hearings and set May 25 for arguments on a preliminary injunction requested by the companies.[8] When the arguments of Pratt and Wolf that the companies *were* engaged in interstate commerce and *were* therefore subject to the Act and the jurisdiction of the National Labor Relations Board proved unconvincing, Judge Kennamer issued a temporary injunction on July 6 that stopped the hearing into the complaints of the International Union's locals. Pratt promptly appealed the decision to the Tenth Circuit Court of Appeals for review.

In the interval between Kennamer's restraining order of May 25 and his July 6 injunction, antiunion factions in the Tri-State took heart, convinced more than ever that the Supreme Court would strike down the abominable law that allowed federal intervention in district labor affairs. Perhaps without thinking, they accepted Wallace's statement of May 25 that Eagle Picher companies were not running from the hearing, because facts [were] on our side. The sole purpose in bringing these court proceedings was to avoid the expense of four or five weeks of hearings, which would in the end be of no avail. It would result in disturbance to the organization [the companies] and would throw several hundred men out of work for 30 days or more, entailing a loss of something like $40,000 a month to common labor alone.[9]

Wallace suggested that the companies were acting in behalf of Tri-State workers in preventing an airing of union complaints.

Five days later the *Metal Mine & Smelter Worker* revealed the true sentiments of the antiunion coalition concerning the complaints, the men who filed them, and the Labor Relations Board. Characterizing the complaints as "ridiculous," the complainants as well-known "undesirables," their lawyer as one who had "flooded the courts with questionable damage suits," and the Act as "unconstitutional," it declared that "a babe could not have had more solicitous nor tender care [than the complainants received from the National Labor Relations Board], and from the smell and cooing that filled the Federal Court room at Miami before the Labor Board began, the Internationalites must have been mewing and puking in "Mother Board's" arms which created a nauseating symphony of sound and stink."[10]

The greatest danger, however, was that some court, perhaps the Supreme Court, would accept the complaints of the International Union, raising the threat that some "two hundred 'smelly' Internationalites" would acquire the jobs of "buddies" and force seven thousand Tri-State Union members to accept "their idea of relations between yourselves and your employers." Kennamer's injunction of July 6 apparently reduced this danger, but looming in the background was Pratt's appeal to the Tenth Circuit Court.

Having checked the investigation of the International Union's complaints of unfair labor practices, opponents of the union settled down for a ten-month respite, free from the fear of federal intervention. But on April 12, 1937, one day following the widespread violence in the district, the Supreme Court shook the antiunion coalition when it issued its decision in *N.L.R.B.* v. *Jones & Laughlin Steel Corporation*. Like the Eagle Picher companies, Jones and Laughlin, which had been charged with unfair labor practices at one of its mills, had argued that its business was manufacturing, not commerce, and that its operations were entirely intrastate in character. Consequently, the efforts of the federal government to regulate labor-management relations at Jones and Laughlin facilities were unconstitutional. The Court, however, rejected these arguments and its own precedents. It ruled that the power of Congress "to protect interstate commerce from burdens and obstructions was not limited to transactions which can be deemed to be an essential part of the 'flow' of interstate and foreign commerce." On the contrary, its authority encompassed intrastate production if it either directly or indirectly affected interstate commerce. Because labor unrest at Jones and Laughlin affected interstate commerce, it was subject to congressional authority. The Court thus removed its previous distinction between direct and indirect effects on commerce.[11] Much to the dismay of Evans and his supporters, the unthinkable had happened. The Supreme Court had upheld the National Labor Relations Act, and, in doing so, had cleared the way for federal intervention in the Tri-State.

Using force and violence, the Tri-State Union had warded off the challenge of Reid Robinson to recapture the mine and mill workers of the Tri-State for the International Union and the CIO. Accepted by business, industrial, and civic leaders and backed by local law enforcement officials, particularly in Oklahoma, the Tri-State Union's domination seemed assured. Now the Supreme Court's decision in the Jones and Laughlin case posed another threat to Evans's organization, for the Labor Relations Act specifically prohibited company unions. It raised the possibility that Judge Kennamer's injunction prohibiting hearings into the complaints of unfair labor practices against the Eagle Picher companies would be overturned. If held, such hearings could expose the true nature of the Tri-

State Union and its relationship with the companies, and could lead to its downfall.

To counter the Court's decision, Evans, Norman, and others concluded that it was now essential to affiliate the Tri-State Union with the AFL. They reasoned that affiliation would effectively block the CIO from the district, destroy the company-union image of the Tri-State Union, and undermine the National Labor Relations Board's developing case against the companies. Most important, they reasoned that affiliation would not produce any substantive changes. It would leave them in control of industrial relations in the district. Developments in the national labor movement made this extraordinary move feasible, producing one of the greatest ironies in American labor history.

The National Industrial Recovery Act of 1933 had encouraged a tremendous upsurge of union membership in every trade but especially among workers in the mass-production industries. American Federation of Labor leaders organized this flood of new recruits into national unions, intending to divide them eventually among the various trades. This procedure provoked opposition from John L. Lewis, president of the United Mine Workers, and other leaders of industrial unions. They believed that because of the changes in American industry that had made the unskilled and semiskilled workers a majority of the labor force, it was imperative to organize on an industry-wide basis. Because employers had been successful in rolling back union membership following the initial upsurge, Lewis and his supporters persuaded the AFL's annual convention of 1934 to authorize the chartering of industrial unions in automobiles, aluminum, rubber, radio, and cement and to begin organizing the steel industry.

Unable to overcome the inertia of tradition and trade interests, William Green, president of the AFL, failed to act. At the annual convention of 1935, reports from the executive council and the resolutions committee revealed that opponents of industrial unionism, who dominated the council and the committee, intended to stand pat in order to protect the jurisdictions of the trade unions. The result was an extended debate over craft versus industrial unionism, a famous physical encounter between Lewis and William L. ("Big Bill") Hutcheson, president of the Carpenters' Union, and a vote that soundly defeated the industrial unionists. Refusing to accept defeat, Lewis met with seven of his supporters, including Thomas H. Brown of the International Union of Mine, Mill, and Smelter Workers, and formed the Committee for Industrial Organization (CIO). In response to this challenge, the executive council suspended these men and their unions in August 1936, and the annual convention of that year also expelled them from the AFL. When reconciliation efforts failed to reunify the two groups, the CIO converted itself into the Congress of Industrial Organizations in May 1938, an action which then appeared to split the labor movement permanently.[12]

Brown's decision to join Lewis's forces greatly influenced events in the Tri-State because the origin of the CIO and the suspension and expulsion of its member unions from the AFL occurred simultaneously with the strike of the lead and zinc workers. Furthermore, beginning in June 1936 the CIO aggressively organized the steel, auto, textile, rubber, mine, and other workers, a move that brought hundreds of thousands into CIO unions and a new intensity to industrial warfare. The unsuccessful struggle to organize the Bethlehem, the Inland, the Republic, and the Youngstown Sheet and Tube companies—"Little Steel"—provoked unprecedented violence that climaxed in the Memorial Day Massacre of 1937. The conquest of General Motors occurred only after the turmoil of "sit-down" strikes and much strife. But the enormous success of the CIO's organizing campaigns also sparked new efforts from the AFL, and soon these two organizations were engaged in a bitter struggle that adversely affected workers throughout the nation.

The militancy, the revolutionary tactic of the sit-down strike, and the presence of Communists or "reds" in the leadership of the CIO greatly disturbed Tri-State Union leaders who had watched from afar. For these and other

reasons they had violently fought CIO penetration of the
Tri-State. At the same time, they recognized that the CIO's
battle with the AFL could be used to their advantage.
Norman recognized the possibilities when he stated to the
Tri-State Union's local at Picher that it was "necessary for
our union to affiliate with some strong national organization [the AFL] in order that we might protect ourselves
against the ravages of John L. Lewis and his Committee for
Industrial Organization."[13] And following the Supreme
Court's ruling in the Jones and Laughlin case, he expected
the Tenth Circuit Court of Appeals to overturn Kennamer's
injunction prohibiting a National Labor Relations Board
hearing on complaints of unfair labor practices. To a mass
meeting of members, Norman stated that the decision had
"made it absolutely necessary for the Blue Card Union to
become affiliated with a federation and affiliation with any
other than the A.F. of L. was unthinkable."[14] Affiliation with
the AFL would undermine complaints that the Tri-State
Union was a company union, thereby reducing the role of
the Labor Relations Board in Tri-State labor relations.

While investigating the violence in Galena, J. S. Parker,
assistant attorney general of Kansas, talked with Evans and
Hickman who confidentially informed him that "there was
a movement on foot to affiliate the Tri-State organization
with the American Federation of Labor. In fact, that is the
intention of the Tri-State Union at present. This affiliation
may come now or it may come within a few days." In
Parker's opinion, if affiliation occurred, it would eliminate
further violence in the district because the CIO would not
"feel strong enough to attempt to continue organization[al]
efforts in the vicinity of Pitcher [sic]."[15] As Parker had
correctly surmised, Evans and the executive committee
moved quickly.

Hoping to exploit the jurisdictional struggle between
the AFL and the CIO, Evans and Norman conferred in
Tulsa on April 14 with G. Ed Warren, president of the
Oklahoma State Federation of Labor and also a representative of the AFL. Warren, whose organization had been
frequently and maliciously attacked in the *Blue Card*

Record, was nevertheless receptive to affiliation. Aware of the Tri-State Union's reputation as a company union, he consulted Green by telephone before negotiating with Evans and Norman a preliminary agreement that placed thousands of Tri-State workers under the jurisdiction of the AFL,[16] workers whom Robinson had hoped to enlist in the CIO. According to Warren, the accord produced the "biggest single affiliation that ever [had] come to the state federation of labor" because the federal charters to be issued made state membership compulsory. He estimated the paid membership of the Tri-State Union, which included many with no connections with the mines and mills, such as merchants, at more than eight thousand.[17]

If Warren, who was certainly familiar with the character and antiunion work of the Tri-State Union,[18] had any reservation about the affiliation, his public statements did not reveal it. In his column in the *Oklahoma Federationist,* he wrote that the CIO "would have done the same thing if given the opportunity," that it "would not [have] refuse[d] to take men simply because they had been members of . . . company unions." Further justifying his action, he declared that:

> I pursued the usual course in such matters [affiliations] and have no apologies to make. Whether or not the "blue card" union was a company union is a matter of opinion. They dealt with 90 percent of the operators in the Tri-State district and had a membership of over 8000. When they came into the A.F. of L. they severed all connection with the company union idea and will as long as they remain in the A.F. of L. obey the laws and the rules of the American Federation of Labor.[19]

In short, the Tri-State Union with its large membership was a plum that Green and the AFL could not reject in the struggle with the CIO. Even the *Blue Card Record* admitted editorially that had not Green been "broadminded and tolerant he would not have accepted us in the Federation."[20]

The Tulsa accord of April 14, although a preliminary arrangement that only the executive council and the annual convention of the AFL could validate, occurred be-

cause it served the interests of the AFL and the Tri-State
Union. It provided that affiliation would be by federal
charter, that "all working contracts . . . would remain in
force," and that no strikes would be called because of alleged violations of contract without prior approval of the
AFL. The AFL assumed jurisdiction over the Tri-State
Union members, while the expenses of affiliation were assumed by the union. With the agreement a tentative linkage was established.[21]

Having scathingly criticized Green and the AFL in their
newspaper over the past two years as the personification of
evil, Tri-State Union leaders realized that their followers
might now find the affiliation with the old enemy in-
comprehensible or at least confusing. It was therefore important to get as large a public endorsement of the affiliation from the membership as possible. Consequently, on
April 16 the *Blue Card Record* announced a meeting to explain and to ratify the agreement. It predicted that the
event would be "the greatest protest demonstration against
the C.I.O." ever held. Two days later, with the mines closed,
six thousand persons jammed into the fairgrounds audi-
torium at Miami to hear Evans, Nolan, and Norman explain
the necessity of joining the AFL.

The responsibility for explaining the apparent about-face
of the Tri-State Union fell primarily upon Norman, whose
remarks were later the source of controversy. According to
Charlie E. King:

> Norman said the Wagner Bill [National Labor Relations
> Act] wasn't constitutional and "we didn't expect that it would
> be passed but as they did pass it we had to do something" and
> that, "As the Wagner Bill was upheld we have to do something,
> but we will yet be Blue Carders. We will print a sign A.F. of L.
> and Blue Carders across that sign and hang it in front of our
> hall so that people will know that we are yet Blue Carders and
> these other men had just as well leave town."[22]

King's recollections were substantiated by John McAlister
who reported that Norman declared that "the blue card
union can't stand the Wagner Act and it had to be changed

and affiliated with someone else." Nevertheless, affiliation "wouldn't change the rulings nor the officers nor nothing of the company, that they would go on just the same as it had."[23]

Concern over the legality of the Tri-State Union under the federal Labor Relations Act and fear of the CIO were the principal reasons given to the crowd. It was expected that affiliation would legitimize the Tri-State Union while producing no substantive changes. The contracts with the companies would remain the same, the headquarters of the union would stay in Picher, and the policies of the past would remain unaltered. Even though a carefully worded resolution prepared by Hickman was adopted that suggested that a complete dissolution of the Tri-State Union was occurring, Norman's remarks emphasized continuity and control by the present leadership.[24] With a strong encouragement from Nolan, who reportedly said "Anybody that is contrary to this agreement stand up and get knocked down, please,"[25] the crowd voted unanimously in favor of the Tulsa agreement. For the first time in more than a half century, a national union had won a form of recognition from the majority of Tri-State miners and millmen.

Nonetheless, the affiliation remained tentative until formally approved by the executive council and the annual convention of the AFL. Hoping to thwart that approval, Reid Robinson urged Green in a telegram to reject the affiliation, pointing out that the Tri-State Union was a company union in violation of the law. He advised the AFL president that an International Union complaint charging that the Tri-State Union was an "employer-dominated" union was then pending with the National Labor Relations Board, and he threatened to amend that complaint to include the AFL as an "employer-controlled and dominated organization" if the affiliation was formalized.[26] On April 23, Robinson and Tony McTeer also conferred with Warren in Tulsa and demanded that he advise Green to reject the affiliation because the Tri-State Union was a company union in violation of federal law. Warren refused. Claiming that the International Union had "tried to en-

F. W. ("Mike") Evans, president of the
Blue Card Union. Courtesy of *Blue
Card Record.*

Joe Nolan, the "Pick-handle King."
Courtesy of *Blue Card Record.*

roll them [Tri-State workers] for two years and couldn't,"
Warren asserted that Robinson's demand was motivated by
a "case of sour grapes."[27]

Eager to enroll thousands of dues-paying workers into
the AFL, Green forged ahead, apparently unconcerned
that for months the AFL had given moral support to the
striking International Union and that he and the AFL had
been attacked and ridiculed by the men he now embraced.
On April 23, he conferred with Evans and Norman in
Washington concerning the future status of the Tri-State
Union and the scope of its jurisdiction in mining and milling. Incredibly, Evans ambitiously hoped to replace the International Union of Mine, Mill, and Smelter Workers and

assume *nationwide* jurisdiction over all mine and millmen! Although no conclusions were reached at this meeting on these points, Evans left with the impression that what he wanted had not been rejected. Furthermore, according to Evans, Green discussed Robinson's telegram and "just laughed" about his charge that the Tri-State Union was an "employer-dominated" union. The meeting was thus very cordial. Norman reported, "Our meeting was an entire and complete success. Mr. Green was tickled to death for us to come into the A.F.L. and we were tickled to death to come in."[28] Next day the AFL granted federal charters to three Tri-State Union locals at Picher, Joplin, and Galena.

On May 16 in Kansas City, Missouri, Evans and Hickman met F. A. Canfield and G. Ed Warren, representatives of the AFL, to work out the arrangement for obtaining an international charter for the parent Tri-State Union. The resulting plan called for a convention of delegates from the newly established federal unions to meet in Picher and elect officers and a new executive committee. They were to modify the union's constitution and bylaws to conform with those of the AFL. Afterwards, a temporary certificate of affiliation was to be issued empowering the Tri-State Union to organize new federal labor unions among lead and zinc miners and millmen in Oklahoma, Kansas, Missouri, and Arkansas, which were to be governed like the other district locals. The new officers and executive committee were to assume trusteeship over Tri-State Union property, continue to pay bills, collect dues, and remit the AFL per capita tax. Because of reports that a "great wave of workers [were] coming from several states . . . which threatened to overrun the district and glut the labor market," on April 21 the dues were increased from one dollar to twenty-five dollars to keep them out.[29] Although Evans and Hickman were "unalterably opposed to ever becoming members" of the International Union, they nevertheless agreed for their organization that in the event of an AFL-CIO reconciliation, it would "not oppose in any manner such a reconciliation, and will, if requested by the [AFL], do everything it can to bring about a settlement of any differences between said lead and zinc mine, mill and smelter workers and the . . . International Union."[30] In any case, jurisdiction over Tri-State workers remained in the Tri-State Union, raising the possibility of future difficulties should reconciliation be accomplished. With this "Memorandum of Understanding," the Kansas City meeting adjourned.

Four days later Evans and Hickman met in Picher with the delegates chosen from the newly chartered federal labor unions to elect officers and an executive committee and to frame a constitution and bylaws. Although no members of the "old" executive committee were elected as delegates, some of them "unofficially" attended the convention. When the twelve members of the old committee were nominated and elected as a slate to the new committee with designated terms, and when they reelected Evans as president, Ray Morris as vice-president, and Hickman as secretary-treasurer, it was clear that the convention was being manipulated to maintain the status quo. (Morris resigned shortly thereafter and was replaced by Joe Nolan, the "pick-handle king.") The convention then transferred all assets of the Tri-State Union to the new executive committee.[31] It also made changes in the constitution and bylaws, but other than making it possible for common labor to sit on the executive committee, no substantive changes were made.[32] Finally, the convention renamed the Tri-State Metal, Mine and Smelter Workers Union the Blue Card Union of Zinc and Lead, Mine, Mill and Smelter Workers, a name change that was long overdue.

Following a conference with Evans in May, the executive council of the AFL issued a temporary charter to the Blue Card Union, effective on June 16, which conferred the right to organize lead and zinc miners in the four states named above and to govern them as though the Blue Card Union was a "National or an International Union." Nevertheless, in reporting to the executive committee on June 15 following receipt of the charter, Hickman expressed disappointment that it did not expressly delegate greater authority over newly organized locals to the Blue Card

Union's leadership. He indicated that the charter provided only that the new union "organize federal labor unions with autonomy except for the loose control exercised by the American Federation of Labor," an arrangement which Hickman thought was contrary to the agreement reached at Kansas City.[33]

When the AFL convened in Denver during early October 1937 for its fifty-seventh annual convention, among its new federal labor unions were No. 20576 (Picher), No. 20577 (Joplin), and No. 20578 (Galena). Serving as delegates from the locals were Evans, a mine operator and businessman; Norman, an attorney for the Blue Card Union; and Nolan, a mine foreman—three tough men who had led the back-to-work movement that had destroyed the strike of the AFL's former union in the Tri-State.[34] Despite their highly publicized strike-breaking role and the fact that none of them were "bona fide wage workers," as required by the AFL constitution, the credentials committee recommended that they be seated. Surprisingly, there was no challenge from the floor. Consequently, three highly visible enemies of the AFL and organized labor sat in the convention, fully empowered to speak and vote on the issues confronting the organization. The *Proceedings*, however, indicate that neither Evans, Norman, or Nolan exploited the opportunity to voice his true opinion about working-class organizations, especially about the AFL.[35]

As extraordinary as the conversion of the Blue Card Union locals to federal labor unions of the AFL and the seating of Evans, Norman, and Nolan as delegates was the convention's confirmation of the charter to the union, which the executive council had granted in response to a petition from the Picher local. The charter gave the Blue Card Union jurisdiction over all mine, mill, and smelter workers in the district, with no indication that its jurisdiction extended elsewhere.[36] Thereafter, new locals would be compelled to affiliate with the Blue Card Union. In effect, this charter transformed the violently antilabor union, the company union of the mining and milling companies, into a respectable affiliate of the AFL. District leaders now believed that the Blue Card Union was acceptable to the National Labor Relations Board as a bona fide workers' union, although affiliation had produced no substantive changes.[37]

The Blue Card Union's affiliation with the AFL revealed the intensity of its struggle with Lewis and the CIO. Green and his associates were fully aware of the happenings in the Tri-State because, although the matter was not discussed extensively in the convention of 1936, Reid Robinson had described the struggle of International Union workers from the floor. Furthermore, Warren, the AFL representative who had met with Evans and Norman to work out the preliminary details of affiliation, knew the history and the character of the Blue Card Union.[38] Consequently, granting the charter was an expedient move, a tactical maneuver designed to counter the International Union and the CIO. In explaining its action, the executive council reported that "inasmuch as the Mine, Mill and Smelter Workers International Union had severed its relationship with the American Federation of Labor, the Council could with perfect propriety respond favorably to the application with the American Federation of Labor."[39] The executive committee expected that somehow the AFL would benefit from affiliating this company union led by proficient and able union-busters. Following the recommendation of the resolution committee, the convention unanimously endorsed the council's action.[40] The AFL was now back in the Tri-State, locked in combat not with the mining and milling companies but with the CIO. Mutual fear and hatred of its rival had produced a marriage of convenience between two heretofore deadly enemies, the AFL and the Blue Card Union, creating some confusion among the latter's rank and file. Reflecting on the alliance, Hickman wrote in 1982: "I felt at the time and still feel that the A F of L had no interest in the BCU except to extend their statistical membership and we had no interest in them except to gain respectability and secure protection from prosecution under the Wagner Act."[41]

Evans and Norman fully expected the affiliation of the Blue Card Union with the AFL to forestall any National Labor Relations Board action against the union based on the charge that it was a company union in violation of federal law. They were to be disappointed. As noted, the Supreme Court's decision in the Jones and Laughlin case had resuscitated the Board, allowing for the overturning of Judge Kennamer's injunction prohibiting a Board hearing on International Union complaints against the Eagle Picher companies. In July the Tenth Circuit Court of Appeals lifted the injunction, which five months later launched the hearings on the International Union's complaints. These now included charges of interference, restraint, and coercion by the Blue Card Union, of an active role by company supervisors in the Blue Card Union, of intimidating and violent acts by the union against International Union members, of refusal by the Eagle Picher companies to hire International Union members, of company support of the *Blue Card Record*, and, after November 9 when the charges were amended, of company domination and control of the Blue Card Union.[42]

With the injunction set aside, the National Labor Relations Board renewed its preparation for a hearing on the complaints of the International Union against the Eagle Picher companies. William J. Avrutis, one of two Board attorneys assigned to the case, wanted the hearings to begin quickly. Conditions in the district were such that the pool of witnesses to support the complaints diminished daily. To Robert B. Watts he wrote:

> Our witnesses have been without regular source of income ever since the strike and poverty has driven many of them out of the district. There is, or shortly will be, a further shutdown of local operations and we may reasonably expect more witnesses to leave. Many have expressed their intention of going away.
>
> Another circumstance not to be overlooked is the prevalence of miner's tuberculosis in conjunction with silicosis, which is methodically cleaning out young and strong members of the mining population in large numbers. I speak from

personal observation. It would be a great error to imagine that this type of illness is long-drawn out and chronic. The passage of days may conceivably deprive us of key witnesses and break down a case having many ramifications, thereby dissipating a substantial portion of the moral effect which properly should follow a successful outcome in this particular case.[43]

Avrutis also was worried that the renewal of the Eagle Picher case would lead to harassment and intimidation of miners and millmen who were willing to testify in support of the complaints.[44] He was determined to build a solid case expeditiously.

The news of the rescheduled hearings against the Eagle Picher companies provoked an outcry from Blue Card Union supporters. Three days before the hearings were to begin in Joplin, Missouri, the *Blue Card Record* declared that "prejudice will run rampant at the trial, yet the board supported by the reddest racketeers in America intends to carry on. American institutions are at stake but there is always a turning of the tables even if it has to be done at the bayonet point by uniformed soldiers who may be our next harbingers of peace if these rackets run on."[45] The Board clearly was not held in high esteem.

In a news story one week later, Hickman claimed that in April when Evans and Norman visited Green in Washington, representatives of the Blue Card Union, the AFL, and the National Labor Relations Board conferred about the role of the union in the Tri-State strike. He asserted that the AFL and the Blue Card Union spokesmen presented proof that the union was "virgin pure insofar as company unionism was concerned," proof that was accepted by the Board, which then exempted the Blue Card Union from the complaints filed by the International Union. Not until later did the Board inform Blue Card Union leaders that their organization was involved in the hearings. According to Hickman, when Green learned that the AFL might also become involved, he "got so mad he could have clipped twenty-penny spikes with his teeth without cracking the enamel, and on the same day issued an official condemnatory order against the personnel of the labor board and raised so much hell with the fair labor standard (wage-hour) law that it has been collecting dust in a labor committee pigeon-hole ever since."[46]

Hickman, reflecting the views of his colleagues, was convinced that "Avrutis (nice sweet bolshevick name)" was conducting a "one-sided investigation with the view of putting the heat on the Blue Card Union." He wrote that "to say that there was even a slight chance for the board to find anything against the C.I.O. would be the same as saying the devil would find something against Al Capone."[47] In a companion piece, the *Blue Card Record* charged that the Board and the CIO had contrived the Eagle Picher case, which rested on the assumption that "local economic royalists [were] working in cahoots with the Blue Card Union to oppose and starve the population." The case, it asserted, was unfair and prejudiced against the companies and the Blue Card Union.[48] Nevertheless, to undercut the charge of company unionism, Evans resigned the union presidency, only to be replaced by Joe Nolan.

The hearings, which began on November 29, 1937, and ended on April 29, 1938, generated more than fourteen thousand pages of testimony, transcripts, and exhibits. Scores of witnesses testified both in support and in opposition to the complaints. To represent their interests, the Eagle Picher companies retained John G. Madden of Kansas City, who pitted his enormous legal skill and verve against Avrutis, trying to persuade the trial examiner of the falsity of the union's complaints against his clients. Writing to "Friend Effie" following the hearings, Avrutis described the closing arguments:

> It [the case] all ended in a blaze of glory, with all the villagers crowding the court to hear their champions espouse their sides. Oratory without end. 'Twas grand and everybody was real serious about it, just as tho we weren't play acting. You should hear John Madden when he pulls out all his tremolo, stops and shivers and vibrates as he pleads his mournful cause! It was all I could do to prevent folks from remembering that there was such a thing as the U.S. Government.[49]

With much gusto, therefore, the hearings closed. When the trial examiner submitted his intermediate report, he confirmed most of the complaints of discrimination and the denial of rights protected by the federal law, and he ordered back pay for more than two hundred claimants and reinstatement for nearly the same number. After a review of the report, the National Labor Relations Board sustained its findings and conclusions, with minor exceptions, in a decision and order rendered on October 27, 1939.[50]

The Board found that the predecessor of the Blue Card Union, the Tri-State Union, was the creature and tool of the Eagle Picher companies and the district operators. It also found that members of the Tri-State Union had not participated in its affiliation with the AFL until after the connection had been made. Acting in behalf of the Eagle Picher companies and other operators, Evans, Norman, Hickman, and the executive committee had "engineered" the affiliation in a "desperate effort to preserve" the Tri-State Union. In effect, they had "transferred bodily" all the policies, members, and assets into the Blue Card Union, a ploy that produced only a name change, that perpetuated the original organization, and that continued the effects of the companies' "illegal campaign." The National Labor Relations Board found that the Eagle Picher companies had "managed and controlled the 'transformation'" of the Tri-State Union into the Blue Card Union, that through Evans and his associates these companies continued to dominate this union, and that the union "represented" the companies, not its Tri-State membership.[51] It therefore ruled that because of the companies' involvement in the origin, administration, and financial support of the two unions, they were guilty of having "interfered with, restrained, and coerced their employees in their exercise of rights guaranteed in Section 7 of the [National Labor Relations Act]."[52] Because similar charges had been filed against dozens of other companies in the district, it was clear that unless overturned on appeal, the decision was a death blow to the Blue Card Union.

Predictably, the Eagle Picher companies appealed the

Board's ruling to the Eighth Circuit Court of Appeals on November 9. In response, the Board filed a petition for enforcement of its order and, with the permission of the court, the International Union also intervened with briefs and oral arguments. On May 21, 1941, the court affirmed the Board's order and issued an enforcement decree.[53]

Included in the order was a special remedy formula that provided that each claimant receive only a part of the back pay that he would have earned had he remained employed. After the Eagle Picher companies offered reinstatement and an amount for back pay to the claimants based on formula calculations submitted to the Board, agents re-examined payroll records and the calculations of the companies and concluded that a different formula should have been used in determining the back-pay compensation of the claimants, one that would enlarge the amount received by each. Consequently, on February 4, 1943, the Board petitioned the Eighth Circuit Court of Appeals to vacate that part of its enforcement decree that concerned back pay and to remand the matter back to it for reevaluation. After hearing arguments, on April 19, 1944, the court dismissed the Board's petition.[54]

Because the National Labor Relations Board did not apply to the Supreme Court for a writ of certiorari, the International Union did so. Although the Board was a respondent, it nevertheless supported the petition of the International Union with briefs and oral arguments. The effort to have the Board reassume jurisdiction for the purpose of enlarging the back-pay compensation of the International Union members failed, for on May 28, 1945, the Supreme Court affirmed the action of the Eighth Circuit Court.[55] The litigation against the Eagle Picher companies thus ended in the highest court of the land.

The case, initiated during the formative years of the National Labor Relations Board, was an important test of the government's powers to intervene in industrial disputes on behalf of labor under the National Labor Relations Act. From the filing of the initial complaints in 1936 until the official closing of the case in 1946 with the last payments to claimants, the labor board warded off every challenge and maneuver to reduce the awards to the strikers whose rights had been violated. After Eagle Picher Lead Company's acquisition in the late 1930s of more than a half dozen former competitors against which charges had also been filed (for example, the Commerce Mining and Royalty Company), the case became further complicated. The National Labor Relations Board nevertheless successfully incorporated these "successor cases" into the original.[56] Before the Eagle Picher case was settled, the International Union filed complaints of unfair labor practices against "some 51 companies in the same area,"[57] most of which complied with the Board's order after the Eagle Picher settlement.

The ploy of affiliation with the AFL thus ultimately failed. Perhaps anticipating the Board's ruling, Green and his associates had second thoughts about their chartering of the Blue Card Union. After 1937, references to the union's locals disappeared from the *Proceedings* of the AFL's annual convention. Exposed by the Board as a company union, the union lost the support of Tri-State operators. For all practical purposes, it ceased to exist as a force in labor-management relations after 1939. Created, managed, and sustained by the companies, the Blue Card Union could not exist independently of them. Each attempt to revive it was met with new International Union complaints to the National Labor Relations Board. The threat of penalties, such as back pay and reinstatement, caused the companies to avoid any overt involvement in union matters. Federal intervention in the district allowed the workers to organize without facing anew the terrorism of the two years between 1935 and 1937.

9

"A Most Tragic Price"

THE decisions of the National Labor Relations Board and the federal courts in the Eagle Picher and other cases assured the demise of the Blue Card Union and suggested that a new day had dawned for the International Union of Mine, Mill, and Smelter Workers in the Tri-State.[1] Although federal power had swept away all legal obstacles there to the exercise of workers' rights contained in the National Labor Relations Act of 1935, a golden era for the International Union did not come about. Its status remained substantially minor despite federal intervention. Out of the conflict to establish federally guaranteed rights had come dissension and division that hung like a pall over the district. Even though they still worked under appalling conditions,[2] most Tri-State workers did not flock into the union; they did not accept it as their spokesman and did not attempt to use it to improve their social and industrial environment. The fight of the die-hard International Union members to establish and practice their legal rights without fear of discrimination, a freedom which through their efforts embraced all Tri-State workers, went largely unappreciated by the thousands who had linked their destinies to the Blue Card Union. They shunned voluntary membership in locals they themselves controlled and which served their exclusive interests. Several reasons explain this apparent paradox.

The collapse of the Blue Card Union following the adverse Labor Relations Board and federal court decisions did not alter the antiunion stance of the major operators nor the organizations, such as the Tri-State Zinc and Lead

Ore Producers' Association, that spoke for them. Federal power had eliminated all legal restraints to the right of workers to organize and bargain collectively through their own organizations, but it had not erased the workers' awareness of the operators' opposition to unionism and their refusal to surrender a paternalistic watchfulness over their employees. Ironically, because hundreds of workers assumed that many operators, especially the smaller ones, were separated from the laboring ranks only by a lucky break and were therefore sensitive to their needs and aspirations, they accepted this paternalism as natural and rarely contested it. The editor of the *Blue Card Record* expressed their acceptance when he wrote: "The producers [operators] are Americans. The most of them were workers once. They understand us and are proud to be served by the best type workers in the world."[3] Sensing the willingness of most workers to defer to their control of district affairs, company officials refused to concede that anyone other than themselves or their representatives legitimately spoke for the majority of Tri-State workers. An example of this assertion of overlordship occurred in April 1940.

Appearing before Secretary of Labor Frances Perkins, who was investigating the deplorable conditions in the Tri-State, James Reed, a delegate of the International Union-CIO who claimed to speak for the workers, stated that as their "representative" he was prepared to cooperate with the operators and officials of Oklahoma, Kansas, and Missouri in a three-point program to improve housing, to build hospitals, and to control the dust in the mines.[4] But in an immediate rebuttal, Evan Just, secretary of the Zinc and Lead Ore Producers' Association who later became the editor of the *Engineering and Mining Journal*, rejected Reed's contention that he spoke for the workers. Just said that: "I want it to go into this record that I am speaking for the operators of this district, and I don't propose to enter in behalf of these operators into some broad compact with this union that only represents an extremely small minority of people in this district's workers [*sic*]."[5] Stating that although he did not wish to stir up controversy, Just added that he wanted it known that "the real workmen in this district are not represented here today, to speak of, and I think that should go into the record."[6] The operators refused to acknowledge that the International Union had any legitimate role to play in the affairs of the district, and they rejected cooperating with it to implement Reed's suggested three-point program for eradicating housing and health problems in the Tri-State.

With such statements from the recognized spokesman for the companies coming less than six months after the decision against Eagle Picher declaring the Blue Card Union an illegal company union, it is little wonder that the workers, fearful of their jobs, failed to rush into locals of the International Union. Such statements served to inhibit or constrain them from exercising their legal rights. Despite the National Labor Relations Board decision of 1939, which Eagle Picher officials quickly challenged in the courts, workers were reluctant to offend the operators whose leadership and values they tended to accept and whose control of jobs left the reins of power securely in their hands.

The opportunity to work had been the most important consideration in drawing the miners and millmen into the back-to-work movement and the operator-dominated Blue Card Union. Its founders clearly understood that in the depression-wracked era of the thirties workers had a compelling need for jobs with reasonably steady incomes and that their need made all other issues—even vital health issues—strictly secondary to them. If joining the Blue Card Union enhanced the opportunity for employment, the majority of workers were more than willing to enroll, gladly surrendering their legal right to worker-controlled organizations in order to put bread on the table and pay the bills. The operators' accurate analysis of the workers' priorities was succinctly revealed in the closing arguments of John Madden, an attorney for Eagle Picher, in the hearings on charges of unfair labor practices against the Eagle

Picher companies. In explaining to the trial examiner why workers had flocked into the Blue Card Union, Madden asked:

> Is that such a mystery . . . ? Is it conceivable that when there are two competitive unions in a single district, and when one union refuses to work and the other union wants to work, that the men who want to work will join the union identified with that program?
>
> Would any working man who wanted to toil join the [International Union] at the present time on this continuing strike? Why certainly, it is too natural, it is the inevitable thing for a man who wanted to work in the back to work movement to join the union in which that movement culminated.[7]

The well-known ties of the operators with the Blue Card Union, which had functioned as a hiring hall for its members, had left the miners and the millmen little choice but to join. With nothing to offer in the short run but increased deprivation and hardship, the International Union was not an attractive option for thousands of workers who rejected the promise of a brighter tomorrow for jobs and survival today. After the strike, the need for jobs remained a restraint on unionization.

Another damaging blow against the International Union after the Board order was the enduring perception among Tri-Staters that it was infiltrated and led by "reds" or Communists. This view had been carefully cultivated and exploited by leaders of the Blue Card Union and the editors of the *Blue Card Record*, who played upon the nativism of Tri-Staters and their sense of pride in being wholly "American." That the leaders of the International Union should be portrayed as radical "outsiders" by Evans, Norman, Hickman, and others made excellent tactical sense. As noted earlier, there was already a strong aversion to "foreigners" and "outsiders," but if the leaders of the International could be successfully smeared as "reds," "radicals" or "Communists," even greater revulsion toward them would be generated among the rank-and-file workers. The leftist leanings of the International under Reid Robinson and other national leaders played into their hands. Consequently, the red-baiting attacks increased following the union's affiliation with the CIO, the Blue Card Union's affiliation with the AFL following the riots of April 1937, and the Supreme Court's decision upholding the National Labor Relations Act.

In an editorial of May 7, 1937, the *Blue Card Record* condemned the sit-down strikes of the emerging industrial unions as un-American, a tactic that Tri-Staters would never engage in because they were "Americans and Americans don't do business that way. We are working for Americans and we think like they do that men should have a fair wage for their service and the producer should have a fair profit for his investment." The message was clear. The leadership of the Blue Card Union was local and thus pure American, whereas the Thomas Browns and the Reid Robinsons of the International Union were nothing more than rabble-rousing "outsiders" who did not understand the Tri-State and its people. They should be rejected. Workers had long been conditioned to accept this conclusion, a fact that also made it easier for them to accept the *Record*'s charge that the International Union was Communist led.

When Chief of Police Joe Pratt of Joplin denied Robinson permission to hold an International-CIO parade, the *Record* supported the decision because allegedly the Communist party had recognized the CIO, which was using Communist tactics, as part of the "movement."[8] And when Robinson failed to rally a large crowd in Picher on May 30, 1937, the *Record* again chortled: "Reid announces he is here to stay, though, and we guess he can, but he must be getting pretty rotten when he couldn't even get the communists from Kansas City to act as a come-on for his crowd, so go ahead you Buzzard, stick around in the district until you stink yourself to death."[9] John L. Lewis, who headed the CIO, was called a "communist at heart."[10] And because of the federal labor board's audacity in holding hearings on the International's charges of unfair labor practices against the Eagle Picher companies, the *Record*

asserted that the members of the Board had "become
C.I.O. brothers in the Bolshevick lodge, in which the Board
allegedly has a lifetime membership."[11]

Thousands of men who had joined the Blue Card Union
in droves to retain or acquire jobs accepted such expres-
sions because they were published in "their" *Blue Card
Record* and were compatible with the district's traditional
xenophobic beliefs. For a Tri-State worker to publicly identify with an allegedly Communist-dominated union led by
"outsiders" and "reds" required great courage. Even if
membership in the union had been a gateway to jobs, after
the Board decision in 1939 few Tri-Staters would have
risked ostracism by their fellow workers to enroll in it because of the radical way the union had been portrayed by
the *Record* during the Blue Card Union's heyday. In the
contest between the unions to control the workers, the
Blue Card Union had won, partly because its local leaders
understood and exploited the psyche of the district. The
operators' pronounced hostility to the International, their
control of the local job market in mining and milling, and
their use and reinforcement of xenophobic attitudes toward outsiders served as powerful inhibitors to unionism
until World War II created a generalized demand for labor and provided external experiences that diluted the
strength of the Tri-State's nativist American sentiment.

In a recent reexamination of the company union movement from 1900 to 1937, Daniel Nelson indicated that a generation of liberal intellectuals and scholars who matured
during the Great Depression had created a commonly accepted negative stereotype of the company union as

> a pale replica of the conventional trade union, created to ex-
> orcise the spector of shared power and higher labor costs . . .
> [and] as a convenient symbol of the cynicism of employers and
> the naivete of workers in the 1920s and early 1930s. . . . Only
> in the late 1930s and 1940s when government and a reinvigo-
> rated labor movement joind hands, did the modern era of in-
> dustrial relations begin.[12]

From his research, Nelson concluded that although company unions did exist that matched the stereotype ("classic

company unions, the bogeyman of the traditional accounts"), there were others "notable for the extent and
character of managerial direction" that "became the back-
bone of the [company union] movement in the 1920s, provided vital services during the Depression, and withstood
the turmoil of 1933–1937."[13] Although the Blue Card
Union provided sporadic assistance to its members and
their families during the depression, unfortunately it substantially conformed to the stereotype that Nelson concluded ought to be modified because he believed it generally distorted the true character of the company union
movement. It was, however, precisely the work of such
unions as the Blue Card Union that created the stereotype.

An earlier analysis explained why Labor Relations Act
workers failed to rush into the International Union after
the labor board and the federal courts had ruled in the
Eagle Picher cases. The analysis also raises a new question
of why the leaders of the Blue Card Union used such extraordinary methods to coerce miners and millmen into
joining their organization which, under the circumstances,
they probably would have joined anyway. The Blue Card
Union was a company union whose leaders, as it has been
shown, resorted to every means to force district workers
into the back-to-work movement and the organization it
spawned. The use of violence, fear, and intimidation, the
corruption of local law enforcement agencies, calling upon
the National Guards of two states to break the strike, with-
holding jobs from workers with needy families, harassing
men from the district, ostracizing and ridiculing opponents by inflammatory rhetoric—all were means employed
to muster the Tri-State labor force into the Blue Card
Union. But were such destructive tactics and measures
really necessary?

Several reasons explain the extreme methods employed
by the Blue Card Union in counteracting the International
Union after the strike began in May 1935. As long as the
union refrained from hampering production in the district,
for reasons already noted, the mine and mill operators were
little concerned about its presence. But when it audaciously
demonstrated its power to shut down operations—even at

a time propitious to the larger companies—they apparently concluded that enough was enough, that their interests were incompatible with those of a union whose leaders boldly claimed to speak for all the Tri-State workers. The roving bands of strikers, some of whom were reported to be armed, that swept over the district shutting down the mines and mills understandably distorted the operators' initial assessment of the actual strength and character of the union, especially its ability to influence the workers. This early misperception of union power ran counter to their later persistent claims that the union represented at best only a minority of the workers. It led inexorably to their backing of the back-to-work movement and the founding of the Blue Card Union to counter an upstart union that threatened traditional patterns of industrial relations and authority in the Tri-State. Shocked by the strike, which occurred in a national context of rapidly changing labor-management relations often marked by violence, Tri-State operators underwrote the Blue Card Union's ready resort to methods successfully used by employers elsewhere to meet labor's challenge to their total authority. Unfortunately, the use of such means in the Tri-State to decimate the International Union locals and to ruin anyone who dared to support them was an extreme case of unnecessary overkill. It only provoked federal intervention on behalf of the striking workers and partially salvaged the dying ember of unionism.

Although the involvement of the National Labor Relations Board in the lead and zinc workers' strike eventually caused the downfall of the Blue Card Union, the immediate effect of federal intervention was negligible. Like employers throughout the nation, the major operators in the Tri-State questioned the constitutionality of the National Labor Relations Act. They resorted to the federal courts to block the proceedings initiated by the National Labor Relations Board's regional office concerning the complaints of unfair labor practices until the issue of constitutionality could be resolved. More than six months elapsed after the Supreme Court's decision in the Jones and Laughlin case before hearings began in October 1937 on the International Union's complaints. These had been filed for more than a year and held in abeyance by court injunctions. Two years elapsed before the Board issued its decision and order validating the complaints and providing relief. By then, although the strike officially continued, it had long been lost.

Nevertheless, the Board's intervention was vitally important. Although a decade passed before all the complainants had received compensatory awards based on unfair labor practices that occurred after the effective date of the federal law, the Board had nonetheless established a permanent federal presence in the district and industrial relations there were never again the same. Furthermore, Tri-State workers who opted for unionization discovered that the Board definitely supported their efforts to create worker-controlled locals to represent their interests. Following the filing of their complaints against the mining companies, particularly Eagle Picher, the resources of the Board's Region 17 office had been vigorously thrown into investigating the charges, causing the opponents of the union to allege that it and the Board were conspiring to misuse federal power in the proceedings. These allegations of connivance found expression in hostile editorials in the *Blue Card Record*.

Internal memoranda between Washington and the Kansas City office and exchanges between George O. Pratt, director of Region 17, and his field investigators confirmed that Board officials considered the complaints of the International Union's members to be extremely important. Their sympathies, as expected under the law, lay with the complainants.[14] Success in the Eagle Picher case was unusually desirable to the Board because of the positive impact it was expected to have upon similar cases in the district, and because the Board was in its formative phase and success was considered essential. Thus there developed a close rapport between local union leaders (for example, Tony McTeer, who pressed for quick action) and Board officials (George Pratt) based upon a mutual desire to uphold the rights of workers embodied in the law. They were eventually successful. Of course, whether workers overcame the informal restraints noted above and exercised those rights was another matter.

The intervention of the National Labor Relations Board was clearly in behalf of the strikers and their desire for recognition and collective bargaining. The military intervention into Oklahoma and Kansas, however, clearly favored the opponents of the union. As was so often the case before the federal government institutionalized labor-management relations in the thirties, the common response of the states to violent labor unrest was to order out the National Guard for selective use against strikers under the rubric of law and order.[15] This pattern unfortunately repeated itself in the Tri-State strike. Following the regrettable beating of Sheriff Eli Dry and his deputies in May 1935, upon the request of local authorities Governor Marland of Oklahoma readily ordered units of the National Guard into the Oklahoma portion of the district where their presence definitely worked against a successful strike. But, when in April 1937, Blue Card Union mobs rampaged through the streets of Picher beating up International-CIO members and destroying the union hall, the governor accepted the advice of a delegation of Picher businessmen that military intervention was unnecessary because local officials, who openly favored the new union and who refused to request troops, could manage without National Guard assistance.

In Kansas, the pattern was similar. Following minor union violence around the Beck Tailing Mill, upon request of local authorities Governor Landon ordered units of the National Guard into the Kansas section of the field, a decision that fully supported the back-to-work movement because of the way the troops were used. To Landon's credit, when substantial violence erupted around Eagle Picher's Galena smelter in June after the removal of the initial contingents, he ordered military units back into the district and imposed martial law. The return of the Guard again aided back-to-workers against the union, however. Furthermore, when the terrible violence directed against union members and union property broke out in Treece and Galena in April 1937, Governor Huxman, Landon's successor, withheld troops, electing instead to rely upon local authorities to protect lives and property. Military intervention in both Oklahoma and Kansas combined with the work of the company union to break the strike by convincing desperate workers that the union cause was hopeless. Thus different forms of federal and state power were employed on opposite sides in the Tri-State strike, the former to support union members in their exercise of federally conferred rights and the latter to aid Blue Card Union supporters in their efforts to deny those rights.

Important contributing factors to the collapse of the strike were the inept leadership and inadequate resources of the union to manage and sustain a massive walkout of thousands of workers and their families already beset by hard times. In their unsuccessful drive to obtain recognition, Thomas Brown and local leaders had patiently exhausted all means. Their failure led to an agonizing dilemma—to risk the gradual disintegration of the local unions, or to risk all on a devastating strike that might bring victory or total defeat. Perhaps from frustration with the operators' intransigence, they chose to strike without properly assessing the chance of success and without considering all the contingencies that a large strike entailed.

If International Union leaders had properly evaluated the many harbingers of defeat, they undoubtedly would have delayed leading the Tri-State workers into the disastrous strike of 1935. The district was a reservoir of unemployed men anxious and willing to work. It included the discards of the Picher clinic and a healthy force of workers who were desperate for jobs. One reason for the rise in union membership between 1933 and 1935 was the inclusion of the out-of-work who expected the union to open the door to jobs. Their loyalty was contingent upon union performance in getting them back to work; their loyalty was therefore easily transferrable to the Blue Card Union when it became evident that it controlled access to jobs.

Not surprisingly, it was unnecessary for the Tri-State companies to go outside the district for strikebreakers. They simply tapped into the reservoir of the unemployed for experienced miners and millmen. With such a surplus of unemployed workers, a strike in May 1935 was extremely ill-advised.

Brown and his associates failed to appreciate how overburdened the local relief systems were when they called the strike. Overwhelmed by the demands generated by the Great Depression, local relief could not readily absorb the additional hundreds who suddenly applied for assistance. Consequently, the advice of union leaders that their striking members "go on relief" for the duration reflected an appalling ignorance of the situation in the district. Their expectation that the AFL and its affiliates would substantially support the strike was unrealistic, considering the growing disunity over industrial unionism and the demands from more highly publicized strikes occurring elsewhere. The carloads of staples, which the strikers expected, never arrived. Few unions outside the district rallied to support the men on the picket lines. The failure of union leaders to provide alternate strategies for coping with the increased deprivation and suffering produced by the strike was a major cause of its failure. It greatly undermined the credibility of union leadership and enhanced the misery out of which the back-to-work movement flourished and the Blue Card Union was born.

The timing of the strike was also an unfortunate error of judgment. Union leaders ignored the historic production cycles in the district whereby a spring shutdown usually allowed a reduction of accumulated inventories. When the strike occurred, ore bins at the larger mines and mills were reported to be full and the work stoppage was, in the short term, compatible with the economic interests of these companies. Instead of timing the strike for the greatest effect, union leaders unthinkingly timed it to produce the least impact on the larger operations. Thus the result was not a quick victory but an extended walkout that worked against success. Under the circumstances, every day off the job created insufferable conditions for more and more strikers and compelled them to desert the union cause.

After the work stoppage began, the failure of union leaders to properly assess the resourcefulness of their opponents became increasingly evident. The skill of the larger operators in maintaining the open shop before the strike failed to alert the leadership that despite federal laws favoring labor, the operators would not meekly concede to the union the equal role in industrial matters that was implicit in recognition and collective bargaining. Failing to anticipate how desperately the operators would cling to their position of dominance and how far they would go to ward off the union challenge, Brown and his associates did not develop adequate counterstrategies to the vigorous tactics of the Blue Card Union. They clearly failed to perceive the potential antiunion leadership among the small operators (for example, F. W. ("Mike") Evans) whose futures were linked to that of Eagle Picher and the larger companies. Nor did they adequately comprehend the deep-rooted antagonism of district residents to "outsiders" like Thomas Brown and Reid Robinson, who presumed too much in claiming to speak for the majority of Tri-State workers. In the absence of material resources to offset those available to the company union, superior union leadership was essential if the strike was to be won. The quality of leadership necessary to win was absent.

In its study of company unions published in 1937, the United States Department of Labor defined the term "company union" to mean "an organization confined to workers of a particular company or plant, which has as its purpose the consideration of conditions of employment."[16] It noted, however, that there were exceptions to this limited definition, that is, a company union under unusual circumstances could embrace the workers of more than one company. The Blue Card Union was such an exception because it was a district-wide organization that embraced the employees of most firms belonging to the Producers' Association. The district-wide character of the Blue Card Union was evidenced from the charges of unfair labor practices filed against more than fifty companies. These complaints, however, were held in abeyance while the National Labor Relations Board focused on the allegations directed against the Eagle Picher companies, major producers in the district that had played a crucial role in founding the Blue Card Union. If they could be forced to comply with new federal law, the other companies were expected to follow suit quickly. Nevertheless, this procedural strategy of the Board did not obscure the involvement of the many companies which, under the guidance of Eagle Picher officials, had helped to organize and sustain the Blue Card Union. It was thus a company union whose members were found in nearly all the mines and mills. The Board found it so.

During the strike of the International Association of Machinists against the Remington Rand Company in 1936, James H. Rand, Jr., devised a package of antiunion tactics that became known as the Mohawk Valley formula. Following its widespread publicity by the National Association of Manufacturers, many employers used the formula to combat militant unions. Its tactics included a back-to-work movement, the condemnation of union leaders as dangerous radicals ("reds," "outside agitators," "Communists"), the use of strikebreakers, the rallying of community support ("citizens alliances," "citizens committee"), the creation of vigilante committees to act against striking workers and to protect property, the mobilization of public opinion through antiunion propaganda in the press, the use of local or state police power against strikes, and the use of threats to move operations elsewhere.[17]

Before the machinists strike, however, most of these tactics had already been successfully employed in the Tri-State. Operating as a front for the mine and mill operators who financially supported its work, the Blue Card Union successfully labeled union leaders as radicals, launched a violent vigilante operation against the strikers condoned by local police and National Guard officers, mobilized public opinion against the International Union with its *Blue Card Record*, and generally tried to root out all vestiges of independent unionism. It was extremely successful. The union went beyond the usual purpose of a company union, i.e., "the consideration of conditions of employment," to become a tool for destroying the locals of the International. Because of the location in a geographically isolated region, the Blue Card Union's trouncing of the International Union went largely unnoticed and unpublicized in the national press. Even so, as a broadly based company union with innovative, even ingenious, leaders, who relentlessly attacked the old union on all fronts, the new union had few parallels in the thirties. It accomplished the extraordinary feat of being chartered by the AFL. For a short while, Blue Card Union leaders dreamed of replacing the International-CIO, thereby having all AFL locals of hard-rock miners and millmen throughout the nation under its jurisdiction. The dream was not realized.

One of the positive results of the strike was that it resulted in a national exposure of the terrible conditions endured by hundreds of Tri-State workers and their families. Following a visit to the district in December 1937, Gifford A. Cochran, secretary of the New York-based National Committee for Peoples' Rights, reported that the district was a "death trap" and recommended that conditions there be investigated. After reviewing the medical literature produced by the various research teams to the district, which Cochran believed substantiated his observations, and after concluding that corrective action commensurate with the extent of the problems had not been undertaken there, the Rights Committee appointed the Tri-State Survey Committee to conduct an investigation and to publicize its findings. The committee consisted of writers, churchmen, physicians, and others, including such well-known persons as Oscar Ameringer, William Allen White, and Bishop William Scarlett of Missouri.[18]

During the spring of 1939, Mildred Oliver, a "trained social investigator," and Sheldon Dick, a "photographer experienced in documentary work," collected case histories, field data, and photographs, while Dr. Anne C. Couch, a trained researcher, analyzed the earlier reports compiled on the health problems in the Tri-State.[19] The result of their efforts was *A Preliminary Report on Living, Working and Health Conditions in the Tri-State Mining Area (Missouri, Oklahoma, and Kansas)*, which the Tri-State Survey Committee issued in late 1939 and which was widely publicized. Dick also produced a documentary film entitled *Men and Dust* about the ravages of silicosis in the district that was made available for private and public viewing.[20] Much to the discomfort of mining and milling officials, the report and the film exposed the lamentable housing, health, and working conditions among hundreds of working-class families that attracted national attention. The distressing revelations also spurred Secretary of Labor Frances Perkins into sponsoring a conference on Tri-State conditions.

Held in Joplin, Missouri, on April 23, 1940, the Perkins conference attracted renowned physicians in the field of occupational health, spokesmen for the Tri-State Zinc and Lead Ore Producers' Association and organized labor, a representative of the Tri-State Survey Committee, and delegates from agencies of the federal, state, and local governments. Evan Just, secretary-treasurer of the Producers' Association, who claimed to have a "100 pecent endorsement" from district operators for his prepared statement concerning silicosis and the work of his organization to control and eradicate it, attacked the veracity of the Tri-State Survey Committee's *Preliminary Report* and Dick's film. He expressed dismay that the film, which he labeled "propaganda" and "pure poison," was being shown throughout the nation, and he charged that the widely circulated *Preliminary Report* was a "very clever and . . . a very vicious distortion of the truth."[21] In a mild defense of the committee, Bishop William Scarlett denied that it had any "axe to grind" or "any intent whatsoever to smear a community [the district]" as Just had alleged. The purpose of the *Report* was "to present conditions as its investigators saw them, conditions which . . . adversely affect[ed] the lives of hundreds of families and which . . . ought to be corrected."[22]

Despite Just's allegations concerning the *Preliminary Report* and the film, throughout the conference testimony from all quarters confirmed the basic contention of the documents that serious problems plagued the Tri-State. Secretary Perkins had also seen firsthand the deplorable conditions that hundreds of people endured when she toured the area with Just and Tony McTeer, who represented the International Union. From the tour and the testimony, Perkins concluded that there was room for improvement.[23] Furthermore, Dr. Alice Hamilton, a pioneer in occupational health who had been among the first to investigate conditions among the miners twenty-five years earlier, stated toward the end of the conference, "I am sorry to say that it [the district] seemed a very familiar landscape to me as I looked over it . . . today—the heaps of tailings (only they are bigger now), and the housing that I saw reminded me of 25 years ago." Although there were some "prosperous little villages" that she did not remember and a common tendency to remember the "worst things one sees," she nevertheless concluded that "the area [was] singularly unchanged in its outward appearance" from what she had previously observed.[24] All the participants, recognizing the existence of grave problems, recommended that Secretary Perkins appoint a small committee to further assess the situation and search for possible solutions. She agreed to do so. Unfortunately, no dramatic changes in housing and health conditions resulted from the conference.

In looking back on historical episodes like the strike of the lead and zinc workers in 1935, it is often difficult to fathom the motives guiding the principal actors. A half century later, Glenn A. Hickman was still certain that he and the other leaders had been justified in marshalling the metal workers back to work, organizing the Blue Card Union, and breaking the power of the International Union in the Tri-State. In April 1982, Hickman wrote

I know it is difficult for you [the author] to understand that I—and I suppose Mike [Evans], too—was proud of the part I played in putting the International Union out of business in the Tri-State district and putting its misguided members, including myself, back to work. You are insulated by forty-nine years of relatively peaceful and respectable labor relations and probably also enamored of the shibboleth "collective bargaining." To really relate to what you are endeavoring to write about you need to have been just emerging from a depression which forced miners to bring boiled potatoes in their lunch pails, to compete daily for a spot on the work force at those mines with rich enough ore deposits that they still could meet their payrolls without going under, then suddenly find your livelihood threatened by an unwanted, no-win strike called and enforced by a mere handful of able-bodied workers joined by a hoard of misfits, thugs and rejects supported largely by local welfare. From this perspective only you could interpret the facts you have assembled—perhaps, even share some of the prejudice which I make no effort to deny or conceal.[25]

Unrepentant and without regrets, Hickman remained convinced that what he, Evans, Norman, Nolan, and the companies did was in the best interest of the workers and the people of the district. But in breaking the strike of the International Union, they destroyed perhaps the last, best hope for large-scale unionism and its promise for improving the life of Tri-State workers.

In June 1938, Hickman surrendered his office in the Blue Card Union to become an assistant personnel manager of Eagle Picher, where he remained on the payroll for many years. He later stated, "I like to think that this came about as a result of my ability and not as a reward for some evil, sinister, and conspiratorial service already performed."[26] After the dismantling of the union, Joe Nolan later went on Eagle Picher's payroll, ending his mining career as a supervisor in a smelter in Illinois.[27] The close economic ties of F. W. ("Mike") Evans to Eagle Picher have already been sufficiently noted.[28] Kelsey Norman and Hickman remained friends after the union had disbanded. Hickman remembered with certainty that Norman "did not do any [legal] corporative or other work for [the] mining companies."[29] For whatever reasons, three of the four leaders of the union linked their economic futures to the company that had provided major support to the back-to-work organization.

Did the refusal of Tri-Staters to embrace the International Union in the thirties really matter? In 1941, Sylvan Bruner, an attorney for the striking miners, answered this question when he addressed the International's annual convention at Joplin. He said:

> I think . . . that the miners in the Tri-State District have paid a most tragic price for their lack of organization. I think I can say, without fear of contradiction, that not only have the miners paid a tragic price, but that their families have paid a tragic price through the lack of organization and through open shop conditions in what is known as the Tri-State District. . . . In other words, what I mean to say is that the hard rock miners in the Tri-State District have paid with their lives and broken bodies for 30 years because they have not realized that they should organize. Thousands of them.[30]

Although few Tri-Staters would have denied Bruner's statement concerning the staggering human costs of extracting and processing the great mineral wealth of their district, the majority would have undoubtedly denied his assertion that the "tragic price" had resulted from their failure to organize. Nevertheless, Bruner was probably right. Without a strong organization, the metal workers were powerless to control the industrial forces that shaped their destinies. For their weakness, they indeed paid "a most tragic price."

Epilogue

AFTER the National Labor Relations Board's favorable order of 1939, which the federal courts upheld, the locals of the International Union of Mine, Mill, and Smelter Workers clung precariously to life, maintaining the fiction of an ongoing strike as their members, who had been awarded back pay and reinstatement, waited patiently for company resistance to end. For reasons already noted, relatively few metal workers then found the union cause sufficiently attractive to join the struggling locals. The attitude of district operators, now reduced in numbers by Eagle Picher's acquisition of its major competitors in the late thirties, did not soften toward the union. To them it remained an outlaw union, especially so because its leftist posture under Reid Robinson, Maurice E. Travis, and others seemed to confirm their frequent charges that it was "red." Nonetheless, with the workers' right to organize and engage in collective bargaining firmly established in federal law, a few companies reluctantly negotiated contracts with some of the surviving and emerging locals. But the old dream of union officials of a district-wide contract was never realized. To help keep the International Union in check, non-union mine and mill operators grudgingly paid their workers the wage scale embodied in union contracts negotiated in the district. They also maintained an informal open-shop posture, capitalizing on the proclivity of the workers to read their desires and follow suit. Between 1939 and the United States' entrance into World War II, International Union locals barely survived, their principal influence being an upward pressure on wages.

In 1943 a report of the United States Bureau of Labor Statistics concerning wages in the nonferrous metals industry revealed the sorry state of organized labor in the Tri-State. As of August 1941, reported the Bureau, "few workers were found in unions" there. Of 3,811 metal workers, 3,533 (92.7 percent) labored in nonunion works, whereas 278 (7.3 percent) toiled in unionized workplaces. The extent of organization in the Tri-State was in sharp contrast with the nonferrous mining districts of the West, where 49.7 percent (9,739) of 19,599 workers belonged to unions, and with the nationwide industry, where 44 percent (11,528) of 26,205 were union members. The small union percentage in the Tri-State indicated that despite the federal government's support of the right to organize and bargain collectively, the majority of metal workers there had concluded that their interests were best served outside the International Union, the "principal union in the metal-mining field."[1]

Nonetheless, in a similar report issued one year later, the Bureau reported that Tri-State union membership in the summer of 1943 had climbed to 23 percent, an increase of 15.7 percentage points over 1941. These data were compiled at the height of World War II and undoubtedly reflected less employer opposition to unionism in the interest of maximizing war production. Even so, in contrast to their counterparts in the metal-mining districts of the West where 60 percent of the workers were organized (an increase of 10.3 percentage points over 1941), wartime Tri-Staters were clearly not inclined to join locals of the "principal union" in the metal-mining industry.[2] Their reluctance had profound membership implications for the union because in 1942 the Tri-State Mining District "alone accounted for over 30 percent of the total domestic zinc production, and for about 7 percent of the entire lead output."[3] The use of federal power to protect workers, the booming wartime economy that stimulated maximum production and employment, and an improved national climate for organized labor did not substantially alter the ingrained skepticism of Tri-State metal workers toward

unions. Nor did the earlier courageous struggle and sacrifices of the International Union diehards in the strike
of 1935.

From the official ending of its strike in 1943 until 1949
when other unions displaced the International Union in
the Tri-State, its membership there remained substantially
below its potential. The sorry postwar state of mining and
milling in the district contributed to the failure of the
union to grow. The rapid wartime depletion of high-grade
reserves and the postwar mineral policies of the federal
government (low tariffs on foreign imports of lead and zinc,
refusal to subsidize production of the district's low-grade
ores, purchase and stockpiling of low-cost strategic metals
from abroad) undermined the local industry and seriously
impaired the union's organizing efforts in the Tri-State.[4]
Furthermore, internal conflicts over the issues of communism, leadership, and program prevented the union from
its best effort there. Making matters worse was the increased competition from affiliates of the AFL and the
CIO to represent district workers. Confronted with these
problems, the union found it difficult to develop a successful organizing strategy for an up-and-down industry
in a district where hostile sentiment toward it remained
substantial.

Buttressed by the National Labor Relations Board decision but with its locals in disarray toward the end of 1939,
the union responded by chartering the Oklahoma-Kansas-
Missouri Federal Miners Union (Local No. 489) at Baxter
Springs.[5] Eagle Picher still remained the nemesis of the
union, however. By 1940 the company had substantially increased its Tri-State properties by acquiring that of several
leading competitors. This development placed even more
of the miners and millmen under its control. In March
1940, the International Union reacted by chartering the
Eagle Picher Mine and Mill Workers Union (Local No.
498) specifically to represent that company's employees.[6]
But even in wartime, the local did not prosper. In April
1943, the union declared it defunct.[7] Consequently, the
workers at Eagle Picher properties were without an Inter-

national Union organization until 1946 when the Eagle Picher Mine and Millmen's Union (Local No. 861) was chartered.[8]

Meanwhile, several of the older locals that were around during the strike of 1935 were declared defunct (the Webb City Miners Union, Local No. 106,[9] and the Treece Mine, Mill and Smelter Workers Union, Local No. 111),[10] while new ones were chartered (the Kansas Exploration and Oronogo Mutual Mine Workers Union at Galena, Local No. 596,[11] the Tri-State Consolidated Mine and Millmen's Union at Picher, Local No. 671,[12] and the Amalgamated Mine and Millmen's Union at Picher, Local No. 856).[13] Several of these new organizations failed to endure, but they and others were part of the explosion of International Union locals established throughout the country in the immediate postwar era. At the time of the chartering of Eagle Picher Local 861 in 1946, organized workers at the Federal Mining Company at Baxter Springs (Local No. 489), and the Saint Louis Mining Company at Galena (Local No. 514)[14] had been working under International contracts for several years. Eagle Picher's workers had benefited from these agreements because the company generally raised its wages to a level close to that paid by its organized competitors in the district.[15] Such raises were expedient measures designed to stifle the workers' demands for unions. The tactic ultimately failed, however, when in 1946 its employees voted to have the International Union represent them in collective bargaining.

For awhile, Local No. 861 flourished, its fortunes largely tied to the ups and downs of the district. Writing to Attorney General Tom Clark in February 1947, J. R. Sadler, president of the local, estimated its membership at "close to 1000."[16] Even so, Eagle Picher was no more inclined to tolerate the union in the forties than it was in the thirties. When negotiations commenced for a new contract in May 1948, the company demonstrated anew that it was not averse to union busting, although perhaps in a more sophisticated fashion.

The negotiating committee of Local No. 861, headed by

Sadler, presented a list of twenty-one demands, some of which it undoubtedly did not expect to achieve (for example, a guaranteed annual wage based on a forty-hour week), and others it was prepared to negotiate. Among the more important initial demands were: a union shop, procedural changes to allow service on grievance committees without a loss of work time, nondiscrimination against employees for past or present union activities, changes in overtime wage rates, a twenty-five cents per hour wage increase, paid holidays and vacations, the right of the union to take up grievances on unsafe working conditions, the elimination of the company's right to unilaterally rule on the qualifications for a job (seniority), paid sick leave, an increase in the company's contribution to the welfare fund, and severance pay.[17] The company's response to these demands was either to reject, ignore, or modify them. The result was a rapid movement toward a strike. On June 26 a strike ballot was conducted at the local's hall in Picher. According to Howard Lee, a regional director for the International, the strike vote carried by 92 percent, a vote that substantially supported the negotiating committee.[18]

The strike against Eagle Picher began at midnight on June 30 and lasted throughout the summer of 1948. Once again union members in the Tri-State were enmeshed in desperate circumstances. After several appeals to the parent International Union for strike relief, several checks for $500 each arrived, but these were not nearly enough to sustain a walkout involving more than six hundred workers and their families.[19] In a bulletin entitled "Why 2,000 Miners and Millmen Are Unemployed," a district appeal was made for money and food for the strikers.[20] Once again Eagle Picher lived up to its reputation as being "one of the toughest companies in Mine-Mill,"[21] forcing Local No. 861 to reduce its twenty-one demands to nine. These now included an 18.5 cents per hour wage increase, extra pay for work on holidays, a 5 to 10 cents differential for the night shift, paid vacations like those provided for workers at its Henryetta smelter, an equal voice in determining workloads, the extension of the previous contract's seniority clause, the arbitration of disputes, an end to the firing of workers who used the courts to seek compensation for accidents or injuries, and a health and welfare benefit plan to cover both workers and their families.[22] The company gave no quarter. After suffering through weeks of deprivation, upon the recommendation of Elwood Hain and Howard Mooney (International Union representatives) the strikers accepted Eagle Picher's offer of a 12.5 cents per hour raise, ratifying the agreement on November 18, 1948.[23] About six hundred and fifty men returned to work with little to show for their effort against the company.

In reporting the end of the strike to national officials, Tri-State representatives of the International Union placed the best possible construction on its outcome. In a letter of November 19, 1948, to Secretary-Treasurer M. E. Travis, Lee, Mooney, and Hain stated that the strike results were a "big gain for the union in the Tri-State . . . because we frustrated the attempts of the company to use it [the strike] to promote secession and union busting."[24] This assessment, however, was far from accurate. During the course of the strike, a back-to-work movement strongly reminiscent of that of 1935 had emerged and climaxed in an independent union called the Tri-State Mine and Millmen's Association. Led by Walter Cherry, who was "known as a company agent,"[25] the association was supported by the company, whose foremen attended its meetings and "tried to get workers to join it." As in 1935, Eagle Picher and the association used smear tactics, charging that the national leaders of the union were Communists.[26] Unlike 1935, the charge in 1948 was partly true. It was the emergence of the company-supported association, the renewed efforts of AFL representatives to raid the membership of Local No. 861, and the charge of communism against the national leadership of the union that made the strike of 1948 so important in the Tri-State. For within a year following its settlement, the fate of the union in the district had been sealed. The passage of the Taft-Hartley Act of 1947 with its provision requiring union officials to sign affidavits that they were not Communists combined with the heating up of the Cold War to help assure the union's demise there.

Even before the strike settlement of November 19, evidence had accumulated that Eagle Picher Local No. 861 was in deep trouble. When Secretary-Treasurer Travis spoke at Picher during the strike, he failed to deny a statement that Eagle Picher had published as a full-page ad in the *Miami Daily News-Record* that there were Communists among the top leaders of the union. His failure made communism in the union a continuing issue after the strike. Furthermore, Eagle Picher allowed Cherry's association a free hand in soliciting members on its properties. And, as of October 20, less than 50 percent of the company's employees had signed union check-off cards. Dissension was rife in Local No. 861, with its entire slate of officers, except one, having contacted the representatives of the AFL's United Cement, Lime and Gypsum Workers' Union about the possibility of affiliation. Assessing these developments, Hain informed Leonard Douglas, a member of the union's executive board, that Eagle Picher would challenge the bargaining rights of the union as soon as the government permitted it. With less than 50 percent of Local No. 861's membership in the union's camp, it was unlikely to win a "no" vote if Cherry's association petitioned for a representation election.[27] The accuracy of this assessment was revealed when, on October 20, William A. Timms, president of Local No. 861, officially notified John Clark, president of the International, that his local intended to withdraw from the organization.[28] After this notification, Hain and Mooney struggled desperately to salvage the most important local union in the district.

Although the union responded to the dismal situation in Local No. 861 by authorizing a monthly budget of $125, principally for "publicity purposes," and hiring Carl Johnson, a loyal recording secretary of the local, for six weeks to help revitalize the union,[29] its efforts proved futile. Throughout the early months of 1949, the semimonthly reports of Hain and Mooney were filled with pessimistic statements about the future of Local No. 861. On January 31, Hain reported that AFL supporters were in the majority at Eagle Picher's Central Mill.[30] Mooney advised on February 15 that the AFL's United Cement Union was attempting to raid Local No. 861, whose officers were aiding the effort.[31] On March 15, Mooney reported that the local was in "very bad shape" with United Cement actively engaged in recruiting.[32] Hain advised on the same day that Cherry's association had allegedly consolidated with United Cement, whose "reps" were working hard to establish a toehold in the union's district locals.[33] On March 31, Mooney reported the likelihood of another AFL petition for a representation election for Eagle Picher's surface workers.[34] Hain complained on April 15 that the failure of the national leaders to comply with the Communist-registration provisions of the Taft-Hartley Act canceled the work of the two "reps" and opened the door for United Cement because, in an election, the union would not be on the ballot as an option.[35]

On April 30, Mooney reported that the AFL had opened a hall in Picher, and it had petitioned again for an election among Eagle Picher's surface workers. The AFL had tried to "work up violence against Mine-Mill people" with threatening signs in their hall windows, and was receiving aid from the company.[36] Hain reported on the same day that local newspapers were carrying stories from the AFL and the association "blasting Mine-Mill for Communist activities" and handbilling the district with antiunion materials.[37] And on May 15, Mooney reported that the National Labor Relations Board had agreed to an election for all workers in the Eagle Picher bargaining unit—surface and underground—for June 1 and 2.[38]

In the Board-sanctioned election to determine which union would represent Eagle Picher's workers, the International Union was severely handicapped. Because its national leaders were in noncompliance with the Communist-affidavit provisions of the Taft-Hartley Act, the name of the union was excluded from the ballot. The workers had three options: one, the company-supported Tri-State Mine and Millmen's Association of Walter Cherry; two, the AFL's United Cement, Lime and Gypsum Workers' Union; and three, "Neither," which was technically a vote for the retention of the union's Local No. 861. Hain's and Mooney's task of explaining to the workers that a vote for "Neither" was a vote for the International was made more difficult by statements from representatives of the other two organizations that a vote for "Neither" was *not* a vote for the union.[39] Furthermore, the 850 employees of Eagle Picher were scattered in eighteen mine shafts, two mills, a powerhouse, and a yard. Although Hain and Mooney attempted to contact each worker by a house-to-house canvass, at meetings of Local No. 861, and by handbills and the *Tri-State Miner* (a bimonthly newspaper published by several locals), they found the task overwhelming. They were not able to dispel the confusion stemming from the "Neither" option on the ballot.[40]

Furthermore, the opponents of the union resurrected the old charge of communism with telling effect. Immediately before the election, representatives of the AFL were guests on a KGLC (Miami) radio talk show. They used the opportunity to engage in red baiting and to assert that a victory for the union would mean an immediate call for a strike. The noncompliance of the International's national leaders with the Communist-affidavit stipulation of the Taft-Hartley Act, which had kept the name of the union off the ballot, confirmed the charge of Communists within the union in the minds of many workers. In reporting to President John Clark about the election, Linus Wampler, an international representative, noted that the results proved that the "red issue" could no longer be dodged by the union.[41]

Further handicapping the union was the long-standing division among Local No. 861's membership and the aggressive raiding tactics of the AFL and the association. Not only were the local's elected leaders working to establish a connection with the AFL's United Cement Union, but, after the election, Wampler charged that Hain had secretly concocted and tried to implement a plan to have Local

No. 861 secede and go independent. Thereafter, the other union locals in the district were to secede and join Local No. 861 in forming a small International Independent Union with Hain holding the reins of power in the background. Mooney also blamed Hain for the internal turmoil, alleging that he had "consistently run down the International Union, its officials and policy to the members."[42] The plan failed when it was exposed, but it revealed dissension and duplicity that were not helpful in the election. Finally, the failure of the national officers to support Mooney after appointing him the administrator of Local No. 861 in the spring of 1949 was used by the association and United Cement to create additional animosity among its members toward the union.[43]

For these reasons, the vote on June 1 and 2 was disastrous for the International Union in the Tri-State. The United Cement, Lime and Gypsum Workers' Union, AFL, received 448 votes; "Neither" (the union), 232; and the Tri-State Mine and Millmen's Association, 50.[44] Mooney grasped the significance of the union's defeat when he reported: "This marks off Local #861, and gives the Gypsum a foothold here in the Tri-State which is regrettable as under the circumstances here with the zinc prices what they are [low] other local unions are going to be attacked by the Gypsum workers."[45] The raids were not long in coming.

By July 1, the Tri-State was prostrate. All the companies were shut down except the Saint Louis Mining Company. Into this extremely precarious economic situation another competitor to International Union appeared, the Gas-Coke and Chemical Workers Union, CIO, which joined the AFL in raiding every organized property. In a hearing on July 1, the National Labor Relations Board granted Gas-Coke's petition for a representation election at the Federal Mining Company of Baxter Springs, a bargaining unit then represented by International Local No. 489. Once again the union was excluded from the ballot because of the non-compliance of its national officers with the Communist-affidavit mandate of Taft-Hartley. The workers thus had three options: Gas-Coke and Chemical Workers Union, CIO; United Cement, Lime and Gypsum Workers Union, AFL; and "Neither." In the election held on July 14, the workers chose Gas-Coke with 72 votes, with United Cement (29) and "Neither" (10) running a poor second and third.[46] It was the second loss for the union within two months.

These defeats ended the history of the International Union of Mine, Mill, and Smelter Workers in the Tri-State. Reeling under the adverse economic conditions affecting the mining industry in the late forties, the Kansas Exploration and Oronogo Mutual Mine Workers Union, Local No. 596 of Galena, had ceased operating as early as February 1949 and was defunct by mid-June.[47] By September 1, Mooney reported that the Amalgamated Mine and Millmen's Union, Local No. 856 of Picher, was down "for all practical purposes" because only the Dines Company was operating. It, too, was expected to close within four months because of a lack of ore.[48] Although the Saint Louis Mine and Smeltermen's Union, Local No. 514 at Galena, enjoyed a brief revival in mid-August after the national leaders of the union had signed the required non-Communist affidavits,[49] the expected surge in new members and organizations did not occur. Thus the union that had begun with such promise in the early thirties was finished in the Tri-State Mining District.

Afterwards, Tri-State production and labor, which had surged to meet the demands of World War II, began to decline steadily because of reduced or exhausted ore reserves and increased foreign competition. In the fifties, the reign of the Tri-State as a principal producer of zinc and lead concentrates ended. With only a short supply of marginal ores in reserve, with the national government turning to foreign sources for strategic metals during the Korean War, and with Congress reluctant to provide essential subsidies to maintain mining operations, the inevitable end came to the prominence of the district as a mining and milling center.[50]

The sights and sounds of a once mighty industry that

Marrion Parsons had observed with wonder as a boy in 1925 disappeared from the Tri-State Mining District, not in a cataclysmic upheaval of labor strife but in the unpublicized and undramatic shutdown of a mine here and a mill there as rich reserves were exhausted. Left behind were the towering chat piles, the concrete pillars of old mills, the rusting machinery, and the worn-out men and women, stark reminders of a vigorous industrial past that consumed the energies and lives of thousands of workers and their families. Left behind, too, was a mind-boggling environmental time-bomb for future generations to defuse. In November, 1981, the Environmental Protection Agency placed the Tar Creek area of the district among the ten "most serious hazards" sites in the United States because of the industrial pollution resulting from past mining and milling.[51] Whether a powerful union movement could have helped to ease the inevitable decline and to enhance the quality of life for all Tri-Staters, then and now, must remain an unanswered question.

Notes

1. No Blacks, No Foreigners, No Unions—No Power

1. Marrion A. Parsons, "I Got Lost in Picher," *The Tri-State Tribune* (Picher, Okla.), August 11, 1983, p. 2.

2. Charles Morris Mills, "Joplin Zinc: Industrial Conditions in the World's Greatest Zinc Center," *The Survey*, 45 (February 5, 1921): 657.

3. Ibid., p. 658. Mills's italics.

4. M.D. Harbaugh, "Labor Relations in the Tri-State Mining District," *Mining Congress Journal*, 22 (June 1936): 19; Arrell M. Gibson, *Wilderness Bonanza: The Tri-State District of Missouri, Kansas, and Oklahoma* (Norman: University of Oklahoma Press, 1972), passim; *Oklahoma Federationist* (Oklahoma City, Okla.) May 1938, p. 13.

5. *Miners' Magazine*, 2 (November 1901): 5–6.

6. There is no satisfactory labor history of the Tri-State Mining District covering the late nineteenth and early twentieth centuries. Vernon Jensen's *Heritage of Conflict: Labor Relations in the Nonferrous Metals Industry up to 1930* (Ithaca: Cornell University Press, 1950) and his *Non-Ferrous Metals Industry Unionism, 1932–1954: A Story of Leadership Controversy* (Ithaca: Cornell University Press, 1954) are institutional studies of the Western Federation of Miners and the International Union of Mine, Mill, and Smelter Workers that do not focus specifically on the district. Although inadequate as labor histories, the best coverage of the early period is found in Gibson's *Wilderness Bonanza*, pp. 201–31, and his "Poor Man's Camp: Labor Movement Vicissitudes in the Tri-State District," *Chronicles of Oklahoma*, 60 (Spring 1982): 4–21; chapter 8 of William James Cassidy's "The Tri-State Zinc, Lead Mining Region: Growth, Problems, and Prospects" (Ph.D. dissertation, University of Pittsburgh, 1955); and John Ervin Brinley's "The Western Federation of Miners" (Ph.D. dissertation, University of Utah, 1972). The following discussion is based primarily on Brinley, pp. 191, 210, 217–19, 222, and 241.

7. The many published accounts concerning the Klan fight in

Oklahoma and Kansas do not mention the role, if any, played by the residents of Cherokee and Ottawa counties in the statewide struggles over the Klan. See Miami (Oklahoma) *Daily News-Record,* June 21, 1936, p. 2; Carl N. Degler, "A Century of the Klans: A Review Article," *Journal of Southern History,* 31 (November 1965): 435–43; Stephen B. Oates, "Boom Oil! Oklahoma Strikes It Rich," *The American West,* 5 (January 1968): 11–15, 64–66; Garin Burbank, "Agrarian Radicals and Their Opponents: Political Conflict in Southern Oklahoma, 1910–1924," *Journal of American History,* 58 (March 1971): 5–23; Charles William Sloan, Jr., "Kansas Battles the Invisible Empire: The Legal Ouster of the KKK from Kansas, 1922–1927," *Kansas Historical Quarterly,* 40 (Autumn 1974): 393–409; Jack Wayne Traylor, "William Allen White's 1924 Gubernatorial Campaign," *Kansas Historical Quarterly,* 72 (Summer 1972): 180–91; David C. Boles, "The Effect of the Ku Klux Klan on the Oklahoma Gubernatorial Election of 1926," *Chronicles of Oklahoma,* 55 (Winter 1977–1978): 424–32; Sheldon Neuringer, "Governor Walton's War on the Ku Klux Klan: An Episode in Oklahoma History, 1923 to 1924," *Chronicles of Oklahoma,* 45 (Summer 1967): 153–79; Charles C. Alexander, *The Ku Klux Klan in the Southwest* (Lexington: University of Kentucky Press, 1965), passim.

8. Mills, "Joplin Zinc," p. 657.

9. Ibid.

10. F. Lynwood Garrison, "The Joplin Mining District's Past, Present and Future," *Engineering and Mining Journal,* 111 (May 21, 1921): 860. For statements from other authors who incorporated into their writings the white, native-born American explanation for the district's historical antiunion posture, see Gibson's "Poor Man's Camp," pp. 4–8; also see his *Wilderness Bonanza,* pp. 201–5, for a similar account of the district's antiforeign and antiblack views.

11. As late as 1931, the following appeared in a brochure prepared for a joint convention of the American Mining Congress and the American Institute of Mining and Metallurgical Engineers: "One interesting feature of the district is the high type of labor. There are no unions. The men are happy, intelligent, and reliable, and thus highly efficient." Otto Ruhl, et al., *The Story of the Tri-State Mining District"* (Joplin: n.p., 1931), p. 21. No other comment about labor appeared in this 43-page brochure. In April 1939, B. B. Brumfield, president of the Picher Chamber of Commerce, observed that the district was populated with "hardy, honest, upright American people—no negroes and no foreigners." Quoted in *Oklahoma Federationist* (Oklahoma City, Okla.) April 1939, p. 7. See also Liston Pope, *Millhands and Preachers: A Study of Gastonia* (New Ha-

ven: Yale University Press, 1942), passim, to compare the condition of the textile workers to the Tri-State metal workers.

12. Malcolm H. Ross, *The Death of a Yale Man* (New York: J.J. Little & Ives Co., 1939), p. 185.

13. Harbaugh, "Labor Relations in the Tri-State Mining District," p. 19.

14. Ross, *Death of a Yale Man*, p. 185.

15. Glenn A. Hickman, Recollections, pt. 1. Transcript in author's possession.

16. Mills, "Joplin Zinc," p. 658.

17. U.S., Bureau of Mines, R.R. Sayers, et al., *Silicosis and Tuberculosis among Miners of the Tri-State District of Oklahoma, Kansas, and Missouri—I*, Technical Paper 545 (Washington, D.C.: Government Printing Office, 1933), p. 5.

18. U.S., Department of Commerce, Bureau of the Census, *Fifteenth Census of the United States: 1930*, vol. 3, pt. 1, *Alabama-Missouri* (Washington, D.C.: Government Printing Office, 1932), pp. 830, 1332, 1334; and vol. 3, pt. 2, *Montana-Wyoming* (Washington, D.C.: Government Printing Office, 1932), p. 554.

19. U.S., Department of Commerce, Bureau of the Census, *Religious Bodies: 1936*, vol. 1, *Summary and Detailed Tables* (Washington, D.C.: Government Printing Office, 1941), pp. 755, 757, 778–81, 804, 806.

20. Ibid.

21. Mills, "Joplin Zinc," p. 663.

22. U.S., Department of Labor, Division of Labor Standards, *Conference on Health and Working Conditions in the Tri-State District, Joplin, Missouri, April 23, 1940* (Washington, D.C.: Department of Labor, 1940), p. 9.

23. Lane Carter, "Economic Conditions in the Joplin District," *Engineering and Mining Journal*, 90 (October 15, 1910): 760.

24. "Editorial Correspondence," ibid., 100 (August 14, 1915): 288.

25. Mills, "Joplin Zinc," p. 688.

26. Gibson, *Wilderness Bonanza*, p. 205.

27. Gibson, "Poor Man's Camp," pp. 9, 11–12.

28. Harbaugh, "Labor Relations in the Tri-State Mining District," p. 21.

29. Ibid., p. 20. The table at the top of p. 234 illustrates how the wage system operated in the district.

30. Tri-State Survey Committee, Inc., *A Preliminary Report on Living, Working, and Health Conditions in the Tri-State Mining Area (Missouri, Oklahoma, and Kansas)* (New York: Tri-State Survey Committee, Inc., 1939), p. 37.

Year	Zinc Concentrate Price	Contract Machine Men, 8 Hours	Shoveler, Per 1,200 lb. Can
1925	$55	$5.00	12½ cents
1927	42	4.25	11 "
1930	31	4.00	10½ "
1931	25	3.50	10 "
1932	18 to 14	2.00	8½ "
1933	31	3.25	9 "
1935	26 to 30	3.55	10½ "

Source: Ibid., p. 20

31. U.S., Census of Partial Employment, Unemployment, and Occupations, *Final Report on Total and Partial Unemployment, 1937* (3 vols., Washington, D.C.: Government Printing Office, 1938), 2: 73; 3: 169.

32. Kansas, Commission of Labor and Industry, *Annual Report* (Topeka: State Printers, 1935), p. 89.

33. Harbaugh, "Labor Relations in the Tri-State Mining District," p. 21.

34. Tri-State Survey Committee, *Preliminary Report on Living, Working, and Health Conditions*, pp. 19–27.

35. Hickman to Reynolds, October 18, 1939, Glenn A. Hickman Papers, Columbus, Kansas.

36. Department of Labor, *Conference on Health and Working Conditions*, p. 9.

37. Bureau of Mines, Technical Paper 545, p. 7.

38. U.S., Treasury Department, *Miners' Consumption: A Study of 433 Cases of the Disease among Zinc Miners in Southwestern Missouri,* Public Health Bulletin 85 (Washington, D.C.: Government Printing Office, 1917), p. 14.

39. U.S., Bureau of Mines, *Silicosis and Tuberculosis Among Miners of the Tri-State District of Oklahoma, Kansas, and Missouri—II,* Technical Paper 552 (Washington, D.C.: Government Printing Office, 1933), pp. 1–2.

40. U.S., Department of Labor, Division of Labor Standards, National Silicosis Conference, *Report on Medical Control: Final Report of the Committee on the Prevention of Silicosis Through Medical Control,* Bulletin 21, pt. 1 (Washington, D.C.: Government Printing Office, 1938), p. 6.

41. See summary of a study made by the Industrial Hygiene Section of the Kansas State Board of Health in Tri-State Survey Com-

mittee, *Preliminary Report on Living, Working, and Health Conditions,* p. 62.

42. See Department of labor, *Conference on Health and Working Conditions,* passim.

2. "Strike Until You Whip Hell Out of This Bunch"

1. William James Cassidy, "The Tri-State Zinc, Lead Mining Region: Growth, Problems, and Prospects" (Ph.D. dissertation, University of Pittsburgh, 1955), pp. 257–61.

2. Ibid., p. 268; Glenn A. Hickman, Recollections, pt. 1. Transcript in author's possession; Marilyn Best, Oklahoma State Department of Health, to Karen Meyer, Park Lawn Health Library, Rockville, Maryland, to Janice Nunnelee, Kent Library (telephone), November 7, 1984.

3. Cassidy, "Tri-State Zinc, Lead Mining Region," p. 268.

4. Hickman, Recollections, pt. 1.

5. Ibid. Hickman pointed out that not all Tri-State workers found to be silicotic or consumptive and refused employment were embittered. He stated: "One of the benefits of the clinic, seldom acknowledged by critics of the period, was the great number who discovered their trouble in its incipient state while there was still time to get out of the mines and thus retain their health. I have a brother among this number. He never ceases to be grateful for the clinic's discovery of his incipiency. He is now 77 [1981] and knows with certainty that without this early discovery he would not now be around." Ibid.

6. Cassidy, "Tri-State Zinc, Lead Mining Region," p. 266.

7. M.D. Harbaugh, "Labor Relations in the Tri-State Mining District," *Mining Congress Journal,* 22 (June 1936): 22–23; Malcolm H. Ross, *The Death of a Yale Man* (New York: J.J. Little & Ives Co., 1939), pp. 189–90.

8. It could not then be satisfactorily determined how many Tri-State workers were enrolled in the International Union of Mine, Mill, and Smelter Workers (IUMMSW), and the number cannot now be precisely stated. The official proceedings of the union's annual conventions held during August 1934 and 1935 in Salt Lake City are only suggestive because they failed to incorporate either a listing of all the locals and their memberships or a treasurer's report indicating per capita receipts from each local. Article II, Section 2 of the union's constitution for 1934 and 1935 stated: "Each union shall be entitled to one vote for one hundred members or less, and one for each additional one hundred or majority fraction thereof,

provided, no delegate shall cast more than five votes, and no proxy votes shall be allowed." Under this formula, Brady, who represented Local No. 15 in 1934 (the only Tri-State local represented), was authorized five votes. In 1935 the delegate from No. 15 again had five votes, whereas each representative from Nos. 17, 110, and 111 was allowed one vote under the formula. As a measure of union strength in the Tri-State, therefore, those delegate votes are virtually useless, although suggestive of membership totals for locals represented in August 1934 and 1935. IUMMSW, *Proceedings*, 31st Annual Convention, p. 5 and 32d Annual Convention, pp. 8–9. Further complicating a precise assessment of union strength in the Tri-State before the strike of 1935 was the deliberate and malicious destruction of union records, including membership rolls, during the riots directed against the IUMMSW's largest locals at Picher, Treece, and Galena in April 1937 (see chapter 7). At best, therefore, estimates of IUMMSW membership before the strike vary substantially.

9. Harbaugh, "Labor Relations in the Tri-State Mining District," p. 23.

10. Arrell M. Gibson, *Wilderness Bonanza: The Tri-State District of Missouri, Kansas, and Oklahoma* (Norman: University of Oklahoma Press, 1972), p. 231.

11. Ross, *Death of a Yale Man*, p. 190.

12. Quoted in the *Joplin* (Missouri) *Globe*, May 9, 1935, p. 2.

13. Harbaugh, "Labor Relations in the Tri-State Mining District," p. 23.

14. Ross, *Death of a Yale Man*, p. 190; IUMMSW, Minutes, Executive Board, April 3, 1935, p. 244.

15. Hickman, Recollections, pt. 1.

16. Ibid.

17. Cassidy, "Tri-State Zinc, Lead Mining Region," p. 269.

18. Tri-State Local No. 15 to [   ] Smith, May 5, 1934, and Smith to Louis Gamble, et al., May 8, 1934, Board Exhibits 13 and 13A, DB 833, Eagle Picher Mining and Smelting Company, Formal and Informal Labor Practices and Representative Case Files, 1935–1948, National Labor Relations Board, Suitland, Maryland. Hereafter cited as Eagle Picher Case, NLRB.

19. See testimony of Ora L. Wilson in Synopsis of Record, p. 3, DB 833, Eagle Picher Case, NLRB; also, *In re* Eagle Picher Mining & Smelting Co., and Eagle Picher Lead Co., and International Union of Mine, Mill & Smelter Workers, Locals 15, 17, 107, 108, and 111 in *Decisions and Orders*, 16 (Washington, D.C.: Government

Printing Office, 1940), p. 741. Hereafter cited as NLRB, *Decisions and Orders*.

20. Board Exhibit No. 11, DB 833, Eagle Picher Case, NLRB.

21. Kansas, Commission of Labor and Industry, *Annual Report* (1935), pp. 69–70; also, *Joplin Globe*, May 9, 1935.

22. Harbaugh, "Labor Relations in the Tri-State Mining District," p. 23.

23. May 9, 1935.

24. NLRB, *Decisions and Orders*, p. 741.

25. *Joplin Globe*, May 9, 1935, p. 2.

26. George O. Pratt to Charles Fahey, June 4, 1937, in DB 4272, Eagle Picher Case, NLRB.

27. *Kansas City* (Missouri) *Star*, May 9, 1935, p. 2; *Joplin Globe*, May 9, 1935, p. 1.

28. Eagle Picher Lead Company v. J. Warren Madden, (Brief) (N.D. Okla., May 22, 1936), in DB 4272, Eagle Picher Case, NLRB. Brief hereafter cited as Eagle-Picher v. J. Warren Madden.

29. Harbaugh, "Labor Relations in the Tri-State Mining District," p. 24.

30. Ibid.

31. F. J. Cuddeback to Alfred M. Landon, July 15, 1935, Governors Papers—Alfred M. Landon, Kansas State Historical Society. Hereafter cited as Landon Papers.

32. Ibid.

33. Interview with Glenn A. Hickman, February 5, 1981.

34. Ross, *Death of a Yale Man*, p. 206.

35. See Eagle Picher v. J. Warren Madden, DB 4272, Eagle Picher Case, NLRB.

36. *Columbus* (Kansas) *Daily Advocate*, May 9, 1935.

37. F. W. Gooch to A. C. Wallace, July 22, 1937, in Eagle Picher v. J. Warren Madden, DB 4272, Eagle Picher Case, NLRB.

38. 136 (June 1935): 295–96; also, Baxter Springs, Kansas, *Citizen and Herald*, May 9, 1935.

39. Testimony of Ernest Berry in Synopsis of Record, p. 63, DB 834, Eagle Picher Case, NLRB.

40. Eagle Picher v. J. Warren Madden, in DB 4272, Eagle Picher Case, NLRB; also, George O. Pratt to Robert B. Watts, June 5, 1936, in ibid.

41. NLRB, *Decisions and Orders*, p. 742.

42. 136 (June 1935), 295–96.

43. Harbaugh, "Labor Relations in the Tri-State Mining District," p. 23.

3. The Rise of the Back-to-Work Movement

1. *Joplin* (Missouri) *Globe,* May 10, 1935, p. 10; *Columbus* (Kansas) *Daily Advocate,* May 10, 1935; and Major Ellis G. Christensen, Activity Report, July 22, 1935, Governors Papers—Alfred M. Landon, Kansas State Historical Society.

2. The old-timer requested anonymity because a discussion of the strike, even after forty years, renewed the bitterness among district residents. *Miami* (Oklahoma) *Daily News-Record,* April 16, 1975.

3. International Union of Mine, Mill, and Smelter Workers (IUMMSW), *Proceedings,* 32d Annual Convention, passim.

4. Edward A. Cassell and J. R. Payne to IUMMSW Convention (n.d.) in ibid., p. 17.

5. Ibid., pp. 20–21.

6. National Labor Relations Board (NLRB), *Decisions and Orders,* 16 (Washington, D.C.: Government Printing Office, 1940), p. 746.

7. Glenn A. Hickman, former secretary-treasurer of the Tri-State Mine, Mill and Smelter Workers Union (T-SMMSWU) (Blue Card Union) to author, April 16, 1982; also, Hickman, Recollections, pt. 2. Transcript in author's possession.

8. *Joplin Globe,* May 18, 1935, p. 1.

9. Ibid., May 19, 1935, p. 1.

10. Ibid., May 21, 1935, p. 1.

11. Ibid.

12. Ibid., May 22, 1935, pp. 1–2.

13. Ibid.

14. NLRB, *Decisions and Orders,* p. 742.

15. Ibid., p. 750; Malcolm H. Ross, *Death of a Yale Man* (New York: J.J. Little & Ives, Co. 1939), p. 194; Synopsis of Record, pp. 4–6, DB 834, Eagle Picher Mining and Smelting Company, Formal and Informal Labor Practices and Representative Case Files, 1935–1948, National Labor Relations Board, Suitland, Maryland. Hereafter cited as Eagle Picher Case, NLRB; interview with Hickman, February 5, 1981; Hickman, Recollections, pt. 1. In response to questions from Eagle Picher laboratory workers concerning Evans's character, Kelsey Norman, attorney for the Tri-State Metal Mine and Smelter Workers Union, stated that: "Evans has the entire respect and confidence of all the men in this district. Twenty Thousand Dollars have been loaned to him at one time by Eagle-Picher with no collateral over his name. . . . His word is good. . . . I will say to you that his integrity has never been questioned. I have known him for 8 or 10 years. My close association has been with him since the union [T-SMMSWU] was organized. The fact that he spent 8 or 9 months in jail in Venita [*sic*] should in no way affect his standing

today. I understand he had a very fine suite at the jail and his most frequent visitors were bankers. I am sure he is the only man in this entire district who could have carried this organization along as he has. He is a man of iron measure." Kelsey Norman to Lab Workers, September 25, 1935, Board Exhibit 76, DB 833, Eagle Picher Case, NLRB.

16. Interview with Glenn A. Hickman, February 5, 1981.

17. Glenn A. Hickman, Recollections, pt. 2. Hickman's testimony in a NLRB hearing in 1937 on the Tri-State strike indicated that he dropped his membership in the IUMMSW because it advocated violence (e.g., dynamiting) and persuaded its members that the operators misrepresented ore prices on which wages were based. See Synopsis of Record, p. 41, DB 834, Eagle Picher Case, NLRB.

18. Hickman, Recollections, pt. 1.

19. Ibid., pt. 2.

20. NLRB, *Decisions and Orders*, p. 743; *Joplin Globe*, May 26, 1935, p. 1.

21. *Joplin Globe*, May 25, p. 2 and May 26, 1935, p. 1.

22. Interview with Hickman, February 5, 1981.

23. Hickman to author, April 16, 1982.

24. Hickman, Recollections, pt. 1. Although secretary-treasurer of the T-SMMSWU, Hickman later stated that he had "always been totally in the dark" concerning "for how much, by whom and for what duration" Norman had been retained. Entries into the financial records of the T-SMMSWU from June 3, 1935 to September 28, 1935 indicate that he received a total of $43.20 for "Expenses" but nothing for salary. Although the records show a $100 "Legal Service" entry, there is no indication to whom it was paid. Hickman's statement and the records strongly suggest that Norman's fees came from sources outside the organization. It is extremely unlikely that Norman provided his wide range of services without appropriate compensation. Ibid., and "Balance Sheet," T-SMMSWU, Board Exhibit 204, DB 833, Eagle Picher Case, NLRB.

25. See Synopsis of Record, p. 9, DB 834, Eagle Picher Case, NLRB, and NLRB, *Decisions and Orders*, p. 745, n. 27.

26. In addition to Evans and Hickman, the executive committee included: Ray Morris (watchman, Eagle Picher Mining and Smelting Co.), William De Witt (ground boss, Tulsa-Quapaw Mine, Eagle Picher Mining and Smelting Co.), Harold ("Boots") Irvin (ground boss, Mid-Continent Lead and Zinc Co.), N.J. Detchemendy (ground boss, Commerce Mining and Royalty Co.), Joe Pruitt (ground boss, Bendelari Mine, Eagle Picher Mining and Smelting Co.), Lawrence Medlin (engineer, Childress Lead and Zinc Co.), John Garretson (employee, Commerce Mining and Royalty Co.), O.A. Jackson (em-

ployee, Childress Lead and Zinc Co.), Newt Keithley (ground boss, South Side Mine, Eagle Picher Mining and Smelting Co.), W.M. Anderson (employee, Commerce Mining and Royalty Co.). NLRB, *Decisions and Orders*, pp. 744–45; and see Articles of Association, Board Exhibit 43, DB 833, Eagle Picher Case, NLRB.

27. Ibid.

28. NLRB, *Decisions and Orders*, p. 745; and see Constitution and Bylaws of the Tri-State Mine, Mill and Smelter Workers Union, Board Exhibit 32, DB 833, Eagle Picher Case, NLRB.

29. NLRB, *Decisions and Orders*, p. 745.

30. Hickman, Recollections, pt. 2.

31. Interview with Hickman, February 5, 1981.

32. Norman Ritter, superintendent of the Eagle Picher Company's South Side and Big John mines, and Oscar Bailey, ground boss at the Tom Brown and Grace B. mines, offered to pay James C. Thompson his wages if he would take a company truck, drive around the district, and "get men that we know to sign that petition to go back to work like the rest of them." When Thompson refused the offer and the request that he join the movement and return to work, Ritter threatened to prevent him from ever working for Eagle Picher again. See Synopsis of Board, pp. 177, DB 834, Eagle Picher Case, NLRB, and NLRB, *Decisions and Orders*, pp. 748–49.

33. Hickman vehemently denied the existence of a conspiracy between T-SMMSWU leaders and officials of the companies. He later wrote: "I get a little sick of the assumption that everything was so precisely plotted and planned." Hickman, Recollections, pt. 1.

4. Pick Handles and Troops

1. *Joplin* (Missouri) *Globe*, May 21, 1935, p. 2.

2. National Labor Relations Board (NLRB), *Decisions and Orders*, 16 (Washington, D.C.: Government Printing Office, 1940), pp. 743–44.

3. *Joplin Globe*, May 25, 1935, p. 1.

4. "American Plague Spot," *The New Republic*, 102 (January 1, 1940): 7–8.

5. *Joplin Globe*, May 28, 1935, p. 1.

6. NLRB, *Decisions and Orders*, p. 744.

7. Hickman, Recollections, pt. 1, Transcript in author's possession; see also NLRB, *Decisions and Orders*, p. 760, n. 57.

8. *Joplin Globe*, May 27, 1935, pp. 1 and 4; *Columbus* (Kansas) *Daily Advocate*, May 27, 1935; NLRB, *Decisions and Orders*, p. 744. How many men participated in Nolan's pick-handle parade remains

uncertain. W.W. Waters estimated the number at "three or four thousand strong." NLRB, *Decisions and Orders*, p. 744. J.A. Long played down the number and the kinds of men who marched, however, when he stated that "by absolute check, only 358 men marched in the parade. Of this number, approximately sixty-five were competent and reliable miners and only approximately fifteen of these were not insurance risks and could be worked. Some of the men in the parade I [knew] personally and they were barred from mining because of inferior clinic cards." *Joplin Globe*, May 30, 1935, p. 1.

9. See Dolph Shamer, *The Story of Joplin* (New York: Stratford House, Inc., 1948), p. 63, and the testimony of Bert Craig, Synopsis of Record, p. 121, DB 834, Eagle Picher Mining and Smelting Company, Formal and Informal Labor Practices and Representative Case Files, 1935–1948, National Labor Relations Board, Suitland, Maryland. Hereafter cited as Eagle Picher Case, NLRB.

10. *Harlow's Weekly* (Oklahoma City), May 18, 1935, p. 3.

11. Sergeant "X," "Show Workers No Mercy, Guardsmen Are Told," *American Guardian*, August 31, 1934, p. 4; *Miami* (Oklahoma) *Daily News-Record*, May 27, 1935, pp. 1, 2; *Joplin Globe*, May 28, 1935, p. 1.

12. *Joplin Globe*, May 29, 1935, p. 1.

13. Ibid., May 30, 1935, p. 1.

14. Ibid., May 31, 1935, p. 1.

15. *Harlow's Weekly*, June 8, 1935, p. 6.

16. *Columbus Daily Advocate*, June 13, 1935.

17. Ibid., June 8, 1935.

18. Dick Helman to Alfred M. Landon (telegram), June 7, 1935, Governors Papers—Alfred M. Landon, Kansas State Historical Society.

19. Shouse and Helman to Landon, June 10, 1935, ibid.; *Kansas City* (Missouri) *Times*, June 8, 1935 (clipping), in Strikes–Clippings, I, 248–49, ibid.

20. Section 48–238, *Kansas Revised Statutes* (1932) stated: "It shall be the duty of the governor, and he is hereby authorized and required, in case of war, invasion, insurrection, or breeches of the peace, or imminent danger thereof, of any forcible obstruction to the execution of the laws or reasonable apprehension thereof, to call upon the national guard to defend the state or aid the civil authorities to enforce the laws thereof." Landon interpreted Section 48–238 to require his honoring the request for troops. (On this point see also the statement of Colonel Charles H. Browne in Kansas, Commission of Labor and Industry, *Annual Report* [Topeka: State Printers, 1935] p. 73.) State Attorney General Clarence V. Beck later pleaded ignorance concerning how the decision to send

troops had been reached when he wrote: "You [the author] will understand that my duty was limited to offering legal advice upon request—and not [to] decide matters of policy." He refused to speculate on Landon's decision or the reasons behind it. Beck to author, August 6, 1975. Beck was, however, very much involved in Landon's second decision to send troops into Cherokee County following a riot at the Eagle Picher Company's Galena smelter. When the request for troops came on that occasion, Beck and Adjutant General McLean conferred, prepared the necessary papers, and then informed Landon, who was at Atchinson, Kansas, to celebrate Amelia Earhart Day. Landon to author, September 1, 1976.

21. Landon to Adjutant General, June 7, 1933, Landon Papers, KSHS.

22. *Kansas City Times*, June 8, 1935 (clipping). Strikes–Clippings, I, 248–49, ibid.; *Miami* (Oklahoma) *Daily News-Record*, June 9, 1935.

23. Italics mine. Burr to Blakeley, June 8, 1935, Landon Papers, KSHS.

24. *Miami Daily News-Record*, June 8, 9, and 11, p. 1.

25. *Kansas City Star*, June 8, 1935 (clipping), Strikes–Clippings, I, pp. 244–45, in Landon Papers, KSHS.

26. Baxter Springs, Kansas, *Citizen and Herald*, June 10, 1935.

27. Ibid.; *Joplin Globe*, June 16, 1935, p. 21. An example of this surveillance occurred on June 19 when Colonel Browne and two officers attended a meeting of Local No. 107 in Baxter Springs where Alexander Howat addressed a crowd of more than two hundred. Howat, who had led the coal miners of Pittsburg, Kansas, on strike in 1919–20, gave a speech which Browne claimed was "radical . . . and highly inflammatory, but not enough to justify arrest. He is a skilled speaker who knows how to rouse the rabble, but he goes just far enough, to make his audience understand what he wishes to infer, yet saves himself from prosecution by a clever choice of words." Browne was obviously prepared to arrest Howat and disrupt the meeting if sufficient cause could be found. Browne to McLean, June 20, 1935, Landon Papers, KSHS.

28. *Citizen and Herald*, June 13 and 17, 1935.

29. Shouse to Landon, June 19, 1935, Landon Papers, KSHS.

30. Douthit to Landon, June 19, 1935, ibid.

31. Quoted in *Columbus Daily Advocate*, June 21, 1935.

32. Landon to author, September 1, 1976. Concerning the financing of the troops in the field, Landon wrote that the expense was paid from a permanent fund created by "an annual appropriation by the legislature to the adjutant general" for emergencies requiring the services of the Kansas National Guard. Ibid. See also the

statement of Colonel Browne in Commission of Labor and Industry, *Annual Report* (1935), p. 73.

33. *Citizen and Herald*, June 24, 1935; *Columbus Daily Advocate*, June 25, 1935.

34. *Joplin Globe*, June 28, 1935, p. 17.

35. Landon to author, September 1, 1976.

36. Federal Writers Project, *Kansas, A Guide to the Sunflower State* (New York: The Viking Press, 1939), p. 440; *Columbus Daily Advocate*, June 28, 1935.

37. See *In re* Eagle Picher Mining and Smelting Co., p. 77, DB 158, Eagle Picher Case, NLRB.

38. *Joplin Globe*, June 29, 1935, p. 1.

39. NLRB, *Decisions and Orders*, p. 747.

40. *Joplin Globe*, June 29, 1935, p. 1.

41. Neely and Shouse to Landon, June 29, 1935, Landon Papers, KSHS.

42. See F.J. Cuddeback to Landon, July 6, 1935, and M.H. Loveman to Landon, July 2, 1935, ibid.

43. *Joplin Globe*, June 20, 1935.

44. General Order No. 1, June 29, 1935, Landon Papers, KSHS.

45. See Respondent Exhibit No. 67, DB 833, Eagle Picher Case, NLRB, for a complete list of the men arrested, the charges, and their sentences. Among these were prominent local International Union leaders. In an extraordinary move, the provost court also suspended Galena Mayor Fred Farmer after finding him guilty of voluntary intoxication, being drunk while driving, falsely claiming to be an agent of Browne, conduct tending to incite riot, and disturbing the public peace. Farmer was an outspoken supporter of the union and the strike. The Kansas Supreme Court overturned Farmer's suspension in November 1935. *Miami Daily News-Record*, July 14, 1935; *Galena* (Kansas) *Times-Republican*, November 15, 1935.

46. *Citizen and Herald*, July 1, 1935.

47. *Miami Daily News-Record*, July 9, 1935.

48. *Kansas City Star*, July 16, 1935, p. 2.

49. The minutes of the Jasper County Court do not indicate how these deputies were selected or paid. See Missouri, Jasper County, Minutes, County Court, vols. 55–57; and the *Joplin Globe*, July 18, 1935, pp. 1–2.

50. For Christensen's reports concerning this period, see Landon Papers, KSHS; *Columbus Daily Advocate*, July 6–15, 1935.

51. Kansas, Cherokee County, Board of County Commissioners, Minutes, vol. P, 613, 624.

52. The role of the Tri-State Union's "squad cars" is discussed in chapter 5.

53. Throughout July 1935, the Bureau kept as many as six men in the mining district working under Head and Watts. C.H. Delaughter to C.W. Daley, July 17, 1935, in F3–17, Box 1, RG 8–J–3, Bureau of Criminal Investigation, Governor's Papers: Governor Ernest W. Marland, Division of State Archives, Department of Libraries, Oklahoma.

54. *Miami Daily News-Record*, July, passim, 1935. The sources of funds to underwrite this enlarged force was uncertain. Although Head had ordered its formation, its financing was a local responsibility. But on July 5, Sheriff Dry announced that the county was unable to pay the expense of the deputies, and the minutes of the county commissioners make no reference to expenditures for this purpose. See Oklahoma, Ottawa County, Board of County Commissioners, Records, vols. 5 and 6, passim. In an extraordinary move, Dry appealed to the public for funds to pay the men who had agreed to "serve without charge to the county." *Miami Daily News-Record*, July 5, 1935. Circumstantial evidence suggests that the companies contributed heavily. See chapter 5.

55. Christensen, Activity Report, July 30, 1935, Landon Papers, KSHS.

5. The Tri-State Metal Mine and Smelter Workers Union and the Companies

1. Glenn A. Hickman, Recollections, pt. 2. Transcript in author's possession.

2. Ibid.

3. See arguments of John C. Madden in *In re* Eagle Picher Mining and Smelting Company, pp. 124–25, DB 158, Eagle Picher Mining and Smelting Company, Formal and Informal Labor Practices and Representative Case Files, 1935–1948, National Labor Relations Board, Suitland, Maryland. Hereafter cited as Eagle Picher Case, NLRB.

4. Evans, testimony, Synopsis of Record, p. 19, DB 834, in ibid.

5. Ibid., pp. 46–47, 54–57.

6. W.P. Howard to William J. Avrutis, December 22, 1937 (copy), Respondent Exhibit 18, DB 833, in ibid.

7. Evans, testimony, Synopsis of Record, pp. 11–13, DB 834, in ibid.

8. Hickman, testimony, p. 47, in ibid. See below for examples of how these funds were used to support Tri-State Union objectives.

9. Evans, testimony, pp. 54–57, in ibid; National Labor Relations Board (NLRB), *Decisions and Orders*, 16 (Washington, D.C.: Government Printing Office, 1940), pp. 750–51.

10. NLRB, *Decisions and Orders*, p. 747.

11. Tables 1 and 2 were compiled from data found in the U.S., Senate, Committee on Education and Labor, *Hearings on Senate Resolution 266* (74th Cong., 1st Sess.) *and Senate Resolution 60*, 75th Cong., 1st Sess. (Washington, D.C., Government Printing Office, 1937–38), pt. 2, 569, 578, and 582; pt. 15–D, 420–24 and 589–643, passim. For the effects of these weapons on humans, see ibid., pt. 2, 420–24 and 589–643, passim.

12. Hickman, testimony, Synopsis of Record, pp. 41–43, DB 834, Eagle Picher Case, NLRB.

13. Ibid., pp. 59–60.

14. Carpenter, testimony, p. 51, in ibid.

15. NLRB, *Decisions and Orders*, p. 747.

16. Keller, testimony, Synopsis of Record, p. 56, DB 834, Eagle Picher Case, NLRB.

17. Waters, testimony, ibid., p. 96.

18. McGregory, testimony, ibid., p. 59.

19. Keller, testimony, ibid., p. 56.

20. O'Dell, Watters, and Windbigler, testimony, ibid., pp. 59–60, 71; NLRB, *Decisions and Orders*, pp. 762–63.

21. Swearinger, testimony, Synopsis of Record, p. 50, DB 834, Eagle Picher Case, NLRB.

22. Meek, testimony, ibid., p. 60.

23. Johnson, testimony, ibid., p. 48.

24. Waters, testimony, ibid., p. 97.

25. Paralee Meek, testimony, ibid., p. 60.

26. Schasteen, testimony, ibid., pp. 167–68.

27. NLRB, *Decisions and Orders*, p. 747; Carpenter, testimony, Synopsis of Record, p. 52, DB 834, Eagle Picher Case, NLRB.

28. Knight, Thompson, and Price, testimony, ibid., pp. 54–55; NLRB, *Decisions and Orders*, p. 762.

29. W.W. Waters, testimony, Synopsis of Record, p. 97, DB 834, Eagle Picher Case, NLRB.

30. Ibid., p. 98.

31. Quoted in the *Miami* (Oklahoma) *Daily News-Record*, April 16, 1975, p. A–2.

32. *Joplin* (Missouri) *Globe*, May 30, 1935, p. 1; *Columbus* (Kansas) *Daily Advocate*, May 30, 1935. Section 12 of the Tri-State Union's constitution authorized the secretary-treasurer to drop from membership any person who incited or participated in a strike. Strikes

were considered detrimental and harmful to the interest of the organization.

33. Italics mine. NLRB, *Decisions and Orders*, p. 777.

34. Ibid.

35. Ibid., p. 799; Eagle Picher Mining and Smelting Co.'s contract (copy), Respondent Exhibit 2, DB 833, Eagle Picher Case, NLRB.

36. *Joplin Globe*, June 7, 1935, p. 1.

37. NLRB, *Decisions and Orders*, p. 781.

38. Ibid., p. 779; Evans's contract (copy), Board Exhibit 33, DB 833, Eagle Picher Case, NLRB. Sylvan Bruner, an attorney for the International Union, later stated: "The head of the union [Tri-State Union] was a man by the name of Mike Evans, a mine operator who employed about a hundred men in the mine. And when the union and the operators rushed in to sign a contract Mike, when they had the Labor Board here, assured me with an absolutely straight face that he could represent the men honestly and impartially. If it was necessary to negotiate a contract to raise the boys' wages $2 a day, he could, as president of the company union, cheerfully arrange to take $200 a day out of his pocket and put $200 a day into the employees' pocket." International Union of Mine, Mill, and Smelter Workers, (IUMMSW) *Proceedings*, 39th Annual Convention, p. 784.

39. *Miami Daily News-Record*, June 5, 1935.

40. Ibid., June 4, 1935.

41. One observer reported seeing a "washtub full" of surrendered IUMMSW membership cards at the Tri-State Union's headquarters. NLRB, *Decisions and Orders*, p. 759, n. 54.

42. *Columbus Daily Advocate*, June 16, 1935.

43. NLRB, *Decisions and Orders*, pp. 759–60.

44. Minutes, Executive Committee, October 30, 1935 (copy), Board Exhibit 94, DB 833, Eagle Picher Case, NLRB.

45. Minutes, Executive Committee, October 23, 1935 (copy), in ibid.

46. Minutes, Executive Committee, January 21, 1936 (copy), in ibid.

47. Minutes, Executive Committee, January 14, 1936 (copy), in ibid.

48. Minutes, Executive Committee, March 10, 1936 (copy), in ibid.

49. Minutes, Executive Committee, June 23, 1936 (copy), in ibid.

50. Minutes, Executive Committee, June 9, 1936 (copy), in ibid.

51. Minutes, Cherokee Association, June 3, 1936 (copy), in ibid.

52. NLRB, *Decisions and Orders*, p. 785.

53. Bulletin Board Notice (copy), Board Exhibit 63, DB 833, Eagle Picher Case, NLRB.

54. Sheppard to MacGregor, telegram (copy), August 28, 1935, and Sheppard to MacGregor, August 28, 1935 (copy), Board Exhibit 67, in ibid.

55. Italics mine.

56. J.H. Baldwin, et al., to Sheppard, August 28, 1935 (copy), DB 833, Eagle Picher Case, NLRB.

57. NLRB, *Decisions and Orders*, p. 786.

58. J.R. MacGregor to Robert Bullard, Sept. 6, 1935 (copy), Board Exhibit 71, DB 833, Eagle Picher Case, NLRB.

59. Sheppard to MacGregor, Sept. 17, 1935 (copy), Board Exhibit 74–A, in ibid.

60. NLRB, *Decisions and Orders*, p. 787.

61. Sheppard to MacGregor, September 23, 1935 (copy), Board Exhibit 73 and Sheppard to MacGregor, September 25, 1935 (copy), Board Exhibit 80, DB 833, Eagle Picher Case, NLRB.

62. Transcription of meeting, September 25, 1935 (copy), Board Exhibit 76, in ibid.

63. Ibid., and NLRB, *Decisions and Orders*, p. 789.

64. Minutes, Executive Committee, October 30, 1935 (copy), DB 833, Eagle Picher Case, NLRB.

65. Minutes, Executive Committee, November 12, 1935 (copy), in ibid.

6. "Purged of the Horrible Stench"

1. Tri-State Metal Mine and Smelter Workers Union (T-SMMSWU) Constitution and Bylaws, Board Exhibit 32, DB 833, Eagle Picher Mining and Smelting Company, Formal and Informal Labor Practices and Representative Case Files, 1935–1948, National Labor Relations Board, Suitland, Maryland. Hereafter cited as Eagle Picher Case, NLRB. According to Hickman, Kelsey Norman "was probably the inspiration for the propaganda sheet which became the *Blue Card Record*" (formerly the *Tri-State Metal Mine & Smelter Worker* before June 6, 1936). Glenn A. Hickman, Recollections, pt. 1. Transcript in author's possession.

2. Charles Windbigler and Evans, testimony, Synopsis of Record, p. 60 and p. 14, DB 834, Eagle Picher Case, NLRB; see also National Labor Relations Board (NLRB), *Decisions and Orders*, 16 (Washington, D.C.: Government Printing Office, 1940), p. 753, n. 41.

3. Minutes, Executive Committee, August 5, 1935 (copy), Board Exhibit 34, DB 833, Eagle Picher Case, NLRB.

4. Hickman, Recollections, pt. 1; NLRB, *Decisions and Orders*, p. 753.

5. Walter Frudenberg and Evans, testimony, Synopsis of Record, p. 251 and p. 16, DB 834, Eagle Picher Case, NLRB; NLRB, *Decisions and Orders*, p. 753.

6. Minutes, Executive Committee, August 5, 1935 (copy), Board Exhibit 34, DB 834, Eagle Picher Case, NLRB.

7. Hickman, Recollections, pt. 1; Evans, testimony, Synopsis of Record, pp. 7–8, DB 834, Eagle Picher Case, NLRB.

8. Hickman, testimony, Synopsis of Record, p. 35, DB 834, Eagle Picher Case, NLRB.

9. Hickman, Recollections, pt. 1.

10. Ibid.

11. Ibid.

12. Quoted from the *Metal Mine & Smelter Worker*, May 30, 1936, p. 8.

13. Quoted in ibid., p. 2. In an interview with the author on February 5, 1981, Hickman described the *Blue Card Record* as a "house organ" that he had not thought important enough to save. Only a few copies are extant. These copies (located in the Tamiment Institute), along with the editorials that were compiled for use in the NLRB's case against the Eagle-Picher companies, and the scattered editorials found in Malcolm H. Ross, *The Death of a Yale Man* (New York: J.J. Little & Ives Co., 1939) and L.S. Davidson's *South of Joplin: Story of a Tri-State Diggin's* (New York: W.W. Norton, 1939), revealed the character of the attacks on the IUMMSW and organized labor.

14. Quoted in Davidson, *South of Joplin*, p. 209.

15. *Blue Card Record*, April 30, 1937, p. 4.

16. Ibid., June 4, 1937, p. 4.

17. Ibid., April 23, 1937, p. 4.

18. Quoted in Ross, *Death of a Yale Man*, p. 201.

19. Ibid., p. 201.

20. *Blue Card Record*, May 14, 1937, p. 5.

21. Ibid., p. 4.

22. Quoted from the *Metal Mine & Smelter Worker* in Ross, *Death of a Yale Man*, p. 198.

23. Quoted from the *Metal Mine & Smelter Worker*, Board Exhibit 172, DB 833, Eagle Picher Case, NLRB.

24. Quoted in Board Exhibit 114, DB 833, ibid.

25. Quoted from the *Blue Card Record*, Board Exhibit 192, ibid.

26. Quoted from the *Blue Card Record*, Board Exhibit 114, ibid.

27. *Blue Card Record*, April 9, 1937, p. 1.

28. Hickman, Recollections, pt. 1.

29. Quoted in NLRB, *Decisions and Orders*, pp. 757–58.

30. Quoted in Ross, *Death of a Yale Man*, p. 199. The IUMMSW

also had its "literary" supporters; however, the circulation of such anti–Tri-State Union pieces as the following was limited.

The local union—pray what is that?
'Tis a scabby gang led by a rat,
They have a den where Mike can snooze,
while the rest of the rats lick his shoes.

"Join our union" lied old Mike,
"We will den together and break the strike."
Ex-convict, bootlegger, liar and thief, he
sneers at the widow woman on relief—The
widows whose husbands have lost their lives
working in the mines to support their wives.
They work in the mines for two dollars or three,
And died a slow death of miners' T. B.
Now, we of the A.F. of L. wouldn't stand for that—
to work and go hungry while the operators get fat.

We will get good wages or they can rot in hell
And we will stick by the A.F. of L.

Quoted in Davidson, *South of Joplin*, pp. 148–49.

31. Ross, *Death of a Yale Man*, p. 199.

32. See chapter 8.

33. Minutes, Executive Committee, April 28, 1936 (copy), DB 833, Eagle Picher Case, NLRB.

34. *Metal Mine & Smelter Worker*, May 30, 1936, p. 1.

35. My account of the picnics relies heavily on the following sources: the *Metal Mine & Smelter Worker*, May 30, 1936; the *Blue Card Record*, May 14 and June 4, 1937; and the *Miami* (Oklahoma) *Daily News-Record*, May 24, 26, 27, 28, 1936; and May 23, 26, 27, 1937.

36. *Metal Mine & Smelter Worker*, May 30, 1936, p. 5.

37. Ibid.

38. See chapter 8 where the affiliation is discussed in detail.

39. *Miami Daily News-Record*, May 27, 1937, pp. 1–2.

40. Minutes, Executive Committee, October 30, 1935 (copy), Board Exhibit 94, DB 833, Eagle Picher Case, NLRB.

41. Minutes, Cherokee Subordinate Association, October 30, 1935 (copy), Board Exhibit 39, in ibid.

42. Ibid., November 6, 1935.

43. Ibid., November 20, 1935.

44. See chapter 6.

45. See Balance Sheet, T-SMMSWU, September 30, 1935 (copy), Board Exhibit 204, DB 833, Eagle Picher Case, NLRB.

46. Ibid., and Minutes, Executive Committee, Aug. 5, 1935 (copy), Board Exhibit 34, DB 833, Eagle Picher Case, NLRB.

47. See Balance Sheet, T-SMMSWU, September 30, 1935 (copy), Board Exhibit 204, in ibid.

48. Ibid.

49. Minutes, Executive Committee, November 12, 1935 (copy), in ibid.

50. Ibid.

51. Minutes, Executive Committee, September 18, 1935 (copy), Board Exhibit 38, in ibid.

52. Ibid.

53. Minutes, Executive Committee, April 28, 1936 (copy), in ibid.

54. Updated Charlie Anderson Memo (cir. July 1, 1936), in ibid.

55. Minutes, Cherokee Subordinate Association, November 6, 1936 (copy), in ibid.

56. Minutes, Executive Committee, July 10, 1936 (copy), in ibid.

57. Ibid., October 30, 1935.

58. Ibid., January 14, 1936 (copy), Board Exhibit 95.

59. Ibid., January 21, 1936.

60. See Balance Sheet, T-SMMSWU, September 30, 1935 (copy), Board Exhibit 204, in ibid.

61. Minutes, Executive Committee, July 10, 1936 (copy), in ibid.

62. Ibid., August 31, 1937, Board Exhibit 98a.

63. See Balance Sheet, T-SMMSWU, September 30, 1935, Board Exhibit 204, in ibid.

64. See case of Lloyd Ray in Minutes, Executive Committee (copy), Board Exhibit 94, in ibid.

65. Ibid., May 5, 1936.

66. Ibid.

67. *Metal Mine & Smelter Worker*, May 30, 1936, p. 8.

7. "Heads . . . Bouncing Off the Cudgels"

1. Cyrus Slater to George O. Pratt, September 30, 1937, Informal Files, Eagle Picher Mining and Smelting Company, Formal and Informal Labor Practices and Representative Case Files, 1935–1948, National Labor Relations Board, Suitland, Maryland. Hereafter cited as Eagle Picher Case, NLRB.

2. National Labor Relations Board (NLRB), *Decisions and Orders*, 16 (Washington, D.C.: Government Printing Office, 1940), p. 862.

3. Ibid., p. 859.

4. Ibid., p. 854.

5. Ibid., pp. 839–78.

6. Ibid., p. 842.

7. Ibid., p. 845.

8. Ibid., p. 846.

9. Ibid., p. 848.

10. Ibid., p. 850.

11. Ibid., p. 852.

12. Ibid., pp. 839–78.

13. Ibid., p. 851.

14. Ibid., p. 863.

15. Ibid., p. 841.

16. Ibid., p. 862.

17. *Kansas City* (Missouri) *Star*, May 17, 1935, p. 1; *Joplin* (Missouri) *Globe*, May 18, 1935, p. 1.

18. Bell quoted in the *Columbus* (Kansas) *Daily Advocate*, June 11, 1935; see also the Baxter Springs, Kansas, *Citizen and Herald*, June 13, 1935.

19. NLRB, *Decisions and Orders*, pp. 777–78.

20. Kansas, Commission of Labor and Industry, *Annual Report* (Topeka: State Printers, 1935), p. 72.

21. Thomas Crowe, president, Kansas State Federation of Labor, to Landon, July 24, 1935; Landon to Crowe, July 26, 1935; Landon to Crowe, July 27, 1935, in Governors Papers—Alfred M. Landon, Kansas State Historical Society; also, see Donald R. McCoy, *Landon of Kansas* (Lincoln: University of Nebraska Press, 1965), p. 195.

22. Christensen, Activity Report, July 29, 1935, Landon Papers, KSHS.

23. Christensen to author, August 3, 1975.

24. M.D. Harbaugh, "Labor Relations in the Tri-State Mining District," *Mining Congress Journal*, 22 (June 1936): 24.

25. George O. Pratt to Tony McTeer, September 4, 1936; McTeer to Pratt, September 5, 1936, Informal Files, Eagle Picher Case, NLRB.

26. McTeer to Pratt, September 5, 1936, in ibid.

27. See chapter 8 for a discussion of the impact that the rise of the CIO and the split in the labor movement had on the unionization of labor in the Tri-State.

28. *Joplin Globe*, April 11, 1937, p. 1; Pratt to NLRB, September 13, 1937; Cyrus Slater to Pratt, September 30, 1937; Daniel House to Pratt, September 29, 1937, Informal Files, Eagle Picher Case, NLRB.

29. Quoted in NLRB, *Decisions and Orders*, pp. 764–65; also, Frank Leuty, testimony, Synopsis of Record, pp. 111–12, DB 834, Eagle Picher Case, NLRB.

30. House to Pratt, September 29, 1937, Informal Files, in ibid.

31. Ray Keller, testimony, Synopsis of Record, p. 87, DB 834, in ibid.

32. Reid Robinson, testimony, Synopsis of Record, p. 75, in ibid.

33. Slater to Pratt, September 30, 1937, Informal Files, in ibid.

34. Quoted in *Miami* (Oklahoma) *Daily News-Record*, April 16, 1975.

35. Hugh Arnold and Edward O. Edwards, testimony, Synopsis of Record, p. 157 and p. 211, DB 834, Eagle Picher Case, NLRB.

36. Lester E. Wakefield and Orville Stever, testimony, Synopsis of Record, pp. 91–92, in ibid.

37. Frank Leuty, testimony, Synopsis of Record, pp. 111–12, in ibid.

38. *Blue Card Record*, April 16, 1937, p. 1.

39. Reid Robinson, testimony, Synopsis of Record, p. 75, DB 834, Eagle Picher Case, NLRB.

40. *Joplin Globe*, April 13, 1937, p. 3.

41. Dee T. Watters, testimony, Synopsis of Record, p. 72, DB 834, Eagle Picher Case, NLRB.

42. Ted Schasteen, testimony, Synopsis of Record, p. 167, in ibid.

43. Marvin C. Forrest, testimony, Synopsis of Record, p. 56, in ibid.

44. Quoted in *Joplin Globe*, April 13, 1937, p. 3.

45. See Pratt to NLRB, September 13, 1937; House to Pratt, September 29, 1937; Slater to Pratt, September 30, 1937, Informal Files, Eagle Picher Case, NLRB.

46. J.S. Parker to Clarence Beck ("Report on Investigation of Mob Violence in the City of Galena, Kansas"), ca. April 15, 1937, File No. 37, "Labor Laws, 1936–1939," Attorney General Papers, Archives Division, KSHS.

47. *Joplin Globe*, April 13, 1937, p. 3.

48. Ibid.

49. Pratt to NLRB, September 13, 1937, Slater to Pratt, September 30, 1937, House to Pratt, September 29, 1937, Informal Files, Eagle Picher Case, NLRB; J.S. Parker to Clarence V. Beck, ca. April 15, 1937, File No. 37, Attorney General Papers, KSHS; E.B. Morgan to Walter A. Huxman, April 14, 1937, in Labor Department Files, Governor Walter A. Huxman Papers, Archives Division, KSHS.

50. House to Pratt, September 29, 1937, Informal Files, Eagle Picher Case, NLRB.

51. Morgan to Huxman, April 14, 1937, in Huxman Papers, KSHS.

52. Quoted in *Topeka* (Kansas) *Daily Capital*, April 12, 1937.

53. Quoted in unidentified clipping, no date, in R.M. McClintock Collection, Division of Archives Department of Libraries, Oklahoma; see also the *Galena* (Kansas) *Times Republican*, April 16, 1937.

54. Morgan to Huxman, April 14, 1937, in Huxman Papers, KSHS.

55. *Topeka Daily Capital*, April 12, 1937.

56. Parker to Beck, ca. April 15, 1937, File No. 37, Attorney General Papers, KSHS.

57. The IUMMSW received permission from Baxter Springs authorities to hold a meeting in July, but when Evans threatened to hold a counterdemonstration, they withdrew it, thereby cancelling the meeting. Elmer Dean (telegram) to Beck, July 23, 1937, in ibid.

58. Parker to Beck, ca. April 15, 1937, in ibid.

59. *Blue Card Record*, April 30, 1937, p. 1; *Galena-Times Republican*, April 30, 1937.

60. See State of Kansas v. Ed. Berry, Order of Dismissal, February 20, 1939, Informal Files, Eagle Picher Case, NLRB.

61. Cyrus Slater to Hugh E. Sperry, October 10, 1939, in ibid.

8. "We Are Yet Blue Carders"

1. Schechter Poultry Corporation v. United States, 295 U.S. 495 (1935).

2. National Labor Relations Act, *United States Statutes at Large*, ch. 372, 49 (Washington, D.C.: Government Printing Office, 1936), 449–457.

3. *Kansas City* (Missouri) *Star*, July 19, 1935; Malcolm H. Ross, *The Death of a Yale Man* (New York: J.J. Little & Ives Co., 1939), p. 196.

4. *Miami* (Oklahoma) *Daily News-Record*, December 22, 1935, pp. 1–2.

5. Ibid.; Ross, *Death of a Yale Man*, pp. 178–81; Pratt to McTeer, August 23, 1936, Informal Files, Eagle Picher Mining and Smelting Company, Formal and Informal Labor Practices and Representative Case Files, 1935–1948, National Labor Relations Board, Suitland, Maryland. Herefter cited as Eagle Picher Case, NLRB.

6. See McTeer, "Charge," March 25, 1936, Informal Files, Eagle Picher Case, NLRB.

7. See Eagle Picher Lead Co., Eagle Picher Mining & Smelting Co. v. J. Warren Madden (Original Bill of Complaints), May 22, 1936, in ibid.

8. See Eagle Picher v. J. Warren Madden (Temporary Restraining Order), May 23, 1936, in ibid. For the lawyers' briefs, transcripts of

testimony, and the NLRB's correspondence and memoranda concerning the early stages of the investigation of the complaints of the International Union against the Eagle Picher companies, see ibid., passim.

9. Quoted in the *Miami Daily News-Record*, May 25, 1936, p. 1.

10. *Metal Mine & Smelter Worker*, May 30, 1936, p. 1.

11. N.L.R.B. v. Jones & Laughlin Steel Corp., 301 U.S. 1 (1937).

12. There are many good secondary accounts concerning these developments; however, the split in the labor movement over the issue of craft versus industrial unionism can best be followed in the AFL's *Report of Proceedings*, vols. 54–58 (Washington: Judd & Detweiler, 1934–1938), passim, and in the CIO's *Proceedings*, vols. 1–3 (Pittsburgh, San Francisco, and Atlantic City: n.p., 1938–1940), passim.

13. Quoted in the *Blue Card Record*, April 16, 1937, p. 1.

14. Ibid., April 27, 1937, p. 1.

15. J.S. Parker to Clarence V. Beck, ca. April 12, 1937, File No. 37, Attorney General Papers, Kansas State Historical Society.

16. *Oklahoma Federationist* (Oklahoma City), April 1937, p. 1.

17. *Columbus* (Kansas) *Daily Advocate*, April 16, 1937.

18. In his presidential address to the Oklahoma State Federation of Labor in 1935, Warren observed: "It [the IUMMSW strike] has been a long, bitter struggle. Most of these men are new in labor organizations but I have never seen better loyalty displayed by them under the most adverse conditions. They have suffered every indignity known by the exploiting employers and have been menaced and abused by professional gunmen, strikebreakers and thugs. Men sworn to uphold the law have used that authority to beat and slug the union men. Ten union men are now bound over on felony charges for trial in the district court of that county [Ottawa], and it is my honest opinion that a fair and impartial jury would not be had in that county who would give them a fair trial." *Oklahoma Federationist*, October 1935, p. 3.

19. Ibid., April 1937, p. 1.

20. Editorial, the *Blue Card Record*, June 4, 1937, Board Exhibit 167, DB 833, Eagle Picher Case, NLRB.

21. National Labor Relations Board (NLRB), *Decisions and Orders*, 16 (Washington, D.C.: Government Printing Office, 1940), pp. 766–67.

22. Quoted in ibid., p. 768, and in testimony, Synopsis of Record, p. 48, DB 834, Eagle Picher Case, NLRB.

23. Quoted in NLRB, *Decisions and Orders*, p. 768.

24. Respondent Exhibit 8–A, DB 833, Eagle Picher Case, NLRB. An editorial in the *Blue Card Record* on May 17, 1937 emphasized

that little had changed. It stated: "Technically we are now operating under the general policy laid down by the American Federation of Labor; really we are still the Blue Card Union in every respect and as such we intend to remain. If the recently negotiated affiliation means the sacrifice of a single iota of the confidence we have established with the employers of this district, it is better that we repent of our action and fight to the end as an independent union."

25. NLRB, *Decisions and Orders*, p. 768.

26. Quoted in *Columbus Daily Advocate*, April 23, 1937.

27. Quoted in ibid., April 24, 1937.

28. Quoted in ibid., April 23 and 24, 1937; see also the *Blue Card Record*, April 23 and 30, 1937. The affiliation, which was mutually self-serving, confirmed a conclusion of J. Raymond Walsh who wrote: "It is the use of the A.F.L., however, that appeals to the anti-union employer. For the C.I.O. represents in his mind the gravest threat. He sees the C.I.O. as militant, radically, genuinely pro-labor. By comparison the A.F. of L. is not only the lesser of two evils, but a possible ally against the labor movement. In this he calculates shrewdly—for the personal hatreds engendered among the A.F. of L. leaders toward their late associates of the C.I.O. have become in many cases more important to them than devotion to the workers' cause." *C.I.O.: Industrial Unionism in Action* (New York: W.W. Norton & Co., 1937), p. 214.

29. *Blue Card Record*, April 23, 1937, p. 1.

30. Respondent Exhibit 12–A, DB 833, Eagle Picher Case, NLRB.

31. Respondent Exhibit 13–A, ibid.

32. See Constitution and Bylaws, Blue Card Union, Board Exhibit 128, in ibid.

33. Certificate of Affiliation, Respondent Exhibit 15, and Minutes, Executive Committee, June 15, 1937, in ibid.

34. In discussing this convention with the author, Hickman recalled that he had also attended and that he had been appointed to a subcommittee to study the problem of silicosis. According to Hickman, the abysmal ignorance of committeemen, especially the chairman, concerning the problem further confirmed his belief that unions were useless in resolving such matters. The author, however, has found no corroborating evidence that Hickman attended the convention. Interview with Glenn Hickman, February 5, 1981; also, Glenn A. Hickman, Recollections, pt. 1. Transcript in author's possession.

35. See American Federation of Labor, *Report of Proceedings of the Fifty-seventh Annual Convention*, 57 (Washington: Judd & Detweiler, 1937), pp. xvi, xxii, 49, 54.

36. Ibid., p. 113.
37. NLRB, *Decisions and Orders*, pp. 768–69.
38. Ibid., p. 766.
39. AFL, *Report of Proceedings*, 57th Annual Convention, p. 113.
40. Ibid., pp. 229, 372–74.
41. Hickman, Recollections, pt. 2.
42. NLRB, *Decisions and Orders*, pp. 752–74.
43. Avrutis to Watts, November 11, 1937, Informal Files, Eagle Picher Case, NLRB.
44. Avrutis to George O. Pratt, October 14, 1937, in ibid.
45. Quoted in "Outline," in ibid.
46. *Blue Card Record*, December 3, 1937, p. 1.
47. Ibid.
48. Ibid.
49. Avrutis to Friend Effie, April 30, 1938, Informal Files, Eagle Picher Case, NLRB.
50. NLRB, *Decisions and Orders*, pp. 727–882.
51. Ibid., pp. 774–75.
52. Ibid., p. 775.
53. Eagle Picher Mining & Smelting Co. v. National Labor Relations Board (International Union of Mine, Mill & Smelter Workers, Locals No. 15, 17, 107, 108, 111, Interveners), 119 F. 2d 903 (1941).
54. Eagle Picher Mining & Smelting Co. v. National Labor Relations Board (International Union of Mine, Mill & Smelter Workers, Locals No. 15, et al., (Interveners), 141 F. 2d 843 (1944).
55. International Union of Mine, Mill & Smelter Workers v. Eagle Picher Mining & Smelting Co., Eagle Picher Lead Co., & National Labor Relations Board, 325 U.S. 335 (1945).
56. See the Formal and Informal Files, Eagle Picher Case, NLRB, for the complete and voluminous records of this case.
57. Paul F. Broderick to Nathan Witt, December 22, 1938, Informal Files, in ibid.

9. "A Most Tragic Price"

1. See, for example, *In re* Tri-State Zinc, Inc., & International Union of Mine, Mill & Smelter Workers, Locals Nos. 15, 17, 107, 108 & 111, Affiliated with the C.I.O. in NLRB, *Decisions and Orders*, 39 (Washington, D.C.: Government Printing Office, 1942), 1095–1107.
2. See U.S., Department of Labor, *Conference on Health, and Working Conditions in the Tri-State District, Joplin, Missouri, April 23, 1940* (Washington, D.C.: Department of Labor, 1940), passim, and Tri-

State Survey Committee, Inc., *A Preliminary Report on Living, Working, and Health Conditions in the Tri-State Mining Area (Missouri, Oklahoma, and Kansas)* (New York: Tri-State Survey Committees Inc., 1939), passim.

3. *Blue Card Record*, May 7, 1937, p. 4.

4. U.S., Department of Labor, *Conference on Health*, pp. 35–36.

5. Ibid., p. 36.

6. Ibid.

7. See *In re* Eagle-Picher Mining & Smelting Company, p. 135, DB 158, Eagle Picher Mining and Smelting Company, Formal and Informal Labor Practices and Representative Case Files, 1935–1948, National Labor Relations Board, Suitland, Maryland. Hereafter cited as Eagle Picher Case, NLRB.

8. *Blue Card Record*, May 7, 1937, p. 1.

9. Ibid., June 4, 1937, p. 1.

10. Ibid., December 3, 1937, p. 4.

11. Ibid.

12. Daniel Nelson, "The Company Union Movement, 1900–1937: A Re-examination," *Business History Review*, 46 (Autumn 1982): 335–36.

13. Ibid., pp. 338–39.

14. See correspondence in Formal and Informal Files, passim, Eagle Picher Case, NLRB.

15. For an example of this tendency, see George G. Suggs, Jr., *Colorado's War on Militant Unionism: James H. Peabody and the Western Federation of Miners* (Detroit: Wayne State University Press, 1972), passim.

16. U.S., Department of Labor, *Characteristics of Company Unions 1935*, Bulletin No. 634, by Florence Peterson (Washington, D.C.: Government Printing Office, 1938), p. 3.

17. Thomas R. Brooks, *Toil and Trouble: A History of American Labor* (New York: Delacorte Press, 1971), p. 190, and Joseph G. Rayback, *A History of American Labor* (New York: The MacMillan Co., 1959), p. 343.

18. Tri-State Survey Committee, *A Preliminary Report*, n.p.

19. Ibid.

20. Garrison Firm Distributors, Inc., New York, 1939.

21. U.S., Department of Labor, *Conference on Health*, p. 19.

22. Ibid., p. 28.

23. *Saint Louis* (Missouri) *Post-Dispatch*, April 28, 1940, "Pictures," p. 3.

24. U.S., Department of Labor, *Conference on Health*, pp. 39–40.

25. Glenn A. Hickman, Recollections, pt. 2. Transcript in author's possession.

26. Ibid., pt. 1.
27. Interview with Hickman, February 5, 1981.
28. See chapter 3.
29. Hickman, Recollections, pt. 1.
30. IUMMSW, *Proceedings*, 39th Annual Convention, 1942, pp. 783–94.

Epilogue

1. U.S., Department of Labor, Bureau of Labor Statistics, *Wage Structure in the Nonferrous Metals Industry, 1941–1942* Bulletin No. 729 (Washington, D.C.: Government Printing Office, 1943), pp. 5–6.
2. U.S., Department of Labor, Bureau of Labor Statistics, *Wages in the Nonferrous-Metals Industry, June 1943*, Bulletin No. 765 (Washington, D.C.: Government Printing Office, 1944), p. 7.
3. Ibid., p. 5.
4. See William James Cassidy, "The Tri-State Zinc, Lead Mining Region: Growth, Problems, and Prospects" (Ph.D. dissertation, University of Pittsburgh, 1955), pp. 285–305.
5. IUMMSW, *Proceedings*, 37th Annual Convention, 1940, p. 118.
6. Ibid., p. 119.
7. Ibid., 40th Annual Convention, 1943, p. 167.
8. Ibid., 43rd Annual Convention, 1947, p. 108.
9. Ibid., 39th Annual Convention, 1942, p. 100.
10. Ibid., 41st Annual Convention, 1944, p. 60.
11. Ibid., 39th Annual Convention, 1942, p. 97.
12. Ibid., 41st Annual Convention, 1944, p. 57.
13. Ibid., 42d Annual Convention, 1946, p. 238.
14. Ibid., 38th Annual Convention, 1941, p. 126.
15. Elwood Hain and Howard Mooney to Members, Local No. 861, March 19, 1949, Elwood Hain Folder, Box 95, International Representatives' Reports, 1949, Western Federation of Miners and Mine-Mill Collection, Western Historical Collections, University of Colorado, Boulder. Hereafter cited as WFM & MM, WHC.
16. Sadler to Clark, February 2, 1947, Box 135, Pres.–Local Corresp. 1944–1947, Local 861, Eagle Picher Mine and Millmen's Union, WFM & MM, WHC.
17. See "Comparison of Union Demands and Company Counter Proposals on Issues in Disputes," in ibid.
18. Sadler, et al., to Members, Local No. 861 (undated), in ibid.
19. See exchange of telegrams and letters between William A. Timms, president of Local No. 861, and M.E. Travis, secretary-

treasurer, IUMMSW, July 22, 1948 to August 23, 1948, Box 142, Secretary-Treasurer and Local Union Correspondence, July 1942–June 1950, in WFM & MM, WHC.

20. Elwood Hain William Timms, Bulletin (undated), Box 44, Vice Pres. [Reid] Robinson, 1948, Misc. General Files, Locals, Staff Canadian Trip, Deportations, in ibid.

21. B.M. Fithian to M.E. Travis, July 19, 1948, Folder 38–Hain, Elwood, Box 82, Secretary-Treasurer, Staff Correspondence, in ibid.

22. See "Why 2,000 Miners and Millmen Are Unemployed," Box 44, in ibid.

23. Howard Lee, Elwood Hain, and Howard Mooney to M.E. Travis, November 19, 1948, Howard Mooney Folder, Box 83, Secretary-Treasurer, Staff Correspondence, 1948–1950, in ibid.

24. Ibid.

25. Linus Wampler to John Clark, president of IUMMSW, ca. June 12, 1949, Linus Wampler Folder, Box 83, in ibid.

26. Howard Mooney and Elwood Hain to Local No. 861 Membership, March 19, 1949, Howard Mooney Folder, Box 95, in ibid.

27. Hain to Douglas, October 20, 1948, Folder 72, Elwood Hain—General, Box 44, in ibid., and Hain, Howard Mooney, and Howard Lee to M.E. Travis, November 19, 1948, Howard Mooney Folder, Box 83, in ibid.

28. Timms to Clark, October 27, 1948, Box 142, in ibid.

29. M.E. Travis to Howard Mooney, December 17, 1948, Howard Mooney Folder, Box 83, in ibid.

30. Hain, Semi-Monhly Reports, January 31, 1949, Elwood B. Hain Folder, Box 95, in ibid.

31. Mooney, Semi-Monthly Reports, February 15, 1949, Howard Mooney Folder, Box 95, in ibid.

32. Mooney, Semi-Monthly Reports, March 15, 1949, in ibid.

33. Hain, Semi-Monthly Reports, March 15, 1949, Elwood B. Hain Folder, Box 95, in ibid.

34. Mooney, Semi-Monthly Reports, March 31, 1949, Howard Mooney Folder, Box 95, in ibid.

35. Hain, Semi-Monthly Reports, April 15, 1949, Elwood B. Hain Folder, Box 95, in ibid.

36. Mooney, Semi-Monthly Reports, April 30, 1949, Howard Mooney Folder, Box 95, in ibid.

37. Hain, Semi-Monthly Reports, April 30, 1949, Elwood B. Hain Folder, Box 95, ibid.

38. Mooney, Semi-Monthly Reports, May 15, 1949, Howard Mooney Folder, Box 95, in ibid.

39. Linus Wampler to John Clark, et al., June 12, 1949, Linus Wampler Folder, Box 83, in ibid.

40. Ibid.

41. Ibid., and Mooney, Semi-Monthly Reports, May 31, 1949, Howard Mooney Folder, Box 95, in ibid.

42. Wampler to Clark, et al., June 12, 1949, Linus Wampler Folder, Box 83, in ibid.

43. Ibid.

44. Ibid.

45. Mooney, Semi-Monthly Reports, May 31, 1949, Howard Mooney Folder, Box 95, in ibid.

46. Mooney, Semi-Monthly Reports, June 15, June 30, and July 15, 1949, in ibid.

47. Linus Wampler to John Clark, June 8, 1949, Linus Wampler Folder, Box 83, in ibid.

48. Mooney, Semi-Monthly Reports, August 31, 1949, Howard Mooney Folder, Box 95, in ibid.

49. Mooney, Semi-Monthly Reports, August 15, 1949, in ibid.

50. Arrell M. Gibson, *Wilderness Bonanza: The Tri-State District of Missouri, Kansas and Oklahoma* (Norman: University of Oklahoma Press, 1972) pp. 266–73.

51. "Who's Who on the List," *EPA Journal*, 10 (November-December 1981): 14–15.

Essay on the Sources

Indispensable to this study of the lead and zinc workers' strike in the Tri-State Mining District were the Eagle Picher Mining and Smelter Company Case Files (Formal and Informal Practices and Representatives Files, 1935–1948) located in the holdings of the National Labor Relations Board (NLRB) (Federal Records Center, Suitland, Maryland). Because archivists there concluded that the Eagle Picher case was one of the most important involvements of the NLRB during its formative years, they have retained nearly all the materials generated by the case. In addition to the official record concerning the complaints of the International Union of Mine, Mill, and Smelter Workers' locals, which included over ten thousand pages of testimony before the trial examiner and most of the exhibits presented by counsel for Eagle Picher and the NLRB, the case files contained the correspondence between George O. Pratt, director of Region 17 where the IUMMSW complaints originated, and the Washington office, between Pratt and his field examiners, between Pratt and the NLRB attorneys assigned to investigate the complaints, between Pratt and local IUMMSW officials like Tony McTeer, and all the informal memoranda, legal briefs, working summaries, and so on. This material was in excellent condition and was unusually revealing about the role of the companies in the strike, the internal workings of the Blue Card Union, the posture of the NLRB in the labor unrest, the uncertain state of labor-management relations in the thirties, and the myriad relationships between the involved parties to the dispute.

The Western Federation of Miners and Mine-Mill Collection (WFM & MM), which is housed in the Western Historical Collections at the University of Colorado, Boulder Campus, contained surprisingly little about the 1935 strike of the Tri-State metal workers. Although containing important pieces of source materials, such as the *Official Proceedings* and the Minutes, Executive

Board, the WFM & MM Collection was not as rich concerning, for example, the organizing of the Tri-State and the strength of the local unions, as expected. The records of Locals 15, 17, 107, 108, and 111 were missing because stolen or destroyed in the riots of April 1937. For the forties, however, the WFM & MM Collection contains much information about the last years of the union in the district. The records include semimonthly reports from international representatives, exchanges of correspondence between local and national leaders, scattered copies of the *Tri-State Miner*, *The Union*, handbills, and fliers. A search continues for records pertaining to the International Union.

A major collection that offers unlimited opportunities for studying the economic development of the Tri-State Mining District are the papers of the Tri-State Zinc and Lead Ore Producers' Association acquired by the Picher, Oklahoma, Museum in 1981. These papers comprehensively chart most of the work of the association from its origin to its demise. They contain invaluable production records for each of its members, complete records of accidents (type, cause, treatment) in each member mine and mill, records of its lobbying activities at the state and national level, industrial maps of the district, the medical records (including x-rays) of workers examined by the Picher clinic during the twenties and the thirties, and other materials pertaining to the district. Unfortunately, the collection contained little information about the strike and labor relations of the thirties, unless in the Minutes of the Executive Committee, which were not available. Nevertheless, it is a bonanza of source materials for future research.

The papers of the Blue Card Union, except those that were incorporated into the official records of the NLRB's Eagle Picher case, have apparently been destroyed. Glenn A. Hickman, secretary-treasurer of the union, professed ignorance concerning the fate of the records, which would have been unusually useful to this study. The records of the NLRB, however, substantially offset this loss.

Useful in examining the role of the state in the strike were the papers of the various governors of Oklahoma, Kansas, and Missouri who held office during the labor unrest. Of these papers, those of Alfred M. Landon of Kansas (Kansas State Historical Society) were the most complete and therefore most useful in revealing the role of the state in the Kansas portion of the Tri-State. Included were the reports of Colonel Charles H. Browne,

Landon's field commander, and Major Ellis G. Christensen concerning military operations in Cherokee County. Unfortunately, a portion of the Landon Papers, which might have provided additional insight about the decision to intervene, was closed to the author. The files of Attorney General Clarence V. Beck were not instructive concerning his role in Landon's decision to intervene following the disturbance at the Beck Tailing Mill. The papers of Governor Walter Huxman, who succeeded Landon (Labor Department Files), contained little to explain the reasons for his failure to send troops following the outbreak of violence in Treece and Galena in April 1937.

Concerning the strike, the papers of Governor Ernest W. Marland (Division of State Archives, Department of Libraries, Oklahoma) were disappointing, especially because of the crucial military involvement of his administration. Little information was found in the governor's files to explain his decsion to send the National Guard in May 1935 and not to send it in April 1937. And in Missouri, the papers of Governors Guy B. Park and Lloyd C. Stark (Western History Manuscript Collection, State Historical Society of Missouri) contained only scattered references to the strike, probably because the major strike activities were in Oklahoma and Kansas. Nevertheless, the absence of substantial material about this major labor upheaval in the Tri-State suggested the low priority that Missouri's governors placed upon the strike.

Because of the large number of striking workers, the sizable territory and the vital industry involved, one might expect a great many references to the strike in municipal and county records. This was not the case, however, The Minutes of the Cherokee County (Kansas) Board of Commissioners (Volumes P, Q, R, 1935–1948) have only scattered but useful references to the strike; the Baxter Springs Record of Council Proceedings (1935–1938) has none; the Galena Clerk's Record (volume 7) provided little usable information. Treece no longer exists as an active municipality with records maintenance. In Oklahoma, the Records (volumes 5 and 6) of the Ottawa County Board of Commissioners contained surprisingly little concerning the labor troubles around Picher. And for the strike period, the municipal records of Picher, the center of the labor unrest, have been lost or misplaced. At Commerce, located near Picher, the Minutes of the City Council were silent about the strike. Cardin exists but had no records of this era. Local records in Missouri provided even less information than those of Oklahoma and Kansas. Volumes 55–57 of the Minutes of the Jasper County Court (the equivalent of the Board of County Commissioners in Oklahoma and Kansas) did not refer to the strike. In Webb City, the Minutes of the City Council for the strike period (1935–1938) were missing. Volumes K and H (1928–1942) of the Minutes of the Council indicated that officials of Joplin refrained from any formal involvement. Of course, the absence of references to the strike in county and municipal records obscured the active role that some local officials played.

In this study of the lead and zinc workers strike, several federal documents were invaluable. Of singular importance were the orders and decisions rendered by the National Labor Relations Board. Foremost among these is Case No. C–73, *In re Eagle-Picher Mining & Smelting Company, a Corporation*, and *Eagle-Picher Lead Company, A Corporation*, and *International Union of Mine, Mill & Smelter Workers, Locals 15, 17, 107, 108, and 111* in *Decisions and Orders of the National Labor Relations Board*, volume 16 (Washington, D.C.: Government Printing Office, 1940). This document was principally a modified expansion of the intermediate report of the NLRB's trial examiner who presided at the hearings of IUMMSW complaints in 1937 and 1938 at Joplin. *In re Eagle Picher* drew heavily upon the official record and informal papers found in the Eagle Picher Case Files in the NLRB archives. Much of what has been written heretofore about the strike has relied substantially upon this document. Although less useful, Case No. C–2130, *In re Tri-State Zinc, Inc., A Corporation*, and *International Union of Mine, Mill & Smelter Workers, Locals Nos. 15, 17, 107, 108 and 111, Affiliated with the C.I.O.* (ibid., volume 39 [Washington, D.C.: Government Printing Office, 1942]) should also be consulted in conjunction with the prior NLRB order of 1939.

Much factual information about the strike and the role of the Eagle Picher companies can be found in the decisions of the federal courts concerning the enforcement of the NLRB's order of 1939 relating to IUMMSW complaints. These decisions were also useful in demonstrating the intermeshing of responsibilities between the NLRB and the federal courts which was required to make the National Labor Relations Act effective in the immediate years following its enactment. The more important of these decisions were: *N.L.R.B.* v. *Jones & Laughlin Steel Corporation*, 301 U.S. 1 (1937); *Lyons et al.* v. *Eagle Picher Lead Co., et al.*, 90 F.R. 2d

321 (1937); *Eagle Picher Mining & Smelting Co., et al.*, v. *National Labor Relations Board (International Union of Mine, Mill, & Smelter Workers, Locals 15, 17, 107, 108, 111 (Interveners)*, 119 F. 2d 903 (1941); *Eagle Picher Mining & Smelting Co., et al.* v. *National Labor Relations Board (International Union of Mine, Mill, & Smelter Workers, Locals 15, et al., Interveners)*, 141 F. 2d 843 (1944); *International Union of Mine, Mill, & Smelter Workers* v. *Eagle Picher Mining & Smelting Co., Eagle Picher Lead Co., & National Labor Relations Board*, 325 U.S. 335 (1945). The legal challenges of Eagle Picher to the NLRB's order prohibiting further unfair labor practices and providing awards to workers victimized by earlier violations can be followed in these cases.

Industrial health problems were mammoth in the Tri-State and attracted federal attention as early as the second decade of this century. Dr. Alice Hamilton, an early pioneer in occupational disease, included the Tri-State in her early investigations of lead poisoning. (Bureau of Labor, *Lead Poisoning in the Smelting and Refining of Lead*, Bulletin No. 141 [Washington, D.C.: Government Printing Office, 1914]). Frederick Hoffman's *Deaths from Lead Poisoning, 1925–1927*, (ibid., Bulletin No. 488 [Washington, D.C.: Government Printing Office, 1929]) also drew data from the Tri-State.

Although lead poisoning was an early problem in the district, silicosis complicated by tuberculosis became the great scourge of workers, making the district a deadly place to live and work. Several federal investigations focused on the Tri-State, from which came several important—and revealing—reports on the ravages of the disease among the miners and millmen. These reports contain extremely useful information pertaining to the lives of the workers in matters other than health. *Miners Consumption: A Study of 433 Cases of the Disease Among Zinc Miners in Southwestern Missouri* (Treasury Department, Public Health Bulletin No. 85 [Washington, D.C.: Government Printing Office, 1917] and *Siliceous Dust in Relation to Pulmonary Disease among Miners in the Joplin District, Missouri* (Bureau of Mines, Bulletin No. 132 [Washington, D.C.: Government Printing Office, 1917]), exposed the gravity of the silicosis problem.

But it was a more extensive, systematic five-year study of the workers in the district between 1927 and 1932 that revealed the devastating impact of the disease. From this investigation, jointly sponsored by the U.S. Bureau of Mines, the Metropolitan Life Insurance Company, and the Tri-State Zinc and Lead Ore Pro-

ducers' Association, came two reports by the Bureau of Mines
(*Silicosis and Tuberculosis among Miners of the Tri-State District of
Oklahoma, Kansas, and Missouri—I & II*, Technical Papers Nos.
545 and 552 [Washington, D.C.: Government Printing Office,
1933]), which were essential to understanding the wretched
health conditions endured by the workers and their families. A
summary of the results of these studies was published as the *National Silicosis Conference, Report on Medical Control: Final Report of
the Committee on the Prevention of Silicosis through Medical Control*
(Bureau of Mines, Bulletin No. 21, Pt. I [Washington, D.C.: Government Printing Office, 1938]). Although not the result of a sci-
entific investigation, the *Conference on Health and Working Conditions in the Tri-State District, Joplin, Missouri, April 23, 1940*
(Mimeograph, Department of Labor, Division of Standards)
was extremely valuable in demonstrating the interrelationship
among poor housing, poor health conditions, and the lack of
medical facilities in the Tri-State. It also contained the contradic-
tory explanations concerning the causes of the difficulties there.
These documents were essential in understanding the deplorable state of health, working, and social conditions that confronted the lead and zinc workers.

Other federal documents that were particularly useful in
providing much general information about the Tri-State worker
were: *Fifteenth Census of the United States: 1930*, especially vols. 1,
3, and 6 (Bureau of the Census, Washington, D.C.: Government
Printing Office, 1931–1933); *Religious Bodies: 1936*, vol. I, *Summary and Detailed Tables* (ibid., Washington, D.C.: Government
Printing Office, 1941); *Sixteenth Census of the United States: 1940*,
vols. 1 and 2 (ibid., Washington, D.C.: Government Printing
Office, 1943); and *Final Report on the Total and Partial Unemployment, 1937*, vols. 2 and 3 (ibid., Washington, D.C.: Government
Printing Office, 1938).

Although the LaFolette Civil Liberties Committee failed to
focus on the violations of the legal and constitutional rights of
the lead and zinc workers, its hearings exposed the nearly total
disregard for workers' rights by American corporations that was
so commonplace in the thirties. Furthermore, fragments and
tidbits of evidence from these hearings revealed that Tri-State
operators and civil officials prepared to use similar drastic measures against striking workers that their antiunion counterparts
had used elsewhere. (Senate, Committee on Education and

Labor, *Hearings on Senate Resolution 266* [74th Cong., 1st Sess.] and on *Senate Resolution 60* [75th Cong., 1st Sess.], Washington, D.C.: Government Printing Office, 1937–1938). Two reports from the Department of Labor's Bureau of Labor Statistics revealed much about the post-strike conditions of organized labor in the Tri-State into the mid-forties. These were: *Wage Structure in the Nonferrous Metals Industry, 1941–1942*, Bulletin No. 729 (Washington, D.C.: Government Printing Office, 1943) and *Wages in the Nonferrous-Metals Industry, June 1943*, Bulletin No. 765 (Washington, D.C.: Government Printing Office, 1944).

With a few exceptions, state publications provided little information concerning the strike in the Tri-State. As an example, in Kansas the *Annual Report(s)* (Topeka: State Printers, 1935–1939) of the Commission of Labor and Industry provided the most direct, yet little, information concerning the labor upheaval in Cherokee County, and the *Biennial Report(s)* of the State Board of Health (Topeka: State Printers, 1937–1944) contained limited information on health conditions there. But information about the strike was conspicuously absent in the *Annual Report(s)* (Topeka: State Printers, 1935–1939) of the Coal Mine and Metal Mine Inspection Office, the *Thirteenth Biennial Report, 1935–1936* (Topeka: State Printers, 1937) of the Adjutant General Department, and the *Thirteenth Biennial Report* (Topeka: State Printers, 1936) of the Auditor and Register of State Land Office.

Invaluable in tracing the divisive issue of craft versus industrial unionism within the American Federation of Labor were its *Report(s) of Proceedings*, especially volumes 54–57 (Washington: Judd & Detweiler, 1934–1937), and the *Official Proceedings* of the Congress of Industrial Organizations for 1938 and 1939 (Pittsburgh: CIO, 1938; San Francisco: CIO, 1939). Although there are excellent secondary works concerning the split in organized labor resulting in the formation of the CIO, the *Proceedings* of the AFL and the CIO were essential in understanding the schism that made possible the affiliation of the Blue Card Union with the AFL. The financial impotence and disarray of the International Union of Mine, Mill, and Smelter Workers at the start of the strike in 1935 can be easily recognized in its *Official Proceedings* (1933–1941) as well as the dire circumstances of the Tri-State locals and their inability to sustain the mammoth strike launched in May 1935. The role of the IUMMSW in the struggle over industrial unionism within the AFL can also be followed in these *Proceedings*. For understanding the organizational twists and turns of the Blue Card Union, the *Proceedings* of the AFL, the CIO, and the IUMMSW were extremely useful.

Regional newspapers varied tremendously in their coverage of the strike, but the *Joplin* (Missouri) *Globe* consistently provided the best and most objective coverage. It should be consulted for the day-by-day developments. Other metropolitan newspapers relatively close to the scene, such as the *Kansas City* (Missouri) *Star* and the *Topeka* (Kansas) *Daily Capital* were episodic in their coverage. Although in a position to provide excellent coverage of the strike, the *Miami* (Oklahoma) *Daily News-Record*, rumored to have been owned by Eagle Picher, carried disappointingly little news of the event, especially news relating to IUMMSW and its activities. Local newspapers like the Columbus, Kansas, *Daily Advocate* and the Baxter Springs, Kansas, *Citizen Herald* were useful sources of information often ignored by the larger newspapers. But even labor-oriented newspapers such as the *Oklahoma Federationist* (Oklahoma City) and the *Missouri Trade Unionist* (Jefferson City) contained little of substance about the strike. The *American Guardian* (Oklahoma City), Oscar Ameringer's Socialist-oriented weekly, which carried stories of embattled coal miners, dock workers, textile workers, sharecroppers, and auto workers throughout the nation, rarely mentioned the struggle of the metal workers of the nearby Tri-State. With one exception, no newspaper in the district took a strong editorial position, either pro or con, on the strike, the desirability of unions, and so on. The exception was the *Blue Card Record*, a company union publication whose poisonous antiunionism has been described in chapter 6. Unfortunately, only scattered issues are extant (Tamiment Institute, New York). Because so much labor activity occurred in other parts of the nation concurrently with the strike of the lead and zinc workers, and because the Tri-State Mining District was relatively isolated, major metropolitan newspapers like the *New York Times* failed to focus on the strike itself. Even the Communist *Daily Worker* virtually ignored the plight of Tri-State workers until the indictment of eleven of them for the murder of Lavoice Miller following the Galena riot of April 1937 and the affiliation of the Blue Card Union to the AFL. These events provoked a short-lived attention to the situation in the district.

The general histories of Oklahoma, Kansas, and Missouri failed to emphasize the events of the thirties in the Tri-State Mining District, often making only casual reference to happenings there. Nevertheless, to place the strike in the sweep of the history of these states, one should consult such state histories as Arrell M. Gibson, *Oklahoma: A History of Five Centuries* (Norman: Harlow Publishing Co., 1965); Edwin C. McReynolds, *Oklahoma: A History of the Sooner State* (Norman: University of Oklahoma Press, 1954); Wayne H. and Anne Hodges Morgan, *Oklahoma: A Bicentennial History* (New York: W. W. Norton & Co., 1977); William Frank Zarnow, *Kansas: A History of the Jayhawk State* (Norman: University of Oklahoma Press, 1957); Francis W. Schruben, *Kansas in Turmoil, 1930–1936* (Columbia: University of Missouri Press, 1969); William E. Parrish, et al., *Missouri: The Heart of the Nation* (Saint Louis: Forum Press, 1980); and Edwin C. McReynolds, *Missouri: A History of the Crossroads State* (Norman: University of Oklahoma Press, 1962).

The most essential published work on the Tri-State was Arrell M. Gibson's *Wilderness Bonanza: The Tri-State District of Missouri, Kansas, and Oklahoma* (Norman: University of Oklahoma Press for the Stovall Museum, 1972). In this work, Gibson superbly traced the history and development of mining technology as applied in the district, which was his major emphasis. Although two chapters of this book concerned the history of labor in the district, there was no expansive development of the strike story. Nonetheless, except for *Wilderness Bonanza*, there has been no scholarly book-length treatment of the Tri-State. In his *Death of a Yale Man* (New York: J. J. Little & Ives Co., 1939), Malcolm Harrison Ross devoted several chapters to journalistic observations about the strike. For awhile, as a member of the NLRB's Region 17 staff, Ross was in a position to observe strike developments in the Tri-State from the perspective of the NLRB. His account was decidedly sympathetic to the union cause. In 1939, Lallah S. Davidson also published her *South of Joplin: Story of a Tri-State Diggins'* (New York: W. W. Norton Co.), a proletarian novel based on the events of the strike. Although a somewhat sensationalized work, it provided powerful and often accurate insights into the troubles of the district, especially the terrible plight of the lead and zinc workers and their families. Morris Wright's *"Takes More Than Guns": A Brief History of the International Union of Mine, Mill and Smelter Workers* (Denver: IUMMSW, 1944) was "brief" and not very instructive.

Various works provided insights into different phases of this study. Vernon Jensen's *Non-Ferrous Metals Industry Unionism, 1932–*

1954: A Story of Leadership Controversy (Ithaca: Cornell University Press, 1954) traced the leftist character of IUMMSW leadership, which helped to explain the frequent charges of the Tri-State operators that the union was controlled by Communists or "reds." Useful in understanding the impact on the Tri-State of the internal struggle within the AFL over craft versus industrial unionism were: Walter Galenson, *Rival Unionism in the United States* (New York: American Council on Public Affairs, 1940) and *The CIO Challenge to the AFL* (Cambridge: Harvard University Press, 1960); Edward Levinson, *Labor on the March* (New York: Harper & Brothers Publishers, 1938); and Raymond J. Walsh, *C.I.O.: Industrial Unionism in Action* (New York: W. W. Norton & Co., 1937). Dolph Shaner's *The Story of Joplin* (New York: Stratford House, Inc., 1948) and Vance Randolph's *The Ozarks: An American Survival of Primitive Society* (New York: Vanguard Press, 1931) and *Ozark Mountain Folk* (New York: Vanguard Press, 1932) provided information and insight into aspects of Tri-State culture.

A number of articles proved useful to this study. M. D. Harbaugh's "Labor Relations in the Tri-State Mining District," *Mining Congress Journal* (June 1936), pp. 19–24, was most helpful in presenting the operators' perceptions of the origins of the strike, the IUMMSW, the attitude of nonunion workers, and so on. A recent article by Arrell M. Gibson, "Poor Man's Camp: Labor Movement Vicissitudes in the Tri-State District," *Chronicles of Oklahoma*, 60 [Spring 1982], pp. 4–20, was essentially a recapitulation of his work on the subject in *Wilderness Bonanza*, which was cited above. And Gibson's "A Social History of the Tri-State District," *Chronicles of Oklahoma*, 37 (Summer 1959), pp. 182–95, is a delightful piece that described the character of the social life in the district throughout its history. In "National Labor Relations Act," *American Federationist*, 42 (August 1935), p. 814–23, William Green elaborated on the National Labor Relations Act and what it meant to labor.

The *Engineering and Mining Journal* contained dozens of articles pertaining to the district; however, most of these concerned mining and industrial developments. Among its most informative articles about the district as it approached its heyday of the twenties were those of H. W. Kitson: "The Mining Districts of Joplin and Southeast Missouri—I, II, and III," ibid., 104 (December 17, 1917), pp. 1067–73; 105 (February 23, 1918), pp. 359–64; and 105 (March 2, 1918), pp. 411–15. Information about Tri-State labor in the *EMJ* was generally confined to editorial comment or letters to the editor. Nonetheless, the *EMJ* did reflect a growing concern about silicosis and accidents as the thirties approached.

In his "Joplin Zinc: Industrial Conditions in the World's Greatest Zinc Center," *The Survey*, 45 (February 5, 1921), pp. 657–64, Charles Morris Mills revealed much about local attitudes toward unions, foreigners, and social conditions in the twenties. Mills's study, combined with Alice Hamilton's "A Mid-American Tragedy," *Survey Graphic*, 29 (August 1940), pp. 434–37, and the "American Plague Spot," *The New Republic*, 102 (January 1, 1940), pp. 7–8, demonstrated the remarkable extension into the thirties of the adverse conditions that earlier affected Tri-State workers and their families. Particularly useful in placing the district operators' reaction to the IUMMSW strike in historical perspective were Allen M. Wakestein, "The Origin of the Open-Shop Movement, 1919–1920," *Journal of American History*, 51 (December 1964), pp. 460–75, and Daniel Nelson's "The Company Union Movement, 1900–1937: A Re-examination," *Business History Review*, 56 (Autumn 1982), pp. 335–37. The latter article was a revisionist piece which stressed the positive features of company unionism.

The most systematic economic examination of the Tri-State Mining District was William James Cassidy's "The Tri-State Zinc, Lead Mining Region: Growth, Problems and Prospects" (Ph.D. dissertation, University of Pittsburgh, 1952). Cassidy's work was an excellent companion piece to Gibson's *Wilderness Bonanza* because it analyzed different dimensions of economic life in the district. However, his chapter on labor, particularly labor in the thirties, must be used with caution. John Ervin Brinley's "The Western Federation of Miners" (Ph.D. dissertation, University of Utah, 1972) provided a rich analysis of the structure and politics of the Western Federation of Miners, a survey of early unionism in the metal mining industry, and a review of the WFM's relationship to the AFL. It also contained useful, although limited, information concerning the early organizing efforts of the WFM in the Tri-State. For the most detailed and critical review of the social conditions in the late thirties, one should consult the Tri-State Survey Committee's *A Preliminary Report on Living, Working, and Health Conditions in the Tri-State Area (Missouri, Oklahoma and Kansas)* (mimeograph, New York: Tri-State Survey Committee,

Inc., 1939) and the film *Men and Dust* (New York: Garrison Film Distributors, Inc., 1939), which was based on the committee's investigations.

Finally, the written recollections of Glenn A. Hickman were extremely useful to this study. Hickman graciously responded to written questions about the strike, the Blue Card Union, the IUMMSW, personalities, conditions, and so on. His answers have been compiled as his "Recollections." These were vitally important in fathoming the motives of some of the men who led the back-to-work movement and the union. Interviews with Hickman also revealed his deep conviction that he, F. W. ("Mike") Evans, Kelsey Norman, Joe Nolan, and others were justified in their actions against the locals of the IUMMSW that broke the strike. The author also profited from correspondence with Governor Alfred M. Landon, Attorney General Clarence V. Beck, and Major Ellis G. Christensen concerning military operations in Kansas.

Index

Union Busting in the Tri-State,

designed by Bill Cason and Ed Shaw, was set in various sizes of Baskerville by G&S Typesetters, Inc., and printed offset on 60-pound Glatfelter Smooth Antique B-31 by Cushing-Malloy, Inc., with case binding by John H. Dekker & Sons.